P9-CCV-191

IF NOT NOW, WHEN?

Most Berkley Caliber Books are available at special quantity discounts for bulk purchases for sales promotions, premiums, fund-raising, or educational use. Special books, or book excerpts, can also be created to fit specific needs.

For details, write: Special Markets, The Berkley Publishing Group, 375 Hudson Street, New York, New York 10014.

IF NOT NOW, WHEN?

Duty and Sacrifice in
America's Time of Need

COLONEL JACK JACOBS (RET.)
AND DOUGLAS CENTURY

BERKLEY CALIBER, NEW YORK

NEWARK PUBLIC LIBRARY
121 HIGH ST.
NEWARK, NY 14513

THE BERKLEY PUBLISHING GROUP
Published by the Penguin Group
Penguin Group (USA) Inc.
375 Hudson Street, New York, New York 10014, USA
Penguin Group (Canada), 90 Eglinton Avenue East, Suite 700, Toronto, Ontario M4P 2Y3, Canada
(a division of Pearson Penguin Canada Inc.)
Penguin Books Ltd., 80 Strand, London WC2R 0RL, England
Penguin Group Ireland, 25 St. Stephen's Green, Dublin 2, Ireland (a division of Penguin Books Ltd.)
Penguin Group (Australia), 250 Camberwell Road, Camberwell, Victoria 3124, Australia
(a division of Pearson Australia Group Pty. Ltd.)
Penguin Books India Pvt. Ltd., 11 Community Centre, Panchsheel Park, New Delhi—110 017, India
Penguin Group (NZ), 67 Apollo Drive, Rosedale, North Shore 0632, New Zealand
(a division of Pearson New Zealand Ltd.)
Penguin Books (South Africa) (Pty.) Ltd., 24 Sturdee Avenue, Rosebank, Johannesburg 2196,
South Africa

Penguin Books Ltd., Registered Offices: 80 Strand, London WC2R 0RL, England

The publisher does not have any control over and does not assume responsibility for author or third-party websites or their content.

This book is an original publication of the Berkley Publishing Group.

Copyright © 2008 by Jack Jacobs and Douglas Century Literary Enterprises, Inc.
Book design by Tiffany Estreicher

All rights reserved.
No part of this book may be reproduced, scanned, or distributed in any printed or electronic form without permission. Please do not participate in or encourage piracy of copyrighted materials in violation of the author's rights. Purchase only authorized editions.
BERKLEY CALIBER and its logo are trademarks of Penguin Group (USA) Inc.

First edition: October 2008

Library of Congress Cataloging-in-Publication Data

Jacobs, Jack, 1945–
    If not now, when? : duty and sacrifice in America's time of need / Colonel Jack Jacobs (Ret.), and
Douglas Century.
        p. cm.
    Includes index.
    ISBN 978-0-425-22359-8
    1. United States. Army—Officers—Biography.   2. Medal of Honor—Biography.   3. Vietnam War,
1961–1975—Personal narratives, American.   I. Century, Douglas.   II. Title.

    U53.J34 2008
    355.0092—dc22
    [B]
                                                                                    2008019835
PRINTED IN THE UNITED STATES OF AMERICA

10   9   8   7   6   5   4   3   2   1

Author's Note

This is the page on which the author asserts that his work is either fiction or nonfiction, probably a requirement dictated by an attorney who spent a great deal of money on his education and needs to repay a very large tuition loan. I suppose a disclaimer does protect the author and publisher from the greed of some real live person who is fuming about being portrayed in a novel as a rapacious villain, but the memoirist is in danger of annoying people in a manner that is peculiar to the genre because it purports to be the truth.

This is a work of nonfiction, and readers may assume that the events are true, the characters real, and the dialogue has been recreated to the best of my recollection. But nothing in life can ever be cleansed completely of fiction because memory is unreliable and selective at the best of times. To those who have been misquoted, misnamed, or mischaracterized, I apologize. I did the best I could with the limited faculties I still possess. Even Mark Twain, whose mind was razor-sharp, observed that when he was younger he could remember anything, whether it had happened or not. When he got older, he said, he could only remember the things that *hadn't* happened.

—J. J.

There is no cure for birth and death,
save to enjoy the interval.

—George Santayana

THE MAN IN SEAT 2B

FOREWORD BY BRIAN WILLIAMS,
Anchor and Managing Editor, NBC Nightly News

My favorite Jack Jacobs story takes place not on the field of battle, but in the office of the chief investment officer of an insurance company in Germany. Jack flew there on business a few years back, hoping to free the executive of twenty million dollars toward a hedge fund Jack was developing back in New York, where he enjoyed a successful career on Wall Street while working for Bankers Trust.

Jack being Jack, he remembers wondering how many of his fellow Jews, perhaps even members of the Jacobs family, had gone to their reward at the hands of the banker's relatives during World War II. At that instant, however, Jack wasn't about moral judgments. His mission was to leave the meeting with a pile of money neatly but figuratively stacked in his briefcase. That was the mission.

So the meeting starts, and during the conversation, Jack was, as he later put it, "absently scratching at a tiny bump" near his nose. As quickly as you can say hemorrhage, Jack breaks something loose that causes "a torrent of venous blood that splattered everywhere," down the front of his clothing, the coffee table and ending up on the handknotted Heriz rug beneath their feet.

Jack remembers it looking like a crime scene. In an attempt to regain control of a business meeting that had taken a sudden and bloody turn south, Jack mumbled an explanation about residual injuries from his time fighting in Vietnam. It was apparently enough for the stunned German: Jack left the room with the twenty million dollars he'd come there asking for. It would more than pay for a new rug. Hand-knotted, no less.

What happened that day isn't at all uncommon for combat veterans: a piece of shrapnel had taken thirty years to come to the surface. The same can be said of the story contained in this book.

Countless business travelers have sat next to my friend Jack for long flights across the Atlantic. If asked, they'd later describe the man in seat 2B as diminutive, smart, a cheerful guy and a wonderful storyteller. They would be stunned to learn he also happens to be a recipient of the Medal of Honor.

That's the thing about Jack. That's also the thing about all the other guys just like him—all of the men alive today who have been awarded the nation's highest decoration for bravery and valor in battle. I have come to know them by serving on the Board of Directors of the Medal of Honor Foundation. At the time of this writing, there are just over one hundred men alive who are members of this exclusive group. Our board is charged with raising money to promote awareness of the Medal of Honor and what it represents. The truth is: I would *pay them* to be on their board. Being around these men—getting to know them—has been among the great ongoing experiences of my adult life.

I've known Jack the longest of any of the recipients, because of our time together at NBC News, where Jack has come to on-air prominence as a military analyst. Like most of the tasks he has tackled in life, it comes to him seemingly effortlessly, and he's awfully good at it. Far from being a pushover for the Pentagon, and despite his retirement rank of colonel following his years of proud service and multiple combat tours, Jack calls them as he sees them, and is an unsparing critic of U.S. policy when circumstances require it.

I also thought I knew him. Because I have read his Medal citation many times over, I rather proudly assumed I knew the details of his Vietnam experience, and of the military engagement that led to the Medal being placed around his neck by President Richard Nixon. While I've flown all over the country with Jack, and spent countless hours happily engaged in conversation with him, it turns out I knew but a fraction of his story.

The living recipients of the Medal of Honor are walking monuments to modesty, Jack chief among them. Most of the warriors I know hate war. Jack's humility and complete lack of swagger are striking. Jack Jacobs is a complete American. He has lived the American experience, while rising out of bed to greet each new day as the sole occupant of a badly broken vessel—his body, like an old house, is full of combat scars and residual shrapnel, and requires constant upkeep: frequent operations to improve plumbing and ventilation. This man who carries around tiny pieces of steel still believes he has grabbed life's brass ring, won the lottery, beaten the odds. He is a patriot of the highest order, in the truest sense of the word, in the tradition of those who have fought hard enough for this place to come down hard on us when they fear we're heading off in the wrong direction.

When I speak to audiences about the lessons I've learned from my recipient friends, I always say the same thing; before I met them I used to think I had an occasional bad day. Never again. Not as long as there are men like Jack Jacobs to remind us all how much a human can endure, and how much this nation means to the people who've fought for it.

One warning: the book you are about to read, at its core, is a story about selflessness, sacrifice, and service, and it collides loudly and rather violently with much of our current culture. We are presently a nation of 120 million blogs and bloggers. Put differently, 120 million of us are enthused enough with our own stories—convinced enough in our own wisdom and wonderfulness of self—to believe there is great utility in posting our every thought, desire, and daily movement on the Internet, presumably for the common good, the benefit of all. Jack was handed a weapon and told to use it on foreign soil to defend his brothers and his country. As you read this, ask yourself which of the two actions you find more heroic.

I'm convinced you'll come away staggered by the diminutive man in seat 2B. I will never view my friend Jack in the same way again. I just didn't think it was possible to admire him any more than I already did.

Courage is the art of being the only one
who knows you're scared to death.

—HAROLD WILSON

PROLOGUE

In the morning heat, moisture on the surface of the Mekong rises slightly over the widening mass of water upriver in Cambodia and then, just after dusk, condenses on its lazy southerly journey through Vietnam. The following dawn, there is always a thin mist skimming the river, even in early March—well before the worst of the wet season, when the torrential sheets of rain have left the landscape a flat carpet of green. That spectral shroud follows the river and dances slowly with it on its trip through the Vietnamese delta, until the wide, muddy Mekong is swallowed whole by the South China Sea.

Just after sunrise on March 9, 1968, a few decrepit and dented assault craft nose slowly through the thin tropical fog, diesel engines chugging cautiously. Lesions of rust leach through the battleship-gray paint of the boats. They are packed with South Vietnamese soldiers bending under the weight of weapons, ammunition, and the weariness of combat. Since the beginning of the Tet Offensive less than two months ago, many of the battalion's troops have been killed or wounded, and only about two hundred soldiers are on the boats.

I am twenty-two years old, rail-thin and infantry dark. At a shade under five feet four, I am shorter than most of the Vietnamese. My journey has taken me from an immigrant Jewish family in Brooklyn, New York, to the 2nd Battalion, 16th Infantry of the 9th Infantry Division of the Army of the Republic of Vietnam, a universe away from home and in fear of my life in an alien land. I look like a child. I am a child.

There are three other Americans serving as advisors with these Vietnamese soldiers, but we aren't temporary interlopers. The 2nd of the 16th is our battalion. We live with the Vietnamese, share their meager rations, fight at their sides, call them friends, and watch them bleed and die.

It begins as just another mission to reestablish contact with the Vietcong unit we have been fighting for months, and when the ragged old boats slide onto the muddy bank, we plan to pick our way slowly, tentatively, from one tree line to another, across wide, open rice paddies that will give any hidden enemy unobstructed fields of fire onto our unit. There are two of us Americans with the lead companies of the battalion. My NCO, Ray Ramirez, is five feet seven inches tall and strong as an ox, a brave, plainspoken staff sergeant with a thick Mexican accent and an even thicker bull neck. Ramirez is from Raymondville, Texas, near Brownsville—he says it's close enough to Mexico to actually be in Mexico.

Ray and I are in the lead boat. With a gentle bump, the groaning old tub finally wedges against the mud on the north side of the river, and we trudge ashore through the eerie morning mist and the thick, smelly muck to the dense undergrowth at the river's edge. We clamber noisily down the slippery embankment of a narrow canal and up the steep opposite side to a vast dry rice field to be greeted by the stinging glare of the newly risen sun. Cautiously, we straggle across the first paddy, almost a thousand meters of open field.

There is no cover here, I think. No concealment whatsoever. We are in the worst tactical position imaginable. We have several hundred troops in the open, marching slowly toward a specific, predetermined point, and we possess no element of surprise. Our only protection is one half-strength, half-trained scout platoon covering our nakedness to the front and flanks. Half of a half. One-quarter *of the minimum protection we need—if it's really there.*

Well, the scouts are somewhere, *but as we will discover to our surprise and great pain, they aren't protecting us. They are to the rear perhaps, at home maybe, but they aren't where they are supposed to be. We are where the scouts are supposed to be. We're the leading edge of what is to become the juicy target of an ambush that was prepared for us by an enemy that has known long in advance that we are coming, and that we are coming in this strength, at this time, to this specific point on the ground. Three hundred enemy soldiers have spent days assembling themselves into the largest, best-armed, most cohesive Vietcong unit in the region. And now they wait—for us.*

This close to the equator, the sun leaps quickly from its berth just below the horizon to its place of business directly overhead. It is an insistent, fiery ball that refuses to relinquish its station until it is forced from the sky. By midmorning, we have been mooching toward our objective for several hours, and the sun has been pounding us, roasting us in our own salty juices that stain uniforms a starchy, brittle salt-white.

Dehydrated now. Tired. Head-heavy. Looking down rather than forward. Searching the ground and not the horizon, tracking the drops of perspiration as they fall and then splatter when they hit the earth. Glancing about for the scouts and hoping that they are protecting us forward and to the flanks. The VC will see the scouts first. Three hundred enemy guns will aim for the center of mass of the scout platoon, and we will maneuver the lead companies to destroy the VC, and Ray and I will survive yet another day and then go home without a scratch.

Though we don't know it yet, two hundred meters ahead of us, about a battalion of Vietcong are waiting for us. They are not waiting for the scouts. They are waiting for me and for Ray. They are patient, quiet, disciplined, concealed.

One hundred meters now. I know how the VC feel, energized with the grisly knowledge that other human beings have only minutes to live and yet don't know it.

I have lain in ambush, too, and I know how the Vietcong soldier feels when he sees Ray and me and the Vietnamese troops move cautiously forward. We are almost close enough, but not quite, and he suddenly realizes that in his excited anticipation he has been holding his breath and needs precious oxygen. A slow, deliberate inhale of thick air, but the sound is startlingly loud to him. We will hear his straining lungs fill, will fall to the ground, and will pour withering fire into his foxhole, tearing him apart. His mouth is cotton-dry, and surreptitiously he tries to swallow, but his throat reverberates deafeningly. The point man will hear him breathe, hear him swallow, hear him blink. The telltale heart is slamming wildly inside his chest. He will be discovered in ambush, and he will become the prey, and he will be destroyed.

Fifty meters. When we get to the tree line, maybe we can take a break, relax, light up, take a drunken slug from our canteens.

All experience inoculates us with the ability to sense the environment in indefinable ways, and nothing is better at honing the senses than armed combat. The wind is a messenger: a whisper, a falling leaf, even silence becomes palpable. They are urgent messages that bypass our consciousness and are transmitted directly to those secret places in the heart that can see what the eyes cannot see, the places that understand passion, euphoria—and danger. The unforgettable smell of death before the first insult to the body. The paralyzing cold of abject fear even in the warm caress of the sunshine.

And in the heat of the tropics, I suddenly feel the cold. It's not a breeze, for the air is calm, even sweet, and just ahead the palm and banana fronds hang limply in the heavy air. But I can feel the penetrating cold of approaching fear, and it is a wind boring through me. An uneventful day so far, and yet my heart is racing. Maybe I can hear the VC breathing, swallowing, blinking, and I don't even know I can hear it.

Suddenly the universe erupts with rifle and machine gun fire, and in seconds dozens of soldiers are thrown to the ground by the enormous energy of high-powered military bullets. My friends don't grasp their wounds and slowly slink to earth in a theatrical, ceremonious ballet. There is no stirring Hollywood score. These notes are the shattering cracks of thousands of bullets and the nauseating thumps as they hit the flesh and bone of my comrades. They are marionettes whose strings have been cut, lying dead or hideously broken. A few of us are lucky so far, and we hug the ground like desperate lovers, unscathed in the initial seconds but scared witless.

We learn as young soldiers that an ambush is best defeated by rushing directly into the teeth of it, by suspending fear and disbelief, by getting off the killing ground, by assaulting directly into the withering fire to overrun the enemy position. And surely there have been ambushes that didn't succeed because soldiers in the killing zone did just this, just as they had been taught.

But today, there will be no concerted effort to rush the entrenched enemy because this is a battlefield on which almost everybody is in the open and already dead or wounded.

We manage to crawl a bit to the left and out of the most direct enemy fire, to a place where there is a tree or two and a bit of protection. Some soldiers, wounded in the first seconds, are on the ground there, their lives leaking onto the dark earth while the enemy fire splits the air and tears into the dirt around us.

Some people say that you can't hear mortar rounds until they hit because mortars are high-trajectory weapons and most of them are

stabilized silently with fins. Unless the firing battery is close enough
for you to hear the rounds sliding down the tube, before they are
propelled out of the barrel in a slow arc to your position, you don't
know you're a target until the rounds hit the ground. Quiet death,
they say.

They're wrong. In the last second before the round hits and disin-
tegrates, before the explosive inside the shell shatters the steel casing
into thousands of jagged, knife-sharp shards, I can hear it whoosh-
ing through the air. After the whoosh comes an explosion so loud
that it overloads my hearing and seems silent.

A quiet, warm, gentle rush of air lifts me, and then I am on all
fours, looking at the ground and the widening lake of my blood. An
82-millimeter mortar round has smashed into the ground a couple
of meters away, killing two soldiers nearby, wounding Ray and me,
and killing two or three more behind us. Shrapnel has torn through
my face and into my skull. I can only see out of one eye.

Then more mortars rain on us all.

There is no fear on earth like the fear of combat, and people who
say they were not scared in battle are either lying or deranged. You
are in fear of losing your life, of losing your limbs, of losing your
courage. In the heat of battle, everyone is scared. But here is the
paradox: when you're hit, when jagged foreign objects rip painfully
through your body, you're surprised, even shocked.

Beside me, Sergeant Ramirez is very badly hurt, with wounds to
his chest that are deflating his lungs, shrapnel in his abdomen, blood
pouring out of his nose and mouth.

Despite his devastating wounds, Ray grabs one of the radios.

"This is Three Two Charlie," Ramirez barks into the handset.
"Three Two Alfa is hit real bad, and I don't think he's going to make
it." He then sags under the crushing insult of his wounds and falls
over, painfully immobilized, eyes lolling backward. I snatch the
handset from him.

"This is Three Two Alfa," I'm saying. "Three Two Charlie is hit real bad, and I don't think he's going to make it."

Someone on the other end of the radio says, quite calmly:

"Hey, you jerks. This is no comedy routine. Get to work."

I patch up Ray as quickly as I can and set him in a place where I hope he'll be safe. But he is badly wounded. My greatest fear is that he won't make it....

CHAPTER ONE

I WAS BORN in the heart of Brooklyn in the summer of 1945, during the waning weeks of the Second World War. Hitler's armies had surrendered almost three months earlier, but the Japanese were still fighting ferociously on the islands of the Pacific. I took my first breath in Crown Heights Hospital on the final day of the Potsdam Conference, where the Allies hammered out the details of how they would administer the edgy, postwar world. Four days later, the *Enola Gay* dropped an atomic bomb on Hiroshima.

My father, a technical sergeant in the U.S. Army Signal Corps, with service in New Guinea and Manila, had accumulated the requisite number of points to go home, but because there weren't enough ships, he was still stuck in the Pacific. The War Department awarded points—for being married, for having children, for being overseas—and when you had enough points, you could go home. Plenty of points, but not enough ships, and so my father sat on some tiny, insect-ridden Philippine island with thousands of others who also had enough points, waiting for a ship to take them home. And they waited.

After a second atomic bomb obliterated Nagasaki, the Japanese finally surrendered, and the war was over. But forgotten on the island, my father and thousands of others continued to wait for ships that didn't come for months, long after troops without enough points had already been delivered to their families back home. It should come as no surprise that discipline on the island deteriorated rapidly, as the soldiers, after months and years away from home, acquired characteristics even William Golding would find repulsive.

When they were finally rescued, their ordeal wasn't yet over. Their ship had two engines and was rated to cross the Pacific in about ten days. But not long after getting under way, it lost an engine, and it took the better part of a month to reach California. Why two engines could get you there in ten days but one engine took three times as long eludes my father's understanding even today.

Insufficient food for such a long voyage was an ingredient for disaster aboard a ship crammed with troops already angry and resentful and of a proven tendency to bloody violence. As soon as the one engine quit, the ship's crew expected riots, mutiny, and murder. But rough seas and soldiers not used to being afloat combined to put most of them on the deck and thoroughly occupied with being violently ill, and thus out of one another's way for the duration of the transit. Meanwhile, my father and a handful of others, impervious to the stomach-churning effects of a rough voyage, ate like kings.

My father was an engineer by training. After graduating from high school, he went to Brooklyn College to study for a degree in electrical engineering and then transferred to the University of Minnesota, which had an ROTC program and a strong engineering school. But by 1944, the armed forces needed every able body they could possibly get their hands on, and so Dad was yanked out of college. When he returned from the war, he went to work as an engineer for Western Electric, which through many corporate evolutions eventually became Lucent. But at the time, after the war and for decades afterward, Western Electric was the manufacturing arm of AT&T

and Bell Telephone. My father became a microwave engineer and was one of the men instrumental in changing the communications system to digital and microwave technology.

When I was a boy, I always thought of my father in those terms—as an electrical engineer and not as a soldier. But he *was* a soldier, just like millions of other people his age. Perhaps the ubiquity of military service in a time of peril made it unremarkable. In the forties and fifties, it was rare to encounter an adult who hadn't been in uniform, and in our neighborhood the vestiges of the war—gasoline ration stickers, amputees, fatherless boys—were constant reminders that the entire, disparate American community had been forged together into an alloy of great strength.

And like most veterans of the Second World War, when he returned home, he quickly and easily slid back into a normal midcentury American life. The ugliness was over, and it was time to move on. If there were anecdotes about the war, they were infrequent. That was partly because the war was still fresh, and human beings rarely find the necessity to reminisce about things until the events are unappealingly moldy and in need of a good airing. Now, my father is almost ninety. He is still in tremendous physical condition, playing paddleball every day, and finally he talks about the war often. When the family gets together now, my father tells war stories, humorous ones mostly, the same stories about the South Pacific over and over and over again. And it's a tribute to their veracity that they never change by so much as one tiny detail.

My parents were Brooklyn born and raised, the children of immigrant Jewish families that came to the United States a century ago, from very different parts of Europe. Both my father's parents emigrated, separately, from a small town called Ioannina in the province of Epirus in northwestern Greece—at that time, part of the crumbling Ottoman Empire. Oddly, they hadn't known each other in Greece but met and married in Brooklyn, where large numbers of Greek Jews had settled at the start of the Balkan Wars and just before World War I.

Their arrival happened to coincide with the much larger—and much better-known—emigration of Yiddish-speaking Jews from Central and Eastern Europe. The proximate causes for the migrations were related. The old world, with its monarchies and artificial alliances, was dying, and rusty, creaking power relationships had become dysfunctional and were coming to pieces. The Ottoman Empire, long a dominant force but now challenged by a new, alien world, was disintegrating. And there were incipient revolutions in Central and Eastern Europe. All of this produced an uncontrollable and growing monster of political and military chaos whose spawn became the First World War. People of all stripes saw themselves entering a fierce, frightening, modern age, but those on the economic and cultural margins saw themselves, quite presciently, as the ultimate losers and started getting out of Europe as fast as they possibly could.

My father spoke nothing but Greek until he was five years old and went to public school in New York City. To say that the new Americans were multilingual would be an enormous understatement. Although my father's generation quickly learned English, Greek—in his case, a dialect of hillbilly Greek found only in the mountains near Ioannina—remained the language of the home and of the adults. But also, they prayed in Hebrew; they understood some Macedonian and Albanian; and because they'd lived for centuries under the domination of the Turks, they could speak a bit of Turkish, too. And it was the experience of living in the dominion of the Ottomans that drove my father's mother to call me "Pasha."

Now, *pasha* is a Turkish title that was granted to high-ranking officials like governors and generals—but in the vernacular, it came to mean "big shot." Not too many years ago, my sister Elissa jocularly complained at some family gathering that I had always been the favorite grandchild. My grandmother, well into her nineties, still with her very thick Greek accent, snapped:

"What you talking about? I like you all the same."

"Oh, yeah?" Elissa said, pointing accusingly at me. "Then why do you call him 'Pasha'?"

And my grandmother's eyes misted with nostalgia. I was the firstborn grandson, and it was a very old tradition to call your favored, firstborn grandson "Pasha." No matter how equal we children were, I *was* the big shot.

My grandmother never became a United States citizen, and she had neither a birth certificate nor even a clue when precisely she was born. Very few people from that part of the world, and almost no women, were issued birth certificates. If I asked her when she was born she could only place it in the context of other things that had happened in the family. "Well, Pasha," she would say, "it was before my mother died but after my cousin was born." And the solution was to celebrate her birthday on the day each year she had to register with the post office as an alien: January first. On her birthday, she would knock back a single jigger of Scotch and, as we knew she would and to howls of laughter from the rest of us, perform some Balkan terpsichorean spectacular on the coffee table.

The Greek Jewish community was highly distinctive and complex. Some families had Jewish surnames such as Levy and Cohen. Others had names that sounded much more typically Greek, like Stavrolakis, Carteris, or Patera, the name of the family that lived next door to her in Williamsburg, Brooklyn. For years and years, I thought that my family was Sephardim, Jews who'd been expelled from Spain and Portugal during the Inquisition and, free to migrate, settled in France and Italy and other places in southern Europe. Many of the Sephardim had been welcomed by Suleiman the Magnificent of Turkey, who'd said to Queen Isabella of Spain: *If you're trying to get rid of your Jews, send them over here—sure, we'll take every one of them.* They were literate, industrious, and well educated, and they became functionaries and doctors and lawyers and other professionals of the Ottoman Empire.

But I learned that my father's family and the community in Ioannina are not descended from those expelled Sephardic Jews at all. We are, in fact, Romaniote Jews. The Romaniotes are historically distinct from both Ashkenazim and Sephardim—they even had their own Greek-Hebrew language, called Yevanic—Jews who have lived in Greece since possibly as early as the Babylonian exile and certainly since the destruction of the Second Temple in AD 70. My father's family came from Judea, most likely 1,700 years ago on Roman slave ships, many of which crashed on the rocks of the northern Mediterranean. A significant number of Jews made it ashore in Greece and settled in communities like Thebes, Chalcis, Corfu, and Corinth and on the islands of Lesbos, Samos, Rhodes, and Cyprus. Ioannina, my grandparents' hometown, was considered the cultural heart of the Romaniote community until the Nazis condemned almost all the remaining Jewish population to Auschwitz in April 1944.

My mother's family, on the other hand, were far more typical of the American Jewish immigrant experience, being Ashkenazim and therefore steeped in the culture of Yiddishkeit. My mother's father came from Czestochowa, Poland, and her mother, who was quite dark, came variously from Romania, Moldova, or Odessa in Ukraine—when we pressed her on her memories, it was not entirely clear where she was from. They all spoke Yiddish as their first language. My mother's family came by ship about the same time as my father's, but they arrived from Eastern Europe when the first serious twentieth-century pogroms, like the infamous 1903 massacres in Kishinev, were shocking the civilized world.

My mother's family, unlike my father's, was very large. We used to have a regular family get-together on my mother's side of the family, and we practically needed to rent Ebbets Field to hold all of them. I have hundreds of cousins, many of whom I have never met. When my mother would bring me to those family circles, I was constantly in a state of confusion.

"You remember Cousin Benny," she'd say.

"Which Benny?"

"You know! Benny-Uncle-Max's."

"Which Uncle Max?"

There were dozens of Maxes and Bennys and Joes, and it was impossible to tell who was who without photographs, a family tree, and a monthly briefing.

Moreover, I found it very strange that most of my mother's relatives, indeed most of the Jews I knew who came from Eastern Europe, had names that were suspiciously Anglo-Saxon. Sure, there were plenty of Samuels, Isaacs, and Solomons, but we were awash in people with names taken from the troop list at the Battle of Hastings. Seymour. Morris. Irving. Murray. Sidney. My own middle name, Howard, is that of the oldest Catholic family in England. And then it dawned on me that they were given these names because their parents wanted everything about their children to be American. They were in the promised land, and they wanted their children to be Americans, too. A name is a distillation of identity, a personal marker that broadcasts who you are before you say a word. In America? Give your kid a proper Anglo-Saxon name. In the generation just before mine, so many Eastern Europeans were given such names that Jews are the only people still named Sheldon.

———————

FAMILY LORE HAS it that my mother met my father at a party in Brooklyn. I take this with a healthy dose of suspicion because everybody embellishes these "how I met your mother" stories. Supposedly, my mother was going out with a guy who was having a house party for some friends, and my father showed up tagging along—a friend of a friend. My parents' eyes met, they got to chatting, and that was the end of whatever was going on between my mother and her old boyfriend.

My parents knew each other for quite a while before they got married. And unlike a lot of young couples in those days, they didn't marry just because of World War II. They were married in 1942, but my father didn't get shipped overseas until two years later, and they made a conscious decision not to have any children until the war was over. Even before he was called up, my father, like everybody else, knew he was going to be sent someplace overseas, and they agreed that raising a child without a father around, if it came to that, was a lousy idea.

In the summer of 1944, my father was sent to Camp Crowder in Joplin, Missouri, for Signal Corps training. And Camp Crowder was about as far—atmospherically and culturally—as you can possibly get from Brooklyn. He wrote my mother a letter saying good-bye and that it looked like his unit was going to ship out very soon. Their pact about children notwithstanding, she wasted no time in sending him a telegram saying that she was coming to Joplin for a final visit. She took the Brooklyn trolley to the subway to the bus to the train, eventually winding up at the front gate of Camp Crowder. The MPs informed my father that his wife had shown up, and they bent the rules by spiriting her inside the camp. My father knew the facility's managers pretty well, and they set my folks up in a set of officer's temporary quarters, really just a tiny room, but at least it wasn't the overcrowded barracks. All of this was strictly against regulations, but it only goes to demonstrate that even in a bureaucracy as impersonal as the U.S. Army, and particularly in wartime when normal situations are enveloped in an atmosphere of desperation, there are always people with empathy. I don't know how long my mother managed to stay at Camp Crowder—it couldn't have been longer than a day or two—but I am the result of that visit. So, although I'm a dyed-in-the-wool Brooklyn boy, I got my start in the Ozarks, and that became a long-standing amusement in the family: that I am literally the last thing my father did before he was sent overseas.

And my sister was the first thing he did when he returned from the Pacific. Again, it was an act of transgression born of passion. My father had finally been transported to Fort Hamilton on 92nd Street in Bay Ridge, Brooklyn, waiting interminably to be mustered out. They wouldn't release the troops until their voluminous paperwork had been processed, a task that had no predictable duration. Could be years. This was annoying in the extreme, since my mother and I—I was now about seven months old—were right there in Brooklyn. So one night my father just went over the fence, asking a couple of buddies to cover for him, spent the weekend with my mother, and sneaked back into the fort. Nine months later, Elissa was born.

PASSIONATE LOVE AFFAIR notwithstanding, among Jewish Americans my parents were considered a highly unusual match. For a Yiddish-speaking Ashkenazi woman to marry a Greek Romaniote Jew was seen as having a mixed marriage. There was, it was said, an argument about whether or not either side would attend the wedding, but in the end they all ended up swallowing their tongues and making nice. I'm reminded of an observation by my friend, a Medal of Honor recipient named Leo Thorsness. Leo was shot down over North Vietnam and spent more than five years as a POW, much of it in solitary confinement, getting tortured every day. Recently, he mentioned to me that he's in a mixed marriage himself.

I had known both Leo and his wife very well for years and had no idea what he was talking about.

"Well, my wife is Swedish and I'm Norwegian," Leo said.

It sounds childishly amusing to most people, but if you go to Wisconsin and Minnesota and talk to folks with deep roots in Scandinavia, they'll tell you that Leo's is most definitely a mixed marriage. People from Denmark tell Swedish jokes, the Swedes tell Danish jokes, and they both unite in telling Norwegian jokes. And in the early to mid twentieth century, things were comparable among the dense pockets of Jewish immigrants in New York City. Much of the nuanced differences among Jews vanished with assimilation into American culture at large, but during the waves of immigration the internecine rivalries among the Jews from Germany, Russia, Romania, and Poland were quite intense. There was an assumed pecking order, with the older German Jewish community thinking they were at the top and the newest immigrants, the Poles and Russians, seen by the Germans as the roughest and most unsophisticated. Of course the vast majority of the immigrants, the entire tenement-dwelling, pushcart culture of the Lower East Side, were deeply steeped in the Yiddish language, Yiddish humor, and Yiddish sensibilities.

One thing that my Ashkenazi and Romaniote sides had in common was that everyone had to be given a proper religious education. They were all observant people, at least in the old country, and that strict orthodoxy was the only way the community managed to stay together in a tremendously hostile environment. It may have been slightly less hostile for the Jews of Greece under the Ottoman reign than it was for the Eastern European Jewish communities who were constantly under threat of Cossack rapists, "blood libels," and other czarist-sponsored pogroms. But by the early years of the last century, it didn't take a genius to see that things were bad and they were going to get worse. And if they were bad and getting worse for everybody in Europe, it was going to be the worst for the Jews.

I have a business partner in London whose family originally came from Russia, and they've been in England for many generations. Somebody asked him recently whether he considered himself English or Jewish, and he replied, "Well, I'm English—as long as you bastards let me stay here." And he's right. It can happen there. It can happen here. It can happen anywhere, and complacency has an unpleasant habit of becoming perilous.

There was no country in Europe in which the Jews were more assimilated than in Germany, and after all, many of them had stopped practicing Judaism for generations. The minute the Nazis came to power in 1933, none of that mattered. Under the Aryan racial laws, it didn't matter if someone of a Jewish background had converted to Protestantism or Catholicism. There are countless stories of Jews, men who'd valorously served as German soldiers and sailors and airmen in 1914–18, being marched up to the gates of the concentration camps still wearing their Iron Crosses on their chests, asking the SS with genuine bewilderment: "What are you doing to me? I am a German. I fought for the Kaiser in the Great War."

Among the best known was Anne Frank's father, Otto, who was born in Frankfurt and had served with distinction in the Imperial German Army on the Western Front, earning the Iron Cross. Of course, none of this stopped the Nazis from murdering his wife and daughters and sending Otto Frank to Auschwitz.

CHAPTER TWO

MY MOTHER GREW up in Crown Heights, just off Eastern Parkway, my father in Williamsburg, on the corner of South 2nd and Roebling Streets. I've never managed to get the straight story about precisely where I lived in my earliest years. I have the impression that during the war, before my father returned from the South Pacific, my mother and I lived with her sister and her family—her husband, Henry, and my cousin Mel, who is seven years older than I. Uncle Henry was glib and slick, and in the 1930s he was almost certainly a flimflam man. He was a short bundle of energy with bright, twinkling eyes, and one can easily see how he would be capable of bringing greedy, unwary rubes into his confidence and fleecing them thoroughly. My uncle sported thick, wavy hair that remained naturally, stubbornly black until he was quite old. He smoked enormous Cuban cigars, lots of them, and still managed to live well into his nineties. For those who eschew the multitude of health fads and exhortations to clean living, Uncle Henry is the poster boy for their valiant resistance, and for them he will be eternal proof that longevity is wholly a function of membership in the Lucky DNA Club.

Everybody's memory is selective, and my autonomic selectivity is among the most arbitrary. We remember only the things we want to remember, and, rather than bringing events and images into sharp focus, we exaggerate them, we combine them, we forget them. President Reagan was notorious for convincing himself that movie plots were reality, that things he *thought* had happened—but hadn't—had actually happened. But we all do that, and there are few things more unreliable than eyewitness accounts, especially accounts by old people about their childhoods. Sixty years after the fact, seminal events fade into the darkness, while trivialities become etched in sharp, meaningful relief.

Unreliable, yes, but my first concrete recollections, very clear indeed, are of living in Queens, where we moved when I was about four years old. It wasn't a *house* exactly—it was a rectangular building called a "Utica hut," about the size of a one-story Army barracks, made of tin-plated steel and with predictable thermal qualities: boiling in summer, freezing in winter, and drafty at all times. During the war, it had probably been a storage shed or maintenance bay or something similar, but after, with the huge housing shortage, all these military tin huts became pressed into service as housing. We shared the building with another family, and our apartments were separated by a thin wall. I don't remember the family at the other end of the hut, and although the adults in the small community commiserated regularly, for a four-year-old the environment was an allegorical Meiji fable. Things happened on the other side of the wall. You could hear them. But you could never know what was actually taking place. There was often a lot of raucous yelling, furniture banging, crockery smashing, and other unpleasant noises emanating from the other side. The parents flogged and subsequently murdered the kids, I concluded, and I passed that end of the hut with enormous trepidation.

The place did have indoor plumbing, at least, but I don't recall taking a bath in anything other than the kitchen sink. It must have had a proper bathtub, but perhaps because I was so small my parents found it much more convenient to wash me as if I were the silverware.

The meager warmth was generated by a kerosene space heater. The heater was a contraption clearly invented by someone with more than two hands, or perhaps two hands and a prehensile foot, and it challenged everyone but an operator with the most finely honed skills and innate sense of timing. The result of error was certain and devastating conflagration.

The process required turning on a valve that released kerosene into the bottom of a combustion chamber. Eyeballing the increasingly deep pool of fuel in the heater, at some arbitrary point you turned the valve to "off." At this point, Catholics and very high-church Anglicans crossed themselves. Then you struck a match and threw it into the pool of kerosene. The match's angle of descent into the kerosene was evidently critical, because often the fuel drowned the flame and failed to ignite.

Try again.

Still didn't ignite?

At this point, even Protestants, Jews, and atheists crossed themselves, and the burning match was very cautiously held to the surface of the kerosene pool, which usually burst into flame. When the pool was nearly consumed, the valve was turned to "on," and you were in business.

If you had permitted an insufficient volume of kerosene to accumulate, it didn't heat the chamber adequately, and you had to start all over again. Too much kerosene, and the flaming fuel overflowed and the place burned to the ground. It required the deftness of neurosurgery, but it was more difficult than neurosurgery and you couldn't go to school to learn it.

Our little tin hut was on the site of what was later the Bulova watch factory, across Grand Central Parkway from the end of the runway of LaGuardia Airport. The world seemed a simpler place then—no extraordinary safety or security measures, no crossing guards, no warnings on packages of peanuts that the package contained peanuts. Only jazz musicians used illicit drugs, and anyone who didn't smoke dope or shoot heroin couldn't be a genuine jazz musician. Similarly, there wasn't a protective fence around the airfield, as near as I can recollect. When I was five years old, I was flying a kite in the bright fall sunshine, and the string broke and my kite lazily drifted off and landed gently in the middle of the active runway. I calmly proceeded to walk across Grand Central Parkway, up the berm and onto the runway, and I retrieved my kite, leaving the runway just as a Lockheed Electra was touching down right at the spot I had vacated fifteen seconds earlier. I casually walked back across Grand Central Parkway to my house.

Now, some people had cars in those days, to be sure, but there weren't a lot of them. There's a classic photograph by Henri Cartier-Bresson, taken from an apartment on Riverside Drive in the years just after World War II, a beautifully composed shot in which you can see a long stretch of the Henry Hudson Parkway, and there are only a couple of cars in the photograph. It was the same on the streets in Queens. The traffic was light enough that I could just walk blithely across Grand Central Parkway, up the slope, and onto the active runway, retrieve my kite, and tread back across what is today one of New York's busiest freeways to the steps of our tin hut. The Utica huts are gone and so is easy access to LaGuardia, where these days you are subject to a full body cavity search and confiscation of your toothpaste. Ain't progress grand?

We lived there for a few years, but at the end of the 1940s, New York City completed a vast number of public housing projects, and we moved to a brand-new apartment in Queens. The subsidized projects were filled with veterans and their families getting back on their feet after the war. Our building was on 12th Street in Long Island City, not far from the 59th Street Bridge that connects to Manhattan.

The project in Queens was my physical home, and day trips to

Manhattan landmarks like Broadway and Radio City Music Hall were stimulating to my young imagination, but the streets of Brooklyn remained very much my emotional touchstone. Until she moved to Long Island, I would often visit my aunt in her old Victorian house on Hart Street. When we lived with her, there was a trolley that ran down Tompkins Avenue, and a trip on it cost a nickel. Nickels, by the way, were made of real nickel then, and quarters were silver, and in a bank I once saw a thousand-dollar bill, a year's wages for most people.

Hart Street had the warm, languid atmosphere of the set of *Meet Me in St. Louis*: fragrant sycamore trees, wrought-iron fences, lawns with tulips in the spring, and the clanking trolley line. The street seemed impossibly wide to me then, and almost bucolic, but to adults it undoubtedly looked like what it really was: a crowded, deteriorating inner-city slum, a place for leaving, not living.

Not long after we moved to the housing project in Long Island City, my aunt and uncle left Brooklyn forever and went to Levittown in Westbury, Long Island. It was the first major postwar housing development, hundreds and hundreds of nearly identical Cape Cods in a planned community. They were much smaller than one thousand square feet and cost less than ten thousand dollars, but to men who had spent the Second World War in tiny foxholes and leaky tents, and had lived the immediate postwar years in crowded apartments, these small houses were indeed palaces.

Levittown was a fresh and startling lesion on the body of Nassau County. Fifty-five years ago, Long Island was dominated by the sound of cows, not cars, a green, agricultural land with most of the place planted to potatoes and alfalfa. I used to spend summers with my aunt and uncle in Levittown, a pastoral paradise in stark contrast to the concrete and housing projects of New York City.

But the city had its own charms: the irresistible draw of stickball in the streets and the Brooklyn Dodgers. My neighborhood had its share of Yankee fans and the occasional misguided soul who rooted for the Giants, but *real* baseball aficionados were devotees of the Bums. I used to ride the subway to Ebbets Field, a rickety wooden stadium full of atmosphere but already decrepit. Everything looks big to children, and we are always amazed when, as adults, we view them again. The enormous schoolyard is really just a postage stamp, and the old street that seemed a grand boulevard is barely wide enough for two cars. Ebbets Field looked small to me even then, and if something looks small to you when you're seven years old then it's pretty small.

In the 1950s, the business model of baseball depended on the Reserve Clause, which effectively locked a player into a team until the team got rid of him. Players were assets and were traded pretty much the same way we kids traded baseball cards. As a result, although players made plenty of money by the standards of the average wage-earner, they weren't paid what they were really worth, but instead were treated as property within the narrow confines of an unregulated monopoly. After a game—most were played during the day—many of the players headed straight for their night jobs. Some were car salesmen, and Carl Furillo, the right fielder known as "the Reading Rifle," was an ironworker who would later help to build the World Trade Center.

Without millions of dollars, baseball players often used public transportation, and if we timed it right, we would find ourselves riding to the stadium on the subway with some of them.

We who were born at the very beginning of the baby boom became part of a modern revolution, as everything in America was rapidly changing. Both the Dodgers and the Giants broke our hearts by leaving New York City in a demonstration that nothing is so iconic that it is indispensable to a modern, vibrant community. One of the best indications that the culture was in a state of turmoil was the character of television programs. Variety shows had been the anchor of network programming almost from the beginning, and their popularity was such that they generated the preponderance of revenues for the networks.

One of the longest running and most successful of the multitude of variety programs was *The Ed Sullivan Show* on Sunday night. It was a vaudeville-style hour that premiered in 1948, hosted by Sullivan, a taciturn and stone-faced newspaper columnist who spoke in a deadpan monotone, an unlikely television star. He occasionally attempted, with no success, to inject some emotion into his delivery but could never avoid sounding like an undertaker and looking like a corpse. Misunderstanding the pronunciation of his name, and having rotten hearing anyway, my Greek grandmother was convinced his name was "Ed Solomon." Thus, as far as she was concerned, he was Jewish, and she never missed a show. It's something of an irony that she thought that Walter Winchell, who actually *was* Jewish, was an Irishman.

On Sullivan's show, the music reflected the times. Initially, they were all big-band swing numbers. But in the 1950s, their popularity waned, and they were replaced with revolutionary rock and rollers like Elvis, Buddy Holly, and, eventually and most shockingly, the Beatles. There was no more obvious evidence that the old cultural universe was dead than the appearance of the new music on staid, provincial American television. The world that we had inherited from the victory in World War II had ended, its old culture irreversibly restructured by technology, vast population shifts, a shrinking world, and the flexing muscles of an impatient generation.

———

MY GRANDMOTHER CONTINUED to live in Brooklyn, and I spent many weekends in Williamsburg, hanging out on the block, occasionally playing stoopball, stickball, and kick-the-can with some of the neighborhood kids. The youths in Williamsburg were a decidedly rougher lot than my friends back in Queens, and I think that even the eight-year-olds wore sleeveless T-shirts, had tattoos, and smoked Lucky Strikes and Chesterfield Regulars. And I was fifty years old before I deduced the reason for my regular visits to my grandmother's place: my parents wanted to be alone. Grandparents are extremely useful in this regard. There are few things that alter a marriage more than a first child, and it is a tribute to the omnipotence of nature and to the unquenchable spirit of the human species that anybody has a sibling.

In Greek, the word for grandmother is *yaya*, but we called her "Nona," Godmother, because the kids next door did. My grandmother's apartment was a cavernous place, and today, with Williamsburg being a trendy home to hipsters, artists, and rock stars, it would probably bring millions on the real estate market. It only had one bathroom, as I recall, but it had three bedrooms and twelve-foot ceilings, beautiful plaster moldings everywhere. My father would take my sister and me to Nona's on Friday night and collect us on Sunday night, but not until after we all had watched Ed Solomon.

Nona's father, my great-grandfather, lived with her, and he was always nattily attired in a three-piece suit and spit-shined French-toe oxfords. He sported a huge white beard and kept in shape by walking a couple of miles a day through the neighborhood. He and Nona both took snuff. They snorted it regularly, often together, as if they were performing some religious ritual. They used the good stuff: black, top-grade Latakia, ground to a fine powder for maximum irritating effect. Taking the snuff was followed by repetitive, almost interminable sneezing, and I couldn't understand why they did it, since it clearly made them uncomfortable and not a little irritable. The snuff stained my great-grandfather's mustache an unappealing yellowish brown, but he was otherwise immaculately turned out. He was "Papoo," a slight corruption of the Greek word for grandfather. Papoo was a tough old guy who spoke only a little English. He had been a baker—perhaps even *the* baker—in Ioannina. Nona once told me a story that, after her mother had died in Greece, Papoo heard that there was a dry-goods business for sale in some isolated town in Albania, about seventy difficult miles away. So he packed every item he owned, cinched them to the backs of donkeys, and he, the donkeys, my grandmother, and her sister, Diana, began walking over the steep, forested mountains to Albania. When they got to Albania they were told that the business had already been sold the day before, and without even taking a rest, let alone remaining overnight, Papoo turned everybody around and walked straight back to northwestern Greece. Now, that's one tough guy.

About the time my great-grandfather was ninety-eight years old, my father and Nona called a doctor to the apartment to give the old man a routine checkup. That was back in the days that doctors would still make house calls. The doctor and my great-grandfather retired to the old man's room, closed the door, and ostensibly the physical exam ensued.

My father and Nona waited in the kitchen, and I, about five, wandered around doing cartwheels and jumping on the furniture and generally making a pest of myself. Sometime later, the pair emerged from the bedroom, and Papoo, now fully clothed and looking as classy as always, sat regally on the couch. The doctor went into the kitchen to give them the results of the exam, and I tagged along.

"So?" asked my grandmother.

"Well, he's in remarkable shape," said the doctor. "He has the body of a much younger man. He's very, very healthy. Remarkable, really."

My grandmother said, "You have to tell him to stop drinking raki."

Papoo didn't drink much of it, but like most of the old-timers, he took a nip a few times a day. The doctor had never heard of raki, the Turkish version of ouzo or sambuca, but he understood it was an adult beverage, and I suppose he figured it was like schnapps. So he said that a little alcohol was good for the old man.

My father laughed, saying, "Did you ever *taste* raki?"

And he poured the doctor a little raki in a used *yahrzeit* goblet, a glass in which once burned a candle for the annual remembrance of the dead.

Raki packs one hell of a kick, and the doctor took a tiny taste and screwed his face into a painful grimace. He tried valiantly to avoid spitting out the sweet, fiery liquid and eventually forced it down with a groan and then a deep aspiration in a vain attempt to quench the burgeoning firestorm in his throat. And the one tiny taste convinced him: he would tell Papoo not to drink raki. I followed him back into the parlor, and he sat down next to my great-grandfather.

"So?" asked Papoo, with a menacingly raised eyebrow.

"You shouldn't drink that raki," said the doctor.

Papoo fixed him with a piercing stare and poked his finger repeatedly into the doctor's chest, asking, "How old are you, sonny?"

"I'm sixty-eight," said the doctor.

Still jabbing his finger to emphasize his words, Papoo said, "Well, I'm ninety-eight. And when you get to be *my* age, you can tell me what to do."

The doctor died later that year. Papoo lived to be one hundred.

———

OUR HOUSING PROJECT in Long Island City was populated predominantly by veterans and their families. I played in the streets with kids whose fathers were ditchdiggers, kids whose fathers were doctors, kids whose fathers were rocket scientists. But from another standpoint, we were not very diverse at all. In our neighborhood everyone was either Catholic or Jewish. Italians, Irish, and Slavs— and Jews. In fact, you identified yourself according to what Roman Catholic parish you lived in—even if you were Jewish. For a while I had a Jewish girlfriend who lived far away, on Tremont Avenue in the Bronx. We had met at some party, and she asked, "Where do you live?" and I said, "St. Rita's," and she knew exactly where that was. New York City was full of people from every imaginable background, but when I was young, it felt primarily Catholic and Jewish. During the Feast of San Gennaro, the patron saint of Naples, my whole neighborhood, dozens of square blocks, was cordoned off for the entire week.

I didn't even meet a Protestant until I was eleven years old. He was a red-haired kid named Billy and had some sort of Welsh surname, Thompson or Evans or something like that. He seemed like a nice fellow and had been in the neighborhood for a few days when we were all playing stickball in the street and someone asked him if he was going to St. Rita's.

Billy said that he wasn't and then volunteered that he was a Protestant.

We were all dumbstruck. "What are you talking about?" There must have been a dozen of us looking at each other incredulously, thinking, "Who is this kid? And what the hell is a Protestant?"

So it was a fairly closed society as far as religion was concerned. However, particularly in terms of socioeconomic strata, it was very, very diverse. That would become evident some years later, in the mid-1950s, when people started to disappear to the suburbs. If you made more than a few thousand dollars a year, you were no longer eligible to live in city housing. And so, the professional people began leaving the neighborhood, to New Jersey, to Long Island, to Connecticut, to Westchester, where they bought their first houses. It was something of an irony that the accumulation of even modest wealth began to unravel the tight fabric of this postwar New York society. It was not necessarily bad, but like all neighborhoods mine was changing, and it was never the same again.

I WAS REARED by a mother and father whose parenting objectives were simple and unambiguous: develop seriousness of purpose and a strong sense of responsibility. Even as a small boy I can remember being cautioned never to bring shame on the family. I didn't want people in the neighborhood to think that I was an idiot, or that my father and mother must be idiots because they raised an idiot. In fact, as I was later to see during my tours of Vietnam, this was very much like the Asian concept of "face." Edwin O. Reischauer, the United States ambassador to Japan for many years, once made a cogent distinction between the Japanese and American attitudes toward proper public behavior. Reischauer said that if an American mother is walking down a busy street and has her son tagging along, and he does something wrong, she'll most likely say: "Don't do that. It's the wrong thing to do." But if a Japanese mother sees a child doing wrong, she'll say: "Don't do that because people will laugh at you and lose respect for our family."

Like many Americans of my generation, I was lucky enough to be inculcated with both of those senses of responsibility. We are a nation of laws and not of men, of course, and that's really the glue that keeps everything together, the notion that what we do, for good or ill, has an impact on all of society, on our neighborhoods, our families, on all of us.

The notion was writ large in my Queens neighborhood, and it was enforced by a platoon of women, the mothers of the children. Someone had to be maintaining a duty roster of mothers because a mother was always watching from a window, keeping an eye on what was going on outside. It didn't matter who caught you doing something wrong. If, from her perch at a window on the fifth floor, Peter Delvecchio's mother yelled at you, "Jack Jacobs, knock it off," you knocked it off, even if your name wasn't Jack Jacobs.

It was unfortunate, though, that my sense of responsibility took some years to develop, and I was at best a difficult, recalcitrant, and recidivist inmate of the prison of childhood.

DESPITE THE CULTURAL imperatives that governed behavior, they were unwritten and largely open to both interpretation and the effects of a rapidly changing society. And of course, we're always at the mercy of our own personalities. Since I was something of an undisciplined character, I was always pushing the envelope of deportment, particularly in school. My idea of having a good time was to get the other children to laugh, and since I was often bored, I spent most of my time in this disruptive endeavor. As you can imagine, I made life extremely difficult for my teachers, not so much because I was causing the other children to be disruptive but because the general atmosphere of school was one of unbending discipline, and I was antithetical to the ultimate goal of complete uniformity. The teachers both created the environment and were its enforcers. Almost all of them came from very structured, traditional European, often Italian, backgrounds and were uncompromising sticklers for adherence to rules. Some had been nuns in teaching orders in the 1920s, had left the Church but stayed in education, and then married in the 1940s. Some had lost their husbands in the war, wore black dresses, and became even more humorless. To them, nothing was funny, which was unfortunate since they encountered in me a rambunctious child to whom *everything* was funny. In a battle of wits I was a contender, but they had the upper hand, and so I won emotional victories but got my ears boxed just often enough to keep me from becoming the grade-school equivalent of Leon Trotsky.

Fifty-five years ago, there was no attempt to align the work to the potential of the student, and so every child performed the same tasks and was given the same amount of time to accomplish them. Furthermore, a lesson was not completed until the last child had done his work or the allotted time—always too long by a factor of about a hundred—had elapsed. We'd get an arithmetic or English assignment that was supposed to take thirty minutes, and I'd do it in twenty seconds and then spend the rest of the half hour goofing off, shooting spitballs, and making snide remarks to my neighbors

while they tried to complete the assignment. Much to my teachers'
chagrin, our desks all had inkwells and girls really did have pigtails,
providing me with the ingredients for further immature behavior. I
knew I was supposed to act more responsibly, of course, but I was a
bit like the fat man who goes to the supermarket when he's hungry
and buys a cartload of Twinkies. He can't help himself, and neither
could I.

I was the subject of frequent, almost continuous, corrective action,
often forced to stand in a corner, which was more boring than the
assignment and consequently propelled me to even greater indisci-
pline. Given the opportunity to hone my skills in the corner, I eventually developed a repertoire of random and annoying noises, most of
them scatological. Trips to the principal's office gave me an opportunity to practice my art as an actor, feigning contrition, seriousness,
and dedication to the unwritten rules of an intellectually strangulated
educational community. These sessions produced a desired effect that
didn't last, and in a few weeks I was again apologizing for some indis-
cretion that I honestly believed was the funniest thing anyone had
ever devised. I harbored the notion of being a research scientist, but a
funny one, a Werner Heisenberg who did shtick.

Because of my antics, my teachers at Public School 83, unable
to effect any long-lasting improvement in my deportment, tried to
enlist my parents in improving my behavior and often sent them letters describing in exquisite detail my most recent misdeeds. I remember one particular letter that was sent by my fourth grade teacher,
Mrs. Savino. She apparently didn't trust me with the envelope and
put it in the mail instead. I can't recall what I had done wrong. When
I got home my mother shoved the letter under my nose. The note
began,

Dear Mr. and Mrs. Jacobs,
Today was the last straw—

—and that is absolutely the last thing I remember, since my mother commenced to administer what the teachers legally could not: a professionally executed right cross. I'm not a fan of corporal punishment, but I must admit that I deserved every licking I got—and also quite a few I never received.

———

WITHOUT WANTING TO, and despite my efforts to avoid it, I never failed to give my long-suffering parents a very hard time. When I was young, I refused to eat anything, and they were worried about my health constantly. My parents tried everything, without much success, and eventually they took me to a doctor who prescribed a diet that consisted principally of heavy sweet cream. This didn't work and resulted solely in the deposit of life-threatening plaque in my coronary arteries.

And I wouldn't sleep either. My mother claimed that it was because I didn't want to miss anything and that I would fall asleep with my right thumb in my mouth and the adjacent index finger holding my eyelid open. Six decades later, one is motivated to stay awake as long as possible, as each day becomes an increasingly larger percentage of the time that's remaining. There will be plenty of time to sleep.

———

I LEARNED EARLY TO enjoy the gift of being small, invariably the shortest person in the class and even shorter than the girls.

When I decided to join the Army, some friends suggested that a military career was more suited for large, beefy men, troglodytes with sagittal crests whose intellectual qualities were secondary to their physical strength. There was a general misapprehension that being a soldier required the ability to bench-press a Buick but to have great difficulty performing simple arithmetic operations, that physical strength and mental acuity were mutually exclusive.

But the physics of anatomy say otherwise. Small animals possess strength way out of proportion to their physical size, and I could always do more pull-ups, push-ups, and sit-ups than everybody else, at least partially because there is so little mass to move around. I use very few resources and thus leave a tiny carbon footprint. And how much legroom do I really need? To me, the middle seat in the last row of economy feels like first class. It is easy to be ignored, overlooked, and dismissed as irrelevant, all extremely useful in many circumstances.

Perhaps the best thing about being small is that in combat, where safety and survival are often the result of blind luck, large objects such as former offensive tackles are at a huge disadvantage. When the bullets and shrapnel start flying around, everybody tries to become as small as possible, and being half the size of a standard human being confers qualities that are difficult to appreciate until the situation makes them glaringly obvious.

CHAPTER THREE

WHEN WE MOVED from Long Island City to New Jersey in the mid-1950s, it was a major inflection point, not just for our family but for the country as a whole. The economy was expanding, and there was a hopefulness that came of a growing economic franchise that managed to survive the inevitable cyclical recessions. Although we were under the constant nuclear threat from the Soviet Union, neither the prospect of an attack nor its hideous consequences made any impression on us. Regularly, we practiced diving under our desks, which the authorities hoped we would instinctively do when we actually got nuked. Even at the time, it was difficult to envision how the old oak desk would protect against massive overpressure and enough radiation to sauté the entire student body. Still, the drill was a bizarre but pleasant respite from the dreary routine of class work, of listening to functional illiterates attempt to read, for example, which possessed some mild amusement value but quickly lost its allure.

By the time I was nine, my father was making three thousand dollars a year, which wasn't a lot of money even back then, but it was sufficient to render us ineligible for public housing. So we were effectively thrown out of the projects, but if people like us were being ejected from public housing, then there were clearly families in worse circumstances.

In a classic demonstration of the law of unintended consequences, it was the GI Bill that had been the engine driving change. It's hard for us as a nation to remember this, but at one point during the 1940s this country had nearly nineteen million young people in uniform, and by war's end we had almost fourteen million Americans who were suddenly being mustered out of the service. And they were all rushing into the weak economy of a country in debt. The workplace that had been dominated by defense manufacturing during the war was, perforce, going to shrink, and there would be no work for the large majority of returning veterans. Millions would swell the rolls of the unemployed, and the economy, unable to cope, would plummet again into a depression. Neither the economic nor the political consequences of the situation could be risked, and something had to be done to delay or prevent certain catastrophe.

The Truman administration is often given credit for the GI Bill, but it was actually the idea of Warren H. Atherton, a California Republican and a consultant to President Roosevelt's secretary of war. His brilliant concept became the Servicemen's Readjustment Act of 1944, and it was the last bit of Roosevelt-era New Deal legislation. The law enabled returning GIs to go to institutes and universities, thus keeping them occupied and off the unemployment rolls. It wasn't cheap, but the government could always print more money, and the negative effect of doing so was calculated to be far less deleterious than the alternative.

So what happened? The program had its desired effect. Averted were the likelihood of millions of unemployed and the dire possibility that a nation that had won the war would be destroyed by the peace. And there was another, unexpected and joyous result. The

American generation that had fought to save the world from fascism became the best-educated cohort in history, and when the veterans were graduated from school they fueled an economic boom never before experienced by any country in the world.

And the results were magnified further by another crucial provision of the GI Bill, one that granted low-interest, zero-down-payment home loans for these veterans. This enabled Americans to own their own homes, and suddenly millions of ex-servicemen's families—families like ours—were being propelled into a genuine middle class that was born during the early days of the automobile and grew to maturity in a great exodus from the traditional urban centers.

———————

NOBODY CAN FORGET his first car. Ours was a 1933 Chevy, which cost less than five hundred dollars when it was new, a fortune during the Depression and the equivalent of more than sixty thousand in today's money. It had an unsophisticated flat-head six-cylinder engine that generated a wimpy sixty horsepower, but it had a running board, and it was the running board that entranced me. I fell in love with that automobile and named her Myrtle. When Myrtle finally crapped out, my father bought a 1941 Plymouth that had been an army staff car, inexpertly painted flat gray with what must have been a four-inch brush. To me, it was ugly and utilitarian, a repulsive and unromantic memento of the 1940s and the period's artlessness. Worse yet, it didn't have a running board, and I flatly refused to ride in it. I wasn't going to ride in anything except Myrtle, and my parents had to drag me kicking and screaming into the car. I eventually got used to the idea that good old Myrtle wasn't coming back, because by the time we moved out of Queens in 1955, we already had an even newer used car, a powder-blue 1951 four-door Nash Statesman. This car should have been a teenager's dream, because although it looked like an inverted bathtub and had the acceleration of a wheelchair, the seats reclined to produce a queen-size bed.

We moved from the projects to Woodbridge, New Jersey, where my parents bought a house for $15,990. It was a neighborhood of new tract houses, thousands upon thousands of them, as in Levittown, and it was one of the first large postwar suburbs that were built in New Jersey.

I arrived in Woodbridge just in time to start sixth grade. My teacher was Mr. Valentine, and I was astounded by the revelation that he had six children. Back in Queens, I'd never heard of, let alone met, an adult who had so many children. During the war, people couldn't afford (and also had the capability to avoid) having six children. New York City was a modern place, and having six children was something that occurred only among those who were insufficiently cosmopolitan to ignore the more inconvenient aspects of strict Jewish or Catholic dictates, or else lived in benighted locations, far from New York, where the denizens could not grasp the relationship between sex and childbirth. I found having six children mindboggling, but Mr.Valentine was merely a devout Catholic. He was a dedicated, motivating instructor, with the physique of a marathon runner, and he wore rimless glasses with octagonal lenses that made him look both studious and forbiddingly stern. When he was disappointed with my performance, he would peer wordlessly over the top of his glasses, and that would be sufficient to alter my behavior and cause me to reconsider my answer. But he must also have had the capability to be an acceptably stultifying bureaucrat, because I understand that he eventually became a school principal.

Another thing that astonished me was the age of some of my classmates. In sixth grade, for example, there was one large, hirsute character, I think named John or something equally unimaginative, who had been left back so many times that he was on the verge of turning sixteen, the age of consent after which he couldn't be kept in school against his will. John was a hulking man-child, maybe six feet tall and a rawboned 175 pounds. He shaved daily and had an Adam's apple, a two-digit IQ, and a grubby-looking girlfriend who wore his ring on a chain around her neck. Alas, the chain collected an unsavory amalgam of sebum, dirt, and dead skin cells, and, like Cyrano's nose, riveted one's unflinching gaze. John drove a car to school every day. To sixth grade.

I entered Woodbridge High School in 1958. We listened to hits by Bill Haley and the Comets, Chuck Berry, and Fats Domino on WABC radio. Most of the girls wore black ballet slippers and swirling gray felt skirts with pink poodle appliqués. The more lascivious among them, the ones you knew were almost certainly going to be pregnant at graduation, wore supertight straight skirts and Orlon sweaters that showed off their Kleenex-filled brassieres to great visual advantage. They invariably went steady with loutish goofballs.

Our high school had been recently constructed, but it was already reeling under the onslaught of twice as many students as it could handle, the effects of the baby boom, the robust economy, and urban exodus. So we had to go to class in shifts: juniors and seniors 7:30 a.m. to noon, freshmen and sophomores noon to 5:00 p.m. Four thousand students went to Woodbridge High. When noon arrived, the majority of the upperclassmen noisily boarded the buses that had just delivered the afternoon shift and went home. Students with cars peeled out of the parking lot, blasting rock 'n roll, and screeched to a halt at the Carvel stand, just yards from the high school entrance. The whole noisy trip took maybe twenty seconds.

And what cars they were! One of my friends had a deep purple '48 Mercury, chopped, channeled, decked, and lowered, with bubble skirts and a continental kit. Another pal had a white, slab-sided four-door Lincoln convertible, the model on which the doors opened from the center; the seats were posh red vinyl. Another friend had a '53 Corvette, the first model, in mandatory red and white livery. The engine was something of an afterthought and was embarrassingly underpowered, and it leaked more gasoline than it consumed. But it was new and rare and a hot-looking car, and all the girls swooned over both it and its owner, a massively overweight sixteen-year-old who was nonetheless the school's most popular kid solely because of his Corvette.

We'd hang out, inexpertly singing a cappella doo-wop, procrastinating doing homework, speaking mostly unintelligible gibberish. Near the end of the afternoon, the guys with cars went to work (they all needed jobs to pay for the wheels), and I headed back to the school to do homework and research, finally returning home on the afternoon bus. In winter, I was never home in daylight.

I had friends on both sides of the scholastic divide and was something of an anomaly. Some of my closest pals avoided lengthy incarceration or reform school only through incredible luck or creative alibi, while others achieved scores of 1600 on the SATs and became successful lawyers and brilliant surgeons.

Finding time for sports was nearly impossible, since I wasted so much of it, and so I never exerted myself adequately to become a proper athlete. But I loved running. I was transfixed by the concept of running, by the idea that you could keep running as long as you wanted to, and that slow, lumbering adversaries would ultimately collapse in ungainly and embarrassing heaps, sweating, panting, uselessly inert. Perhaps it was the inchoate concept of escaping from predators that interested me. In any case, somebody my size and build had the potential to be a great distance runner, but there were no great distances to run in high school, and I was dedicated mostly to constructing rude innuendos and improper suggestions and not to the hard work it would take to be good at organized athletics. Later, in the Army, I discovered that I could run enormous distances such as marathons, relatively fast, but as in most of my endeavors I never pursued it sufficiently to reach my potential. Maybe next year.

In addition to track, I loved boxing, and I was at least as good a fighter as I was a runner. I blossomed into a decent amateur featherweight, at 112 pounds, and every few days I'd train and spar, and if I

happened to get a black eye I'd tell my mother that I fell, or that Pau-
lie Pastafagioli and I got into a tiff, but everything was now okay. A
long time ago, back in the 1920s and 1930s, boxing had been a sport
dominated by legendary Jewish champions like Benny Leonard, Bar-
ney Ross, and Ruby Goldstein, but by the 1950s, at least in New
York and New Jersey, the fight game was mostly an Italian scene.
Still, the shoddy but delicate spectacle transfixed me.

I was blessed with some natural characteristics. I was very quick,
had good footwork and fast hands, and, though I didn't pack a heavy
punch, it never bothered me to go toe-to-toe and trade right hands
with an opponent, even if he was much bigger than I. If he surged
toward me like a scaled-down Rocky Marciano, I didn't mind getting
pounded, because I was a pretty effective counterpuncher and I usually gave better than I got. Boxing then still had some of the glowing
aura of its halcyon days, and many adults really took to Muhammad
Ali when he first came to prominence as Cassius Clay. Big and strong
as he was, they saw in him a throwback to the master boxers, surgical technicians like Benny Leonard and Sugar Ray Robinson. Enthusiasm for boxing had some element of nostalgia for the old, simpler
days. The world was changing, but even the novelty of Cassius Clay
was enough to stop time.

For my buddies and me, the trip to the gym was a male rite of passage. You learned the jab, the right cross, the left hook, and the footwork, and if you got proficient enough, you got booked for amateur
bouts: three-minute rounds, two minutes apart. Now, if you've never
boxed, you cannot understand how excruciating it is just to hold your
hands up for three minutes, let alone stick and move around the ring
with any degree of skill. I'm grateful for the sweet science. It gave me
enormous confidence and not a little audacity, and many years later
it would prove to be very useful when I was in the Army, at Fort Ord,
California.

I probably would have developed into a better athlete had I not also
had so many other interests, but academically I finished fourteenth in a

high school class of about nine hundred, more a testament to efficiency than to intelligence or even scholarship. Many of my classmates were genuinely brilliant, and four of them in particular were close friends who wrote for the high school's literary magazine. In English class, we had been studying modern and contemporary poetry for some time and were generally unimpressed with the genres. Poetry appeared to us to be a refuge either for people with a terminal case of irrelevance or those with an inability to write complete sentences. One afternoon, we thought it would be a jolly jape if we wrote some nonsense poetry, not unlike the rubbish we had been studying, and submitted it to the literary magazine for publication.

We quickly generated some ridiculous doggerel that sounded just sophisticated enough to be something other than pure trash. But it *was* pure trash, and we were worried about the reaction of our English teacher, Miss Baum, who was the magazine's faculty adviser and a notoriously serious person. She was a sturdy woman who had been graduated from Misericordia, a college of the Sisters of Mercy, and I assumed that attendance there required both penury and chastity of its students, at the time all women. We feared she would hold us accountable for being outrageously satiric if we used our real names, and so we devised a nom de plume for the piece: Q. Peaux Etune. Miss Baum was dogged in the way that only Ahab, detectives, crazed fanatics, and those trained at Misericordia can be, and she eventually figured it out. She was not amused.

Of the five of us, four were Jewish and one was not. The Q stood for *quatre*, "four." *Peaux* is French for "skins." And by *Etune* we really meant *et une*, "and one." Foreskins plus one. That was our great witticism, supremely silly and sophomoric, but it is a tribute to our lack of development that the five of us gather from time to time, over forty-five years later, and still find our cleverness and the episode an example of avant-garde brilliance.

CHAPTER FOUR

NOTWITHSTANDING THE OCCASIONAL attitude adjustment administered by my mother, my parents gave me wide latitude in my social life
primarily because, despite my immature classroom shenanigans, they
never had to tell me to work hard. I always managed to achieve very
good grades and was embarrassed and disappointed when I received
something other than a top mark. When I didn't perform particularly well, it was difficult to make excuses, since it was obvious to
even the most casual observer that I was to blame for the shortcoming. I found others' explanations—that Mike left his homework at the
prison where he was visiting his brother, that Brenda's mother had
died again—possessed of a certain creative merit, but not for me.

My decision to attend Rutgers University was a function of several factors. For one thing, it was a fine school, founded in 1766 and
academically the equal of many more prestigious institutions, but it
was not so selective that acceptance required recommendations from
Albert Einstein and George Washington. For another, as a state university, it had the advantage of costing only two hundred dollars a
semester. This was not very much money even in 1962, when you

NEWARK PUBLIC LIBRARY
121 HIGH ST.
NEWARK, NY 14513

could still buy a car for two hundred dollars, although it was often in poor shape, the body consisting of more putty than steel and the engine consuming more motor oil than gasoline.

Rutgers had an early admissions program, and this suited me, since acceptance would obviate the necessity to fill out more than one application. Applying to one school was tedious enough, but anyone with his eye on several universities was destined to be enslaved by the labor-intensive, pedestrian, dehumanizing process. Because no two applications were even remotely similar, it took a herculean effort and a pathological attention to detail to complete a number of applications. Only those who possessed a stultifying fastidiousness could hope to complete multiple applications that didn't look like they were dashed off by someone who hadn't completed grade school. It actually took less effort to earn a degree than to apply in the first place, and with little patience to spare, I just applied to Rutgers, hoped for the best, and resolved that if I was rejected I would instead lead the louche life of an artist or a writer. So I applied to Rutgers, was accepted, and, unlike my high school classmates, spent no time driving myself crazy with worry and anticipation. I thus learned the important axiom that even difficult problems often have uncomplicated solutions.

That fall, when I got to the Rutgers campus in New Brunswick, I was shocked by how different it was from high school. I started out in chemical engineering, but I discovered after a semester or two that it wasn't for me. I was interested in the subject matter, but the course work required a high level of commitment to rote and a capacious and easily recalled memory, neither of which I possessed. I was a lover and a poet, not an engineer. Among other things, freshmen in the College of Engineering were required to take a five-credit calculus course, which consisted of an hour and fifteen minutes, every day, five times a week. To my dismay, the instructor I drew was the head of the math department, and his classroom had blackboards very nearly around the entire perimeter. Try to envision this: the professor wordlessly entered the room, grabbed a piece of chalk, and started writing equations. And he'd silently write equations, unintelligible to me, on each succeeding blackboard, all around the room. When, an hour and fifteen minutes later, he arrived at that point where he had entered and had completed the circuit, he'd merely leave, never having said a word. I fell behind quickly and never recovered.

To be an engineer you also had to take two-credit physics. Now, physics is not all that difficult, and because it was only two credits, there were only two forty-minute periods a week and no lab work. I couldn't envision what one would do in a lab of a basic physics course anyway. Drop stuff and see if it breaks? Heat water and verify that it boils? These are things that previous generations determined with little experimentation and even less lab work. Given that most of the knowledge was for all intents and purposes intuitive, I managed a satisfactory grade in physics, but if I was surprised about one thing, it was the amount of work that was required of me on my own.

In my freshman year, I lived on the third floor of a dormitory, in a garret about the size of a broom closet, with a roommate who claimed that he was a direct descendant of William of Orange, whose statue dominates the Rutgers campus. It didn't do him any good, however, and he made it through one year and then disappeared, never to be heard from again. There was a three-man room on the floor below, and its denizens, an odd assortment, became my friends for the short time they attended Rutgers. One of them looked exactly like John Lennon. He was a very pleasant chap, and he played the guitar, too, but he possessed no creativity or talent of any kind and thus in all important respects was nothing at all like John Lennon. He, too, was gone before the end of the academic year. One of his roommates majored in English, but he had no clear understanding of literature generally, which was something of a handicap. Like most people, he found *Paradise Lost* to be an impermeable bore, but he also had trouble with simple declarative sentences, and this proved to be a fatal intellectual deficiency. After spending a few months drinking beer he also departed, becoming, it is said, a policeman. The third guy was absolutely brilliant but had no discipline whatsoever, was drunk most of the time, and finally got thrown out of school before the end of freshman year, having failed every subject. At least he was consistent, but he was a disappointing waste of talent, smarter than all of us combined. There's always the possibility that he finally discovered his forte elsewhere and has since invented the Internet.

Another member of this friendly, underachieving mob was a fellow named Al Tannenbaum. J. D. Salinger was all the rage then, and his *Nine Stories* contains one called "Down at the Dinghy," in which the protagonist is an odd woman named Beatrice Tannenbaum. She was known by everyone as "Boo Boo," and so was Al. He despised it, of course, but the groundswell of opinion could not be stanched, and Boo Boo he was until he, too, left Rutgers, chucked out by an insensitive and humorless administration that found no redeeming value in Boo Boo's pranks and misadventures.

Alone among us, I was graduated in four years, but Boo Boo—now resurrected as Al—reapplied and ultimately earned a degree in philosophy. Spinoza and Locke seem like odd training for it, but they evidently prepared Al very well for his career as an award-winning photographer, with covers on *Time* and *Newsweek*. A few years ago, I saw him again for the first time in almost four decades, and he hadn't aged a bit, although this is not necessarily as attractive as it sounds, since in college Al already looked like he was sixty years old.

———————

THE SUMMER BEFORE I got to New Brunswick I decided to enroll in the Reserve Officers' Training Corps. Rutgers had sent me an information packet, which I read voraciously and in an almost euphoric state, preplanning my whole four years, deciding that I would eventually take Seminar in Advanced Polymorphous Materials, Synthesis of Dimethyltetraethylyglucosamine 101, and so on. I was going to have an absolute blast becoming a chemical engineer. It was a bit like the mental process people employ when they buy lottery tickets. The chances of winning approach zero, but a ticket is a cheap thrill, and the higher the jackpot the more value one gets from squandering the dollar. There are few things that generate more dopamine in the brain than daydreaming about buying everything you've always wanted and realizing that you'll still have a hundred million dollars left over.

And the Rutgers packet included a pamphlet on ROTC. The program was an elective, no longer mandatory as it had been for decades, but there were two things that motivated me to join. First, we were only seventeen years removed from the end of the Second World War, and the notion was powerful in me that everyone had an obligation to make some contribution to the defense of the Republic. Second, after two years in the program, you began receiving a small stipend: twenty-seven dollars per month. Now, this wasn't a lot of money even in those days, but it was more than zero dollars per month, and it was from an employer who would never miss a payday and was disinclined to fire you. For some students, the disadvantage of having to spend two years in the Army after graduation was sufficient motivation to quit the program, but for those of us who found military service to be an honorable endeavor, getting even paltry wages was a magnificent bonus.

This was 1962, and the prospect of having to fight seemed vanishingly small. The United States may have had a few advisers in Vietnam, but we students certainly didn't know about it, and, despite the highly publicized defeat of the French there only a few years before, many people would have been hard-pressed to find the place on a map. Indeed, few people, including the national leadership, had much of an idea about how one should employ the military instrument of power, save in a total war like World War II in which the strategic objective was the unconditional surrender of the enemy. If recent events are any indication, not much has changed in forty-five years.

Only two months after arriving at Rutgers, however, we got our introduction to the real world. The entire population of the dormitory crammed into the basement and in front of the only television in the place to watch President Kennedy as he announced that unless the Soviet Union removed its missiles from Cuba, we would destroy them, and that we had already begun blockading the island. All of us were convinced that we were going to war. We had seen Khrushchev on television, pounding his shoe on a podium and vowing to bury the United States, and it was clear that he was a mental case in the tradition of Stalin and similar unhinged dictators. In our judgment, he thought he had nothing to lose, and it is often the best policy not to contend with such maniacs unless their absolute destruction is the objective.

But such was our lack of sophistication that this trepidation did not translate into a fully baked scenario that made any sense. We didn't think about a nuclear exchange, about the deaths of our friends and families, about the extermination of the human race. We had a vague and immature view that we were going to be inducted into the Army the very next day, and after some perfunctory weapons training we were going to invade Cuba and perhaps physically dismantle the missiles, with simple hand tools, we deduced.

But perhaps because he wasn't the lunatic we thought he was, Khrushchev backed down and took the missiles out of Cuba, and that was the end of the crisis. The sending of thousands of American troops to Vietnam in the succeeding years seemed to us like a natural concomitant of that defining event in 1962, and it was astonishing how inexorably things snowballed during my college years. By the time I was commissioned in the Army four years later, we had already been significantly involved in Vietnam for two years. I was eventually to go to Vietnam, as was everybody else who believed that their citizenship carried the obligation of service and that twenty-seven dollars per month was quite a bit of money.

———

WE SUFFERED THROUGH ROTC drill on Wednesdays. It was quite a sight to see 1,500 students marching in a park near the campus, but the exercise didn't produce anything other than groups of college students who could assemble themselves into ragged units of breathtakingly poor marching skill. The disutility of such activities remained with me, and I never enjoyed participating in parades and don't much care to watch them, either. Properly conducted, to some people a parade can be an exciting thing to watch, but the same can be said for an autopsy.

We spent a good amount of class time on military history, and that had positive value of some consequence, but it did dawn on me that many battles, campaigns, and wars contained the same lessons. This resulted in two conclusions. First, there seemed to be a relatively small and finite number of inexorable military truths, universal constants whose mastery should form the basis for success in nearly every combat situation. And second, because all this stuff was a matter of public and historical record, there is no earthly reason to make the same mistake twice. My early naïveté was clearly boundless.

The military professors were active-duty Army officers, captains mostly, who were assigned to ROTC for tours of three years. Some of them were of dubious utility, with marginal qualities of leadership, but the majority of them possessed impressive powers of intellect and a low threshold of pain for foolishness. These people had a mature take on life and were an important additive to the proper and thorough liberal education I was receiving. These were educated men, easy to approach and free with their wit and cynicism. It was from them that I learned the wisdom of Santayana's observation that skepticism is the chastity of the intellect, and that it is shameful to surrender it too soon.

———————

A PERSUASIVE ARGUMENT can be made to restrict marriage to people over the age of eighty-five, and having been married at eighteen I am powerfully qualified to make the argument. By my sophomore year, I ceased to have a social life at Rutgers, spending what little spare time I had working to support a wife and a daughter. This lifestyle teaches great lessons of discipline and restraint, but it is otherwise not recommended. The experience led to my advising my children to resist the temptation to get married at an early age and instead to search for the ideal spouse, one who is both incredibly rich and incurably ill.

When I got married, I left the old gang at the dormitory and moved into married student housing across the river in Piscataway. As Yogi Berra said, it was déjà vu all over again: these were exactly the same kind of quarters as my family's Utica hut, where we had lived just after World War II, and it came completely equipped with an identical recalcitrant kerosene space heater.

I was scrambling to make ends meet, going to school full-time and always holding down at least one full-time job and sometimes two part-time ones as well. For years I worked nights as a broiler chef. But I also was a door-to-door salesman, pitching everything from magazine subscriptions to kitchen utensils, delivered furniture, and spent time in a slaughterhouse. At the time, the long-term value of my diverse employment was not evident, but the principal utility of living like this is that one develops many different skills, some of them useful. If you need a calf butchered and the pieces of the disassembled animal sold door-to-door, I'm your man. And call me first if you've thrown your brother-in-law out of the house and you need help muscling his stained, threadbare couch down the stairs and to the toxic waste dump.

By my senior year in 1966, my life had become almost intolerably hectic and disorganized, and I hadn't given much thought about what I was going to do for a career, how I was going to employ my political science degree, which now didn't seem as useful as my ability with a skinning knife. When I was nearing graduation day in June, I realized that I desperately needed a job. I was about to receive a commission in the Army Reserve, but I was not slated to report for active duty until the following year. So I approached the senior ROTC instructor, the professor of military science. He was an ancient, white-haired colonel who, as near as I could determine, had fought in the Revolution.

"Sir, I really need to come into the Army right now," I said. "Not next year. I need to come in right away."

He said I could enter active duty immediately, commissioned as a second lieutenant, but I'd have to be a Regular Army officer, and that entailed being committed to three years of active duty, not two years. But when you're a kid, what difference does it make? Two years, three years, three million years—it's all the same. To a twenty-one-year-old, time is irrelevant. It disappears over the horizon to infinity, and you don't have an appreciation for time until you get to be old. Because they are afraid they'll never wake up, old people often don't sleep well at night, and they know that you can cheat the Angel of Death by taking short naps in the daytime, when the Angel of Death is ostensibly occupied in China, where it's nighttime. But at the age of twenty-one, you're going to live forever, and you can sleep all day if you want to.

When you have nearly completed the ROTC program and are approaching graduation and commissioning, you request a specific branch assignment. There are many occupational specialties whose smooth integration into the whole of the Army produces the well-oiled military machine we know well. Soldiers and contractors have to get paid, and so there is a Finance Corps. The Army is a large bureaucracy, there is plenty of paperwork to do, and so some officers join the Adjutant General's Corps. The Army can't fight without supplies, and so the Quartermaster Corps is critical to combat success. Indeed, among many of my brethren in ROTC, the large majority of them selected noncombat branches, almost certainly because for some of them these administrative specialties afforded far less chance of becoming a casualty. Let's face it: some people talk a convincing game, but they shrink at the point of decision, when, in the harsh glare of sunlight, the consequences of their selected course of action appear overloaded with personal danger. This does not make them bad people, but it is instructive of the axiom that you should believe half of what you read and none of what you hear.

The essence of the Army is the infantry and so it was my first choice. To me, it made little sense to be in anything else. My second choice was armor, but I had enough trouble keeping my beat-up Volkswagen running and was not too keen on the prospect of all the maintenance. And in any case, although a tank afforded lots of battlefield protection against small arms, climbing into one would immediately turn me into a gigantic, sixty-ton target, much easier to hit and destroy. No, I'd rather take my chances scooting around the battlefield, protected only by a thin shirt and an insubstantial helmet made of recycled tuna cans.

With so many people avoiding the opportunity to get shot at, you would think that the Army would leap at the chance to thrust a young idealist like me into the fray as quickly as possible. You would be wrong. As if to demonstrate at the very outset that neither logic nor empathy were strong suits in the Army decision-making apparatus, I was selected to be commissioned in the Transportation Corps. Beginning what would become twenty years of dynamic tension and a difficult relationship with the Army, I announced that I was not going to take the oath unless I was commissioned in the infantry. Having learned its lesson, that it was dealing with someone who could charitably be described as single-minded, the Army relented, and on the first of June 1966, I was commissioned a Second Lieutenant of Infantry.

The Army also gave me my first choice of assignment, the 82nd Airborne Division, based at Fort Bragg, North Carolina. Although the 82nd was the preferred unit for many people because it was, and still is, an elite, spirited organization with a proud combat history, sadly it was money that motivated me the most here, too. A new lieutenant earned a bit over $200 per month, but jump pay was an additional $110 monthly. It did not take a certified public accountant to calculate that jumping out of airplanes provided me an instant 50 percent increase in salary. The realization that gravity did almost all the work made the whole thing that much more appealing. While it's exhilarating, the act of jumping out of a military airplane and landing without injury is actually quite uncomplicated and can be learned relatively easily. By the time I had been a paratrooper for less than a year, my daughter had a new brother, I now had four mouths to feed, and the decision to jump for dollars appeared to be even wiser than I had originally calculated.

ONCE I HAD accepted the commission, my toughest task was still ahead: telling my parents. The difficulty lay not merely in telling them that I was going to dedicate myself to military service for the next three years. Indeed, the concept of serving the community in some fashion was deeply ingrained in Judaism and in my family. During the war, my father had done his bit, and although he found neither the vermin-infested wilds of the Pacific Theater nor the prospect of being killed in action to have any lingering attractiveness, he did harbor the common patriotism that swept the country when times were difficult. No, the objection was guaranteed to be a superficial one, but it promised to be deeply felt anyway. I drove the half hour to their house, asked them to sit down at the kitchen table, and then told them that I was not going to law school or to get a degree in accounting. I was going to spend the next three years in the Army, and I was guaranteed to fight in Vietnam.

What seemed like a long and painful silence probably lasted only a few, fleeting seconds.

"Are you out of your mind?" asked my father.

"Are you out of your mind?" asked my mother, as if my father hadn't already broached the possibility. Perhaps the shock of it had rendered her deaf.

"You must be out of your mind," she said. Evidently, I was not required to answer. And it also seemed that being out of one's mind was a state that someone out of his mind could easily recognize. "Why, yes," I guess I was expected to say. "I *am* out of my mind. How kind of you to notice. May I have some more coffee, please?"

And from their point of view, there was something seriously wrong with a bright young boy who could have become almost anything admirable and remunerative, say a banker, and instead chose to sleep in the rain and make no money and get shot when he wasn't required to do so. Without a general mobilization, it made no sense for me to be a soldier, and almost anything else was preferable. Hard at work was a deep ambivalence about being a soldier.

On the one hand, service, particularly military service in aid of countrymen, was something of a Jewish commandment, an obligation to one's fellow man. There is nothing more important than contributing in some way to the community as a whole, and in perilous times that meant its defense. During World War II, over half a million Jews served in the American armed forces, more than fifty thousand of them becoming casualties.

On the other hand, there was something of a deep-seated, subconscious, and persistent mistrust of any military establishment, since it had figured so heavily as an instrument of Jewish misery. In Eastern Europe during the reign of the czars, Jews had been forced into the indefinite service of a people who were murderously anti-Semitic, and they were the subject of isolation, ostracism, and periodic genocide. And in the memory of many Americans still alive today, almost the entirety of European Jewry had been exterminated by the Germans by using the efficiency of its military machine. It's not surprising, therefore, that people who had proudly and bravely served the United

States would be less than enthusiastic about military service at a time when it was optional, when the barbarians were not at the gate.

There was something else at work in forming the prevalent attitude, and it was typical of immigrants generally. In this new land, Jews had surmounted the obstacles faced by all immigrants and had prospered, through education, through hard work, through sacrifice. Long hours, low pay, and little opportunity were every immigrant's lot. Now, just two generations later, with every opportunity open to me, I chose to be a soldier?

I was staring down at the kitchen table, trying desperately to avoid my parents' disappointed eyes, and then, courageous at last, I looked up at them, and their faces had that sad, shocked expression that said they would have preferred I become a trash collector, or a grave digger, or a Catholic. No, I was supposed to be a banker, and it was something of an irony that, when I called twenty years later to say that I was going to retire from the Army to become a banker, my parents were horrified, saying that I had to be out of my mind to leave the Army, where I had such a good career.

CHAPTER FIVE

To BE OF any military use whatsoever, newly commissioned officers must undergo further training. During the previous four years,
my instruction had consisted of some military history; eight weeks
of basic training at Fort Devens, Massachusetts, in the summer
between my junior and senior years of college; and lots of marching.
All the marching would have been useful if it were still the eighteenth
century, when the primary military tactic was to advance and fire
in large and regular formations until most soldiers were slaughtered
and the survivors, if any, ran away. In the modern Army, the idea
behind marching is that, among other things, it teaches some measure of discipline, which I suppose it does, but it mostly taught me to
loathe marching.

Although training at Fort Devens the year before my commissioning required some drill, it was perfunctory and used almost
solely as a method to move my unit from one training site to another,
or to the mess hall, or to and from church. I had always believed
that organized religion provided not only a philosophy for living but
also a measure of comfort and reassurance in a difficult world, but

at Devens, I also learned its practical value on the very first Sunday. Cadets were placed in formation according to religion, one for Catholics and one for Protestants, and each was marched off to church, disappearing down the dusty company street to the barking cadence of an NCO. We Jews remained behind and were forced to labor in productive and character-building details such as painting the rocks around the perimeter of our ancient wooden barracks and cleaning the latrine. A bit over an hour later, the Catholics marched back into the area, the first to return from church and clearly the most efficient at delivering the Word of God. This was not surprising: they had had centuries' more practice at it. Not particularly enamored of the prospect of more Sunday slavery, the next week we merely joined the Catholic formation, becoming the front men in what all of us, Catholics and Jews alike, thought was an honorable and ecumenical enterprise. The benighted members of the cadre were presumably at a loss to determine what had happened to all the Jews.

Much of our training that summer was to make us familiar with the panoply of weapons available to the modern infantryman. We spent quite a bit of time with the M1 rifle, learning its curious method of loading, which required more manual dexterity than the average college student possessed. The procedure required a soldier to hold open a heavily sprung bolt with the heel of the hand while simultaneously pressing a loaded clip down into the rifle's mechanism with the thumb of the same hand. If you can't picture how this is done, you are not alone, since neither could we, and the incorrect performance of this chore resulted in the thumb's being crushed against the chamber of the rifle by the powerful sliding bolt.

We threw hand grenades, learning for the first time how important it was to stay away from people who couldn't throw the grenade very far, as well as the impossibility of pulling the pin with the teeth without ruining thousands of dollars' worth of orthodontia. We fired the .45-caliber pistol, in inexperienced hands far more dangerous to the shooter than to the intended target. And we were each given the chance to fire one round of the 3.5-inch rocket launcher, the antitank weapon then current in the Army inventory. It was an unsophisticated weapon, dating to the Korean War, but we were even more unsophisticated, and I for one found it impossible to hit a stationary tank hull one hundred meters away. Indeed, I only barely qualified with most of the weapons, and this was to be a portent of things to come. In actual combat against an armed enemy, I discovered that I am far better using weapons like machine guns, effective because they produce a huge volume of fire and are not dependent on the questionable marksmanship of the operator.

By the time I was commissioned a year later, we had been pouring American soldiers and marines into the war in Vietnam for two years, and the facilities for training newly minted lieutenants from ROTC were inadequate. It would make little sense for a platoon of about forty enlisted soldiers, including grizzled sergeants who were veterans of previous wars, to be led by a young lieutenant with a deeper understanding of urban planning than of loading a rifle. But training and logistics had a habit of lagging behind the strategic or tactical plan. While there are vestiges of that still, the huge logistical footprint in Iraq makes it look as if the tactical plan is the servant of the support base, rather than the other way around.

Typically, the first step was to attend the Infantry Officer Basic Course at Fort Benning, Georgia. But the Army school system was in disarray. So, instead of following the logical progression of going through basic course, airborne, and other schools and *then* going to a unit as a well-trained lieutenant, I got orders to head straight from Rutgers to the 82nd Airborne Division at Fort Bragg, North Carolina. It was the first week of June 1966.

The day after I was commissioned, I left our hovel in the married students' housing area and began a three-day drive to Fort Bragg. It was not a smooth trip to North Carolina. At the time, I owned a 1958 Volkswagen Bug that looked like a misshapen, radioactive, white potato. The guy from whom I'd bought it several years before had worked for the New Jersey highway department, and when his wife badly dented one of the fenders he repainted the whole thing in reflective highway paint. The Bug was the ugliest vehicle then on the road, but it had the albedo of a glacier and glowed in the dark, and I never had a problem finding it in a crowded parking lot.

Back in those days, the interstate highway system was still in the process of being constructed and was primitive and discontinuous. Whole swaths of the country were traversed with U.S. routes going directly into towns and villages, and the journey was frustratingly punctuated with stoplights. A trip from New Jersey to the South took forever, and you were always subject to local jurisdiction. Instead of state troopers, myriad local cops and sheriffs cruised the roads and lurked in ambush behind billboards, setting speed traps for unsuspecting suckers like me. Unless it was going downhill, my old VW couldn't manage more than fifty miles an hour, but with a cacophony of screaming sirens and flashing cherry lights, I was pulled over by a towering, 250-pound, red-faced cop in Caroline County, Virginia. He claimed I was speeding at some rate that my car couldn't possibly achieve, said I was under arrest, and told me to follow him to the nearest town. We pulled up to a ramshackle building that turned out to be the town hall. Inside, he introduced me to an even heftier, older gent—the justice of the peace. The judge found me summarily guilty of speeding and fined me forty dollars, a week's gross pay and an enormous sum to me. Worse, I didn't have forty bucks on me. The judge rolled his eyes and, in a deep, slow drawl, asked me how much money I had. I dug into my pockets and came up with twenty-three dollars and some change.

"Okay, boy," the judge said. "That'll do. Jes' hand it over."

I said that I needed some money to get down to Fort Bragg. The cop and the judge put their heads together, whispered between themselves, then separated, and the judge announced that I could keep ten dollars for myself. Right in front of me, the judge and the cop split my fine, and each man pocketed his share.

Walking me back to the door, the cop clapped me on the back as if I were an old pal of his, wished me luck in the Army, and waved me out of the building.

WHEN I ARRIVED at Fort Bragg, I reported to the division's head-quarters and, after completing several reams of paperwork, each page of which required substantially the same information, received an assignment to a Charlie Company of the 2nd Battalion (Air-borne), 505th Infantry. My company commander was a captain named Hunter Shotwell, a 1963 graduate of West Point. He had been a hockey and lacrosse player and had the false teeth to prove it, those two sports existing principally as excuses for people to hit one another with sticks. Shotwell had just returned from his first tour in Vietnam, where he had served with the 199th Light Infantry Brigade. He later returned to Vietnam and was killed in action.

Being one of only two lieutenants in Charlie Company, I became many soldiers' rifle platoon leader, instantly responsible for every-thing in the lives of men older than I. Nothing gives young people more responsibility and authority than the Army, experience that is almost impossible to duplicate outside the military service. The nature of military life consists of vital tasks like setting objectives, allocating resources, and solving problems, all things which can be accomplished by most young enlisted people but evidently devilishly difficult to do by elected officials and highly compensated business executives. This is even more startling when one considers that often the best performance from our young troops occurs when people are trying to kill them, which led an old friend to propose that such intense motivation would serve to improve the performance of gov-ernment leaders and business executives and, if nothing else, would weed out those among them who were in poor physical condition and couldn't run very fast.

After some months as a platoon leader, Captain Shotwell told me that the battalion commander wanted me to be the S-3 Air, the battalion's air operations officer and effectively the deputy to the operations officer. This was a staff job. I didn't yet know much about the trajectory of my military career, but one thing I did know was that I didn't want to be the S-3 Air, to me just another subordinate staff officer in a vast military bureaucracy. Although very few soldiers had any college education at all, and many did not even finish high school, these people were the backbone of our defense, knew they were doing important work, and were wonderful human beings whom I found engaging. My intellectual taste ran to simple, comfortable constructs, and nothing was more comfortable than leading soldiers and doing soldierly things and living among people who were performing very difficult tasks at the lowest level in pursuit of an ideal. Being on staff was life as a bureaucrat, and bureaucracies are organized to do routine things in a routine way. They are committees, notoriously inefficient and obstructionist enemies of the people. I wanted to be a platoon leader, I liked being a platoon leader, and I wanted to continue being a platoon leader.

And that's exactly what I told Captain Shotwell.

"Sir, I don't want to be the S-3 Air," I said.

"No, Jacobs, you're going to be the S-3 Air," he said.

"Well, sir, I don't want to be the S-3 Air."

"Look, the battalion commander says you're going to be the S-3 Air, and you're going to be the S-3 Air."

I said that I wanted an appointment with the battalion commander, so that I could plead my way of out of what I considered a horrid fate. Shotwell laughed uproariously, and when he quieted down, he said, still chuckling, that he'd arrange an appointment for me.

After physical training the next morning, I reported to the battalion commander, a lieutenant colonel named Hans Druener. He had been an enlisted glider pilot on D-Day, survived the crash of his plane, received a battlefield commission, and ultimately, as a company commander, made the jump into the battle at Nijmegen in Holland. The disastrous operation, known as Market Garden, became famous through the popular book and film *A Bridge Too Far*. Druener was a tough old paratrooper, and when I reported to his office he wouldn't return my salute, wouldn't put me at ease, and simply sat at his desk, glaring. This wasn't going to end well.

"What do you want?"

"Well, sir," I said, "I understand that you want me to be the S-3 Air."

"That's right. What about it?"

"Well, sir, I'd prefer not to be the S-3 Air. I want to keep being a platoon leader."

"What?! Get the hell out of here."

I saluted smartly, executed an about-face, and marched out of his office, secure in the understanding that in that short interview I had just learned a number of critical lessons it took many people years to learn, including the startling realizations that sanctimony gets you nowhere and that groups are successful when each person does what he must do rather than what he wants to do.

ABOUT A MONTH after I arrived at the 82nd, I finally received orders to go to jump school at Fort Benning, Georgia. I had spent about four weeks in an airborne unit without being airborne qualified, not a pleasant experience. The purpose of the course is ostensibly to teach soldiers how to jump from military aircraft, but it's much more a vehicle for instilling esprit de corps and teaching the value of discipline.

I was at Jump School during the hottest weeks of the Georgia summer, and we trained even on the Fourth of July. We would break for ten minutes every hour, drinking gallons of water so that we wouldn't become dehydrated and drenching ourselves from hoses to cool our roasted bodies. It was so hot that, just minutes after the break was over, our uniforms would be bone-dry from the heat.

The course was divided into three one-week blocks of instruction. During Ground Week, we did lots of moderately slow running, but it was less to get into Olympic-level physical prime than to bring into some semblance of reasonable shape those who arrived morbidly obese or addicted to five packs of Camels a day. We also practiced parachute landing falls from low platforms over and over again, enough for the task to become literally automatic. And we spent time in an apparatus called the swing-landing trainer. Suspended in a harness oscillating over the ground at a height of as much as ten feet, the object was to prepare the jumper to hit the ground at unanticipated angles. The instructor would select the point at which he released the suspension line, and invariably it would be at the extreme of the arc, when there was no angular momentum. This would cause the jumper to plummet straight down and test his ability to perform a proper landing under the most difficult circumstances. At the time, it seemed that the sergeant who controlled the time of release and thus the difficulty of the landing was selected for the task because he was pathologically sadistic and probably even on bail, but when we eventually jumped from an airplane in flight and hit the ground, the misery he inflicted on us became fully justified.

For those who performed adequately, Tower Week followed, and the essence of this training was to practice a good body position as we exited the aircraft. The importance of exiting properly could not be overestimated, since a poor body position often resulted in parachute malfunctions and subsequently injury or death. The height of the tower, thirty-four feet, was selected because, evidently, the height is inherently scary and imparts even more fear than jumping from an altitude of thousands of feet. I never had much fear of heights, but I knew plenty of troops who were unmoved by the prospect of jumping from a plane at 1,250 feet but were petrified by the thirty-four-foot tower jump. A jumper donned a parachute harness, but the risers were attached to a wheel that rode a cable, so that after he exited the tower, counted to four, and practiced checking for malfunctions, the pulley carried him about two hundred yards to a berm, where he was disengaged from the harness. Because a good, tight exit position was crucial, it took five successful exits to merit continuation in the program, recycled to the following week if found wanting, and eliminated if failed again.

Initially, we derived most of our entertainment from watching others exit the tower, as inexperienced jumpers invariably struck wildly comical poses while trying to adopt a proper exit position and, hurtling to the ground, flailed ineffectually like maniacal windmills. It was like an early version of bungee jumping, but at a height low enough to see every detail, including the diabolical scowl on the cigarette-lined face of the mean NCO who would find the exit unacceptable.

Tower Week also included one jump from a 250-foot tower. The tower was a world's fair relic, and it had four arms. Suspended from each arm was a cable, at the end of which was a steel hoop the same diameter as a T-10 parachute. Cams around the hoop temporarily secured a parachute in whose harness was strapped a student. Three arms were used at a time, and one was empty because the prevailing wind would otherwise carry the released jumper into the tower. When all three jumpers were in harness and their parachutes cammed up, they were slowly hoisted and then stopped about ten feet from the very top of the arm. On command through a loudspeaker, each jumper in turn detached a thin safety strap and dropped it 250 feet to the ground. He was then yanked up the remaining distance to the top, jerked to a stop, and the inertia released the cams, the inflated parachute and the parachutist. The jumper floated freely to the ground, and he was graded on his control of the canopy and on the quality of his parachute landing fall.

Occasionally, a jumper would be so inept as to steer his parachute into the tower, not a pretty thing to witness. Or he would execute some painful and embarrassing pantomime of a parachute landing fall. All these misadventures were madly entertaining, principally because they were happening to somebody else. The popularity of today's reality television shows demonstrates conclusively the satisfaction that results from seeing other people in difficult circumstances, not because people are inherently cruel but because when the show is over, the viewers are still fine. All that is required from us is sympathy, and it's easy to be sympathetic because it costs us nothing. When it comes time to sacrifice, however, the price is no longer zero, and that is when the value of one's character can be calculated.

The last week consisted entirely of live parachute jumps, one a day for five days, and those who survived all five jumps were graduated and received the jump wing insignia. After all the intensive training, all the screamed criticism from the instructors, all the days devoid of any rest but that required to prevent the students from succumbing to heat stroke, Jump Week was something of a vacation. Down to the airfield, wait for your aircraft, suit up, and jump. The instructors became noticeably kinder, now that we were one of them.

If a paratrooper had any fear remaining, he tried not to show it, although most soldiers harbored at least a little trepidation, even when they reported to their airborne units and jumped regularly. But once the soldier was in the aircraft, hooked up and ready to jump, it was really too late. I remember being on a jump with paratroopers who included our battalion's chaplain, a streetwise New York Catholic priest who was the jumpmaster. We were shuffling to the door to jump out of the aircraft and the young, fully qualified airborne soldier who was directly in front of me balked at the door of the aircraft, ashen with fear. Even his lips were white. "I don't think I can go, Father," he screamed to the chaplain over the roar of the engines.

"Son, you can't *not* go!" he yelled, put his boot on the kid's backpack, and promptly kicked him out the door.

———————

BACK WITH THE 82nd Airborne at Fort Bragg, I was sent to Jumpmaster School myself, a one-week course that taught how to control an entire aircraft full of paratroopers, from gearing up on the ground to assembly after the jump. Among the most important things to learn was proper inspection of a jumper's gear, and there was only one correct way to wear a parachute backpack and a reserve and connect the straps. Instructors donned equipment, usually with one or more intentional errors, many difficult to find, to test each student's ability to correct the rigging mistakes. On the final exam, one missed error was enough for dismissal from the program, hammering home the point that proper rigging is crucial to surviving the jump, that when lives are in the balance, a leader must know what he's doing.

At the end of the week, the student was also graded on both how he performed inside the aircraft—controlling the preparation for the jump, hanging outside the plane while in flight to observe the drop zone—and also on the ground. You still had to jump after your troops and land properly, and one improper landing earned you a prompt dismissal.

In a standard military parachute jump, one of the riskiest things to do was to land standing up, dangerous to attempt and almost guaranteed to snap a jumper's legs. For most paratroopers it was impossible anyway. But not for me.

Being very light and pretty strong for my size, I could always slow my descent almost to a stop by controlling the parachute canopy. I could be the first jumper out of the aircraft and the last to land. My jumpmaster exam was on a late afternoon with relatively brisk winds, but not high enough to cancel the jump, and I managed a perfect stand-up landing. I was very satisfied with myself, but with the canopy deflating around me, I saw that the ground instructor, clipboard in hand, was just a few feet away, scowling and ready to mark me deficient in landing and propel me ignominiously out of the program. Looking squarely in his eyes, I belatedly threw myself onto the ground in one of the most exaggerated parachute landing falls ever seen. He let me get away with it, probably because the outrageous acting was of such elevated intrinsic value that it redeemed even my substandard performance. There is, after all, something to be said for amateur theatrics, and we can see them every day in the public arena, especially in an election year. That some politicians manage to survive, even prosper, performing the equivalent of my theatrical landing is a tribute to the flexibility of the democratic process and the inventiveness of its practitioners. Without the histrionics, the hyperbole, and the outright falsehoods, we would be led by humorless bureaucrats, and Leno and Letterman would be bereft of material.

IN THE MID-1960s there were many different types of military aircraft, and we jumped them all. My first jump was out of a Korean War–vintage C-119, an old twin-engine, twin-tailed rattletrap that was so underpowered it was something of a miracle that it ever got off the ground. C-119s were in the Air National Guard inventory and were piloted by men who'd taught Orville Wright how to fly. We also jumped out of a variety of aircraft that were created, it seemed, merely to permit the use of yet another curiously inapt name: Caribou, Otter, Beaver, none of which can actually fly in nature. We jumped out of World War II–vintage C-47s, which were already old when I was born, and more modern C-130s and C-141s. And we jumped from helicopters. The chopper pilots needed flying practice, and every Saturday, riggers would lay out many dozens of parachutes and reserves in the headquarters area, and anybody from the unit who wanted to jump could do so. The helicopters would fly out to one of the drop zones at Bragg, you'd make the jump, and a truck would pick you up and bring you back for you to do it all over again, as many times as you could until the helicopter pilots had to call it a day.

It defied logic that the military establishment would find it useful to have so many different aircraft. It wasn't necessarily that they were designed and built at different times, because many of them were contemporaneous. And they weren't necessarily for markedly different tasks, either, because many of them could perform the same job as similar aircraft with more or less the same success and efficiency.

Decisions like this are made jointly between the interested military service and the Congress, and both are bureaucracies and not in the business of setting strategic plans and following them. The Congress, in particular, is highly motivated to satisfy the desires of its members, which means that the parochial interests of their constituencies often come first. Thus, there is little logic and even less efficiency in programs, authorizations, or appropriations, which is why you can have the deplorable circumstance we have today: the Navy and the Air Force receive from the Congress more major weapons systems than they want or need. To be sure, the executive branch and particularly the Department of Defense do a poor job of planning, coordination, and execution, but the Congress hasn't been much of a check on foolishness and actually adds to it.

———

THE 82ND AIRBORNE Division was full of crusty old characters. During those early years of the war in Vietnam, the senior ranks of both officers and noncommissioned officers were dominated by World War II veterans whose experience was acquired in the extreme violence of a conflict whose desired end state was the unconditional surrender of our adversaries. When you fight a war in which nothing is out of bounds and the survival of your nation is in the balance, you acquire a persistent state of mind that finds limited or unconventional war a great discomfort. And yet, experience in World War II did not prevent an astounding anomaly: extremely high-ranking officers, those who advised the president on the conduct of the war in Vietnam, making inept decisions that produced an incremental commitment of forces and debilitating restrictions on the employment of the military instrument.

My battalion's command sergeant major, whose name is lost in the haze of memory, proved to be one of the more remarkable characters I would meet in the Army. In the Second World War, he fought in three different armies. When he was sixteen years old, in the Hitler Youth, he had been impressed into service in the Wehrmacht, fought on the Eastern Front against the Russians, and was wounded and captured. The Russians then made him fight on the Eastern Front against the Germans. Wounded again, he was repatriated by the Germans and then fought in the Wehrmacht again, this time on the Western Front against the Americans. You can see where this is going: he was wounded yet again and finally captured by the Americans. When the war was over and we emptied the POW camps, the MPs told him he could go home to Hamburg. But he said that he didn't want to return to Germany, that he wanted to come to the United States. They struck an agreement: he could come to the States, but only if he enlisted in the U.S. Army. He agreed, moved to America, and ended up my command sergeant major twenty-one years later. Perhaps because he had spent so much time in combat as a young man and therefore understood the complexity of the military profession, he had a high tolerance for the errors of youthful leaders like me. And because my initial service was so fraught with these errors, he was invariably pulling me aside to deliver the kind of counseling that can only be proffered by someone who had fought for the Wehrmacht, the Soviet army, and the U.S. Army, all in the same war. He was stocky and had cancer and was nearly crippled from his many wounds and from years of jumping out of airplanes. Moreover, as the highest-ranking NCO in a battalion of seven hundred men, he had his hands full. But he was gentle and avuncular and always had time for me.

He and my battalion commander weren't the only exemplary soldiers at Fort Bragg, and the 82nd Airborne Division has always had an indefinable, elite mystique. It had attracted extraordinary people since its inception during the First World War before it became an airborne division. Among its famous alumni were Medal of Honor recipient Sergeant Alvin York, who was cited for leading an attack on a German machine gun nest and killing twenty German soldiers and capturing 132 others, and General James Gavin, who was the youngest division commander in World War II.

After serving as a platoon leader, attending Jump School and then returning for a while to my unit, I was sent back to Fort Benning for Infantry Officer Basic Course. By then, I had already received enough on-the-job training, guidance from the command sergeant major, and admonitions from my battalion commander to make IOBC a superfluous bore. Among the least enjoyable aspects of the course was the ineptitude of the cadre. Using a pedagogical technique that works only occasionally but never when the task is important and time is of the essence, the Infantry School decided that the student company should be led by the students. This guaranteed that there would be no shortage of unintelligible orders, wasted time, and general disorganization.

One particular evening is instructive. We had been in the field all day and much of the night on some tactical exercise that could have been accomplished in about half the time it actually took. Finally, we were in front of the barracks, and it was just before one in the morning. We were scheduled to depart again in just a few hours for another day of training, we were still in formation, and we hadn't been released because the student chain of command couldn't calculate what time we needed to be awakened. Making this determination isn't difficult, of course, but that assumes a level of intellectual acuity way in excess of that possessed by these leaders. At this rate, of course, there would be no need to awaken us anyway, since it didn't look like we were going to get any sleep. It was possible that the intention of the Infantry School was to permit such foolishness to continue long enough for the remainder of the students to become incensed and get the student leadership to shape up. But we lacked the ability to do so, since in garrison we weren't issued live ammunition.

In the early spring of 1967, my entire brigade of the 82nd received orders to go to Vietnam. Most of the troops were very pleased, since serving in combat with such an elite organization was the dream of every infantry soldier. My excitement was short-lived, however, because almost immediately following the euphoria of the deployment warning order, I was alerted that I would be going to Vietnam all right, but as an advisor.

This was hideous, morale-crushing news, disastrous from every angle of analysis. I would not be with American troops but with the Vietnamese army, which was poorly trained, insubstantially led, and inadequately equipped. Furthermore, duty as an advisor was viewed by the U.S. Army hierarchy as being far less valuable to the war effort than combat with an American unit. This meant that, in competition for promotion and schooling, my service as an advisor would be far less creditable, and my career was thus at a competitive disadvantage. And the worst aspect? No jump pay. I could kiss $110 per month good-bye.

Once again, I wasted little time raising a stink, and I called Infantry Branch, the sadists who had selected me to be an advisor. I spoke to the laconic major who was responsible for picking me for this odious duty, and we engaged in something of a circuitous exchange, with my saying, over and over, "I want to stay with my unit," and the major saying that I was going to be an advisor. As a simple functionary in an insensate system, he could have kept this up for weeks, and he was surely programmed to do so in the recognition that callers like me, who were not satisfied with their assignments, would eventually tire of the enervating discussion and surrender peacefully. The illogic of separating me from my unit, however, prompted me to ask *why*, forcing him to admit that it was a purely arbitrary decision, leading me to conclude that it also could be arbitrarily reversed.

"Lieutenant Jacobs, we need advisors and you're going to be one of them."

"Why can't you get somebody else to be an advisor?"

And his startling response: "Because you're uniquely qualified."

"Uniquely qualified? Sir, in what way am I uniquely qualified?"

"You've got a college degree."

And that was that. The discussion was over. He could have said just as easily that I was selected because I had black hair or that I liked chocolate ice cream or I drove a VW. The lesson was that there *was* no real reason. Like combat, like life, it was the luck of the draw, and I had drawn the advisor card, just as surely as some men are dealt the cancer card while others die at one hundred after being shot by an irate husband.

THE UNITED STATES had had advisors in Southeast Asia for years before we committed combat units to the region. On February 12, 1955, President Eisenhower's administration sent the first group of advisors to train the Army of the Republic of Vietnam (ARVN). Many of those were veterans of the OSS in World War II and had years of experience working with indigenous fighters, but twelve years later, by the spring of 1967, advisors were merely rank-and-file officers and NCOs who were only unlucky. In the interim, the Army had established a training program that consisted principally of five weeks at Fort Bragg in a course of study called Military Assistance

Training Advisor. Course work in the morning consisted of information about the structure of the Vietnamese army, the demographics of the country, a bit of history, the nature of the Vietcong, and pitfalls to avoid. The latter were mundane observations about drinking responsibly with your counterpart and how not to offend Buddhists. Vietnamese language classes were in the afternoon. A few of us were selected to attend a subsequent eight-week language course at Fort Bliss in Texas, and, this being the Army, we were not chosen because we demonstrated a facility for language but probably instead because we were selected at random by a bureaucrat with a perverse sense of humor.

During the advisor course, one thing was made abundantly clear: in Vietnam we were engaged in an unconventional war, one for which few of the lessons of World War II and Korea applied. The template for a war of this type was the British success in Malaya, but there were truths to be learned from the American Revolution, too. All wars are ugly, but Vietnam had already proven to be frustrating as well, and it was clear to everyone that we would be there for a long time. But in typical American fashion, the Department of Defense ignored many of the lessons that had been learned about counterinsurgency. In other conflicts, it had been proven conclusively that the prevailing side achieved success by isolating areas and securing them. Instead, we launched a strategy of attrition.

Robert McNamara, Lyndon Johnson's secretary of defense, had no practical experience as a war fighter. Although his background was impressive—he had an MBA from Harvard, worked for the accounting firm Price Waterhouse, and became the president of the Ford Motor Company—there was really nothing in his background that would recommend him to be the defense secretary in a time of a national security crisis. During the Second World War, he had served in the Office of Statistical Analysis. It was not a position that would portend anything other than a career as a bureaucrat, and a bureaucrat he certainly became. He, his staff, and their successors inflicted on the United States a series of policies with no military coherence, and it was startling even then that uniformed leaders such as the Joint Chiefs of Staff and senior field commanders, all of whom had extensive combat experience, put none of this hard-earned knowledge to work. Otherwise intelligent and dedicated general officers, William Westmoreland and Creighton Abrams included, passively rolled over when commanded to do so by no-talent civilian leaders. And the most infuriating thing about the entire tragedy is that our leaders, both civilian and military, seem to have gleaned absolutely nothing from the experience. We have made many of the same strategic and tactical mistakes in Iraq.

Our mission as advisors in 1967 was to do exactly what American advisors are trying to do in Iraq now: train the local army to assume all security and nation-building duties and permit us to go home. We never managed to do it effectively in Vietnam, and we are unlikely to be given enough time to get it done completely in Iraq, either. Among other things, it takes more than simply sending over advisors, regardless of how well trained, qualified, and committed they are. It takes the dedication of all executive departments in an organized, centrally directed, and concerted effort. That's not something one sees in Iraq.

———

IT ALWAYS SEEMED a bit curious that we would leap at the opportunity to fight in Vietnam. True, we were in a period of intense international competition with, and under clear threat from, the communist world, and so the imperative of fighting communism in Southeast Asia was compelling. Fail to defend South Vietnam against the communists, and, with assistance from Russia and China, the whole region would soon be communist.

But among many complicating details that most people tended to forget was that we had switched sides. During the Second World War,

when we had been allied with the Soviet Union and were all trying
to destroy the Axis, the United States had placed American advisors
with Ho Chi Minh to help fight the Japanese in a bloody conflict that
had already been raging for ten years. We had been striving mightily
to be an isolationist country, protected from war by two vast oceans,
but by the time we finally joined the Allies, millions of people had
already been slaughtered in Asia.

Combat in Southeast Asia was very much different from that on
the European continent, and the demographic environment favored
the enlistment of the indigenous population to fight the Japanese, and
the terrain in Vietnam favored the conduct of unconventional warfare. And so we dispatched officers like Colonel Edward Landsdale
of the Office of Strategic Services to advise and assist Ho Chi Minh.
When the war was over, Ho asked for our continued assistance, this
time to eject the French from Indochina, and we refused.

For people who remember those days, our refusal was the only
response that made sense using our cramped calculus. Old enemies—
Japan and Germany—had become allies; and allies—China and the
Soviet Union—had become enemies. Ho Chi Minh, a nationalist,
was also a communist, and we could not abide supporting him. It
also looked to us as though he was a close client of China, although
by 1968 all evidence pointed to a nasty break in the relationship, and
not long after that the two fought a war. Nevertheless, the communist world looked to the American leadership like a monolithic and
uniformly antagonistic adversary, and our intelligence capability, no
better then than it is now, concurred.

An odder reason for not working with Ho was that his objective
was the ejection of the French. The colonial system that had served
the European powers for almost two centuries was in the process of
disintegrating, falling to the local wars of revolt begun by idealists
and despots alike. Our decision in Vietnam had its roots firmly in the
soil of French colonialism. France, an ally during the war, had done
almost nothing in its own defense, and President Charles de Gaulle,

whose principal personal characteristic was an attitude of ungracious sanctimoniousness, would later pull French troops out of NATO. Not much of an ally. So for us to make a decision about Vietnam based on the aversion to alienating de Gaulle and the French made positively no sense. Ho Chi Minh was a communist, but he also was a nationalist. At the time, our aversion to the first trait trumped our sympathy for the second, and we chose not to help Ho get rid of de Gaulle, especially regrettable in view of how the ungrateful egomaniac treated our friendship.

The French did help us in one way by giving us an excellent example of how *not* to fight in Vietnam. Following a poorly conceived strategy and employing bankrupt tactics, the best soldiers the French could muster were ultimately surrounded at Dien Bien Phu by the communists and were routed in 1954. As had often been the case before, the French leadership didn't have much of an idea what it was doing, the valiant French paratroopers could not compensate for their execrable generalship, and they were destroyed.

Frankly, however, we didn't know what we were doing either and astonishingly learned nothing from the French debacle. In the final analysis, we suffered from a succession of fools dictating our foreign and military policy. These were patriotic and dedicated people with laudable records of previous public service but who otherwise had little to recommend them. Overmatched by circumstances they didn't understand, blinded by the cataracts of predisposition and invalid assumption, and ignorantly buoyed by the American ability to field powerful but irrelevant technology, we were our own worst enemy. And, as with the French, the sacrifice of more than fifty-eight thousand young people was insufficient to overcome the ignorance at the top of the hierarchy.

A fine example is a conversation, now declassified, that records a discussion about the number of additional troops General Westmoreland once requested for Vietnam. The Pentagon said it could spare fewer than half of what Westmoreland requested, but he accepted them anyway. Either Westmoreland's request was the right number or the Pentagon's was the right number. They couldn't *both* have been right.

But they could both be wrong, and they were in this case. The proximate cause of our failure in national security was, and is now, that the American leadership has often had trouble being clear about its objectives—in Korea, in Vietnam, in Iraq—except at the grossest level of abstraction. The unlikely person who best articulated the painful but simple lesson in all this was Lewis Carroll: *If you don't know where you are going, any road will take you there.*

MY OWN ROAD to Vietnam was, if nothing else, at least clearly delineated. In June 1967, I left Fort Bragg and headed west for Fort Bliss, Texas, where I was enrolled in the eight-week Vietnamese course at a hastily organized rump annex of the Defense Language Institute, whose premier location was in the far more salubrious Monterey, California. Fort Bliss is in west Texas, on the border with New Mexico and surrounded by the Chihuahuan Desert. This place is beautifully ugly in a way that only wild, scorched North America can be.

The course was one of total immersion, eight hours a day, and that seemed to produce acceptable results. Most of us acquired a working fluency that would help us avoid the most embarrassing and dangerous errors to which people are prone when they are speaking a completely foreign tongue with native speakers who are armed with deadly weapons.

My off-duty hours were spent speaking English and going to the dog track across the border in Juárez, Mexico, with my friend Jim Echols. Jim was a 1965 graduate of West Point and was to be assigned to the Vietnamese Airborne Division, the choice assignment for advisors. He saw the most intense combat of the Tet Offensive and survived the war, but he was later killed in an air crash back in the States.

Chief among the attractions of Juárez were impossibly tough but tasty steaks, undoubtedly carved from beef that had died of old age, overwork, or a matador's sword. Properly chewing these steaks required either the teeth of a wild predator or an infinite amount of time, but they came with decent fries and a salad and cost a dollar. Every night, Jim and I each voraciously consumed one of these old hunks of meat, supposing, quite correctly, that there wouldn't be much steak where we were going.

Chapter Six

By the summer of 1967, some young people, those with plenty of time on their hands but with an intense purposefulness, donned tie-dyed clothing and flocked to Haight-Ashbury. Others of us, equally focused, packed our duffel bags and shipped out to Vietnam.

The point of embarkation was Travis Air Force Base in Vacaville, California, but all Army personnel first had to report to Oakland Army Terminal for processing. I flew from Newark to San Francisco, where a bus took to Oakland anybody with a uniform and a lost expression. The main edifice at the terminal was a huge hangar that contained cots as far as the eye could see. Waiting to be called for the trip to Vietnam often took many days, as the Army's appetite for nearly half a million individual replacements every year was not matched by an ability to manage the complex logistics needed to satisfy it. Thousands of troops milled about, waiting, playing cards, sleeping, getting into fights.

Because I was an officer, I had an assigned room, microscopically small, that I shared with another lieutenant. Finally manifested on a chartered flight, I and three hundred others were packed into buses in the middle of the night and driven laboriously from Oakland to Travis Air Force Base. Once on the tarmac, we were subjected to some insanely complicated process of loading us into the cabin and our name-tagged duffel bags into the cargo hold, all in the same sequence. This was meant to produce the swift location of our bags when we eventually debarked in Vietnam, but it resulted instead in much shucking and jiving, hours of loading and reloading, and the generation of an intense hatred of all things organizational among those who had not already developed it.

It's difficult to describe what a twenty-two-hour voyage on an ancient Boeing 707 was like. The plane was the width of a commuter aircraft but longer, and ours was configured to hold three hundred troops, six across, in extreme discomfort. If *my* knees were jammed against the seat ahead of me, it is difficult to envision the contortions required of a normal-sized human being to prevent complete loss of circulation and subsequent spontaneous amputation of the legs. Remarkably, there was less grousing among the troops than I had expected. Perhaps it was because we were on our way to an adventure, for almost all of us the defining experience of our lives, and for many of the kids this was their first ride on an airplane.

For me, however, the trip was a tutorial in impossibilities: couldn't sleep, couldn't read, couldn't stretch.

The length of the trip, which intensely magnified the discomfort, was a function of the relatively short range of the airplane. We had to refuel in Hawaii and again at Clark Air Force Base in the Philippines before landing in Vietnam. On its final approach to Bien Hoa Airfield, our plane broke through the fluffy low-hanging cotton, and we were treated to a scene of startling beauty. It was that lush time of the year in Vietnam between the rainy season and the dry season. The sky was the deepest blue, and below the thick clouds we could see Technicolor bursts of luxurious green. As we descended rapidly and banked toward the runway, I did not know that this was the last truly benign moment I would know for many, many months.

We landed roughly on the runway and bumped to a stop, the ground crew rushing toward us with a gangway. Squinting in the bright sunlight, we filed down the steps, one or two of the engines of the aircraft still running at a deafening volume: this was a "hot refuel." Dump the passengers, change the crew, reload with soldiers for the return to the United States. Not far away, there was a long line of ragged GIs who'd finished their one-year tours of Vietnam, all impatient to cram into this thin metal tube and get home.

As we came down the gangway, all new uniforms and fresh faces, we passed close to these shaggy, unkempt veterans. They were just like us except that, to a man, each looked like he was a hundred years old.

As we were passing, they were yelling out, in a collective sing-song, like taunting kids on a playground, "You'll be sorreeeee..."

And they knew what we didn't then: in a couple of weeks we, too, would be a hundred years old.

———

We were herded onto buses, and most of the GIs were driven down a bumpy road to one of the permanently temporary camps that served as replacement depots, where soldiers would be outfitted with weapons and equipment, given a hot meal and their units of assignment, and then hauled off to somewhere up-country. The lucky ones wouldn't get home for another year.

We advisors, a few lieutenants, captains, and NCOs, clambered aboard a separate bus whose windows sported tough wire mesh to protect against hand grenades that we were told were occasionally thrown by Vietnamese children, although I never met anyone who was in a vehicle when it was attacked in this way. The bus brought us to downtown Saigon, a noisy, sprawling city, hazy with the blue smoke of motorbike exhaust, the Saigon we had expected to see, complete with moldy French colonial architecture. Many buildings were ringed with barbed wire and sandbags, and they added to both the excitement of the place and to the air of faded, inelegant shabbiness that most former colonies possessed.

Our destination was Kelper Compound, the processing center for advisors, and it was composed of a few seedy buildings that contained a multitude of tiny rooms, temporary bedrooms for advisors while they waited for their assignments. The building could have been a hotel once, or an apartment building, but it resembled nothing so much as a flophouse. The ground floor of the principal building contained a few decrepit offices for the cadre and a filthy cafeteria that sold unsanitary omelets, slices of iridescent ham, and fly-specked mysteryburgers. Rat, perhaps, or some assortment of ground pet, but decidedly not beef. I knew what beef tasted like, and this wasn't it.

A loudspeaker blared a continuous loop of "Ode to Billie Joe," whose novelty evaporated after only two renditions. Even today, when the heat index exceeds ninety degrees, I can't get the blasted song out of my head.

Upon our arrival, we received a number of forgettable briefings and were given some forms to complete. They seemed to be placebos, since, although several of them purportedly were instrumental in arranging pay, I didn't get paid for some months afterward. I concluded that none of the forms had anything to do with anything and served only to keep us busy while we waited for our assignments.

Every morning there was a formation, and in a lugubrious monotone a bored clerk read the names of the people who had received assignments. When the formation was dismissed, those whose names had been called went gleefully to a nearby bulletin board, on which was posted the unit of assignment and the time of departure to the airport. Having your name called meant going up-country, to the unknown, to combat, to danger and perhaps death. But even the prospect of fear and misery was preferable to hanging around the squalor of Kelper Compound.

On the second day we were issued weapons and magazines,

load-bearing equipment, suspenders, web belt, canteen, everything we would need in the field except ammo. They gave me a slab-sided .45-caliber pistol and a .30-caliber carbine, an old weapon that fired an ineffective pistol cartridge that propelled a bullet so lacking in penetrating energy that it would bounce off the quilted clothing of Chinese soldiers in the Korean War. The .45-caliber pistol, however, was another story and was as powerful a sidearm as we had in the inventory. It was ineffective, too, but only because of my ineptitude, as I would discover later.

For the better part of a week, my name did not get called. I hung around Kelper Compound, sharing with three other lieutenants a tiny room that was barely large enough to accommodate a prostitute and her client. And my luck being what it was, this microscopic accommodation was located directly above the exhaust of the diesel generator that produced electricity for the compound. It was a hideous place. Too hot, too humid, too noisy, too smoky, too crowded, and suffused with a stultifying boredom that drove everyone to accept any fate other than the prospect of remaining there another minute.

Finally, blessed relief, release from the purgatory of slow but certain diesel exhaust poisoning, parole from the sentence of eternal damnation for eating the ground flesh of impermissible animals: in formation one morning the clerk read my name. I was going to leave Kelper, directed to report at 8:00 p.m. with equipment and duffel bag, ready to be transported in some circuitous way to the headquarters of a Regional Force battalion. RF units were part-time soldiers, poorly equipped and incompletely trained, but they were the future of Vietnam. They would wrest control of the countryside and thus eliminate the appeal and domination of the Vietcong. It was an awful assignment, full of impossible challenges and unbearable frustrations, but it was my ticket out of Kelper Compound.

That afternoon, I wrote letters home that captured the ecstasy of my relief at leaving Saigon, and that night I cheerfully posted myself in formation with all my stuff, as directed. The clerk read everybody's name from his clipboard...except mine. The clerk dismissed the formation, and everyone else moved to load the buses, leaving me standing alone, a forlorn, confused little boy.

"Uh, Sergeant, what about me? Jacobs."

He looked at his clipboard. "Sir, you're not going tonight," he said.

"What do you mean?"

"I mean you're not going tonight," he repeated, enunciating deliberately, as if he were speaking to someone who was very hard of hearing and had recently emigrated from Bulgaria.

"But why not?"

"Sir, I have no idea, but your assignment's been canceled." And he casually sauntered off, going to some secret place known only to military clerks in Saigon, where they breathed real oxygenated air and ate real hamburgers made from real cows.

A miserable night, the heat and exhaust magnified by being left behind. This was unbearable, being left behind, even by people I hardly knew. Brand-new advisors arrived every day, and they left me behind, too. It crossed my mind that I had been forgotten by the Army, perhaps expunged in some mysterious fashion from the rolls, never to receive an assignment. The unobservant clerks would never realize that I'd become a nonperson, because I would have become part of the squalor, blending into the mildew that coated the walls. I was disappearing.

But several days later, I had a new assignment: the 2nd Battalion, 16th Regiment of the 9th Vietnamese Infantry Division, a frontline unit. That was the good news. And the reason that I was going to the 2nd of the 16th and not to the RF unit was the bad news. A night or two earlier, one of the 9th Division's battalions had been overrun by the Vietcong, and the entire American advisory team had been killed in action. Captured, bound, shot in the head like animals, and left there to be discovered, so that the lesson of the VC's fury would not go unnoticed. Advisors in the other units were then shuffled around to fill the gap left by this tragedy, and the organization was now short of advisors. This was not information that filled me with effervescent confidence, and while I was pleased in a professional sense that I was now going to be a real combat soldier, the circumstances left me with a nagging suspicion that I would ultimately wish I were back at Kelper Compound, listening to Bobbie Gentry, breathing diesel fumes, and eating ratburgers.

MY DESTINATION WAS Sa Dec, the city where the 9th Vietnamese Infantry Division was headquartered, in IV Corps, in the Mekong River delta. The delta is a vast alluvial plain, with scarcely more than a foot in elevation from the South China Sea inland to the border with Cambodia and beyond. Flat and flooded and as wet as a sponge in the wet season. Flat and hard and as dry as dust in the dry season. Sa Dec was south of the river, and the aircraft, a Caribou, was to take a number of us to various locations in IV Corps. A bus took us from Kelper to Tan Son Nhut Air Base, actually within the borders of the city of Saigon, and we were loaded aboard the ungainly-looking Army airplane.

The CV-2 Caribou was a twin-engine cargo aircraft with a high wing and a higher tail. In those days, the Air Force complained bitterly and constantly about the fact that the Army had fixed-wing aircraft as well as helicopters, the argument being that fixed-wing aircraft like the Caribou did not belong in the Army. The Defense Department eventually agreed, transferring the Caribou to the Air Force, and it should come as no surprise that the Air Force promptly retired the aircraft. There is a certain puerile, playground mentality that pervades the relationships among the armed services. It is a bit better these days, but in general the business of defense, particularly in the arenas of manpower and the budget, is perceived as a zero-sum game. As the infamous observation says, "It's not enough that I succeed. My competition must also fail."

———————

OUR CARIBOU PLIED a regular circuit, taking off from Tan Son Nhut and making the rounds in IV Corps, dropping off all the men and equipment that it needed to drop off down in the delta. The first place that it was scheduled to land was a city called Can Tho, the IV Corps headquarters. The two old engines made an intolerable din, and the spare, uninsulated cabin merely amplified the noise. With the same resonant frequency as the rotating propellers, the fuselage threatened to disassociate itself into its component rivets and sheet metal. Mercifully, the flight was not very long.

We banked sharply as we smoothly lost altitude on final approach to Can Tho's airfield, and the main landing gear hit the perforated runway and rumbled loudly. The pilot slowly dropped the nose to complete the landing, and—of course—the nose gear abruptly collapsed, sending the wheel skidding off somewhere. In a civilian aircraft, this would be known as a plane crash, but in the military service it was undoubtedly classified as a "malfunction-induced landing inadequacy." The pilot handled the mishap very well, controlling the Caribou to a slewing, awkward stop at the end of the runway. It could have been much worse, and nobody aboard was hurt. We staggered out of the aircraft, a bit woozy, and it was perfectly clear that the first stop was also the last stop. Of the half dozen passengers, I was the only one whose destination was elsewhere. Everybody else was now where he needed to be.

I turned to one of the pilots. "Say, how am I supposed to get to Sa Dec?"

"Hey, it's not my problem, buddy."

"But I have to get to Sa Dec."

"What can I tell you? *This* aircraft is not going to Sa Dec. I recommend you hang out here and try to hitch a ride on a helicopter."

I glanced around. No other aircraft of any kind.

"There's a helicopter?"

"No," said the pilot quite deliberately, "they come here all day. You just have to *wait* for one." It was clear that he assumed he was speaking to a child, emphasizing the important words in the sentence in an exaggerated fashion. And off he went, accompanied by the copilot and crew chief, to a shack on the other side of the field. I trundled after them, under the burden of about three-quarters of my own weight in weapons, helmet, bags, and assorted junk I eventually threw away. After several months of combat I learned the value of ammunition, hand grenades, and cans of Vienna sausage and the extraneous disutility of almost anything else.

At the flight shack, there was a weather-beaten NCO behind the worn plywood desk, a cigarette dangling precariously from his lips and another behind his right ear. Lounging around outside were a few Vietnamese soldiers, smoking unfiltered Ruby Queen cigarettes and appearing to serve no function other than being local color. Every once in a while a helicopter would land and the pilots would come to the shack to get cans of Coke and talk to the NCO behind the counter, who said nothing in response and as near as I could tell was a deaf-mute. I'd try to talk the chopper pilots into taking me the thirty miles to Sa Dec, but one after another, they said they couldn't help me. They would remount their Hueys, crank up the rotors, and lift off, eventually becoming tiny specks against distant, billowy clouds. Initially, a bit of panic gripped me, since I was supposed to be in Sa Dec, and I was decidedly *not* in Sa Dec. Early in Army training, you learned that your location was important, and if you were anywhere other than where you were supposed to be, you were in big trouble. But, after a while, I became resigned to the fact that I wasn't in Sa Dec, that I may never get to Sa Dec, that perhaps I would spend my entire year in Vietnam hanging around this flight shack, just as I had feared about being stuck in Saigon. And I began to take some perverse delight knowing that I was not where I was supposed to be. This realization was particularly attractive to someone like me, who harbored something of a creative but rebellious nature that, without constant control, always threatened to evolve into a pernicious destructiveness. I found myself grinning quite inanely about this when yet another chopper landed.

Two warrant officers hopped out of the slick, came to the shack, and grabbed a couple of sodas. I made a fast pitch.

"Hey, any chance you guys are going to Sa Dec?"

"Nope."

"See that busted-up Caribou? That was my aircraft. That was supposed to get me to Sa Dec, but the nose wheel collapsed, and now I'm stranded. I need a ride to Sa Dec. How about it?"

They talked it over for only a few seconds, gulping down their Cokes, then turned to me with a nod. "Sure, why not? We'll take you up."

They let me hop in their Huey and flew me into Sa Dec, where I was quickly processed and then sent out to meet up with my battalion near its base in Cao Lanh, far across the river from Sa Dec. I wasn't there long before we received the order to provide security for a Regional Force unit that was building an outpost about five miles away.

The entire trip from home in New Jersey to my unit in Cao Lanh seemed like a disjointed, uncoordinated, and unsupervised odyssey, more the result of happenstance than of planning. But as I discovered in the ensuing months, that's exactly what combat is like. And so is much of life, too.

———

VIETNAM WAS UNUSUAL in that it was exactly as I'd pictured it. Very few places are like that. We've been spoiled by the skill of photographers and cinematographers, whose job it is to create a mood and, often, a falsely romantic picture, reinforcing the stereotype. This produces a startled, almost heart-stopping disappointment when we see the real thing. Travel to the pyramids at Giza, and from one angle the scene looks just like the picture in an encyclopedia. Smack in the middle of the trackless, wind-whipped desert, there are the Sphinx and the pyramids, and you feel like you're stepping into an old Ronald Colman movie. Execute an about-face, and what do you see? Strip malls, fast-food joints, bumper-to-bumper traffic, and clouds of smog, because that's what Giza *really* is: just a suburb of Cairo, one of the most populous cities on earth. But from the photos in history books, you never get a sense that the monuments are in a metropolitan area of seventeen million people. They've cropped that out of the picture, given you just a narrow-angle shot, managed your expectations.

Not so Vietnam. It was one of those few places where expectation meshed precisely with what was presented in real life. When I caught up with my unit, it was pulling security on a canal, in the midst of dense jungle. The thick, dark green growth of palms and banana trees was like something out of Joseph Conrad. The climate was hot and muggy, just as I had expected. It takes time to adjust to a new environment, but the place seemed so familiar that I had an easy acclimation to the sounds and smells of the place, and to the rich pictures I saw.

But as for being a soldier, I had much to learn, even in such quotidian matters as sleeping and bathing. The first night I chose to sack out in my hammock, which, in a stroke of what I thought was brilliance, I'd strung between two small trees located the perfect distance apart. The Vietnamese troops watched me doing this with strange, almost bemused expressions, whispering among themselves, but I paid them no mind and proceeded to ease myself into the hammock and in a few seconds a deep and restful sleep. At first light I awoke to the sound of roaring laughter and found my backside drenched. The trees had collapsed and I was sopping wet because I'd fallen deep into the rice paddy and was sinking deeper by the minute. Only then did I learn that I'd strung my hammock between two banana trees. They have no bark, no wood. They aren't really trees at all but instead like overgrown leaves of grass that sprout berries we eat as bananas, and they can't support anything, even a small and inconsequential soldier. Light as I was, my weight had pulled both of the trees together, lowering me slowly into the water overnight, and the Vietnamese thought this was the funniest thing they'd ever seen. Crowded around me, they howled with laughter, gesticulating wildly, while I lay in the cold cocoa water.

More than forty years later, I'm over it now. Indignities are odd things. There is an inverse relationship between the intensity of the indignity and the time elapsed since its occurrence. Spectacularly embarrassing things are almost unendurable two minutes after they occur but are not only bearable but actually quite amusing years later. Perhaps humans can live with tribulation because of our ability to find redeeming value in our own ignominy and, occasionally, humor in our folly.

My worst indignity occurred the day after I slept in the banana trees, and it had the extra added attraction of being hazardous to my health as well. I had been in the field for two days, and while I had never been a particularly fastidious person, I felt desperately in need of a bath and decided to take one in the canal we were guarding. I stank—badly—and I was starting to offend myself, and I knew that the next level of offense was to smell so awful that I couldn't tell. I figured there shouldn't be any problem in hopping into the water and soaping up.

The South Vietnamese units, both regular and regional forces, were quite unlike the American army in that the men generally had their entire families in tow with them wherever they were stationed. So here at this canal, there were hundreds of kids, mothers-in-law, wives, and grandmothers going about their daily chores and, when they weren't doing something productive, just standing around and gawking. The protocol was intuitively obvious, even if I hadn't already been so instructed: I whipped off my shirt, boots, socks, and uniform and waded out in the canal in my boxer shorts. The canal bank was wet, thick in mud, and it dropped off quickly to deep water. Attempting to stick close to the bank of the canal, I was neck deep in the opaque canal only three feet from the bank, mud sucking at my ankles.

After the catastrophe with my hammock the day before, it was no surprise that all eyes were on me as I started soaping my face, washing my hair, dunking my head under the water. Just then, in my left-side peripheral view, I spied a very old woman, doubtless a soldier's mother-in-law or grandmother, walk out to a little promontory on the bank, about ten feet upstream from me. In a single practiced, nonchalant movement, she proceeded to pull down her pajama bottoms and hang her backside over the edge of the canal. *Upstream* from me. Now, I hadn't been in country for very long, and I had never encountered this behavior before, even in Brooklyn, but my instinct drove me to conclude that nothing good was going to come of this. And from the old, toothless, frail woman surged a deafening, reverberant noise not heard on the earth since the Jurassic Age, the exhaust sound of a hundred flatulent farm animals and concurrently the undigested remnants of her previous week's breakfasts, lunches, and dinners. Very loudly, she had launched a dauntless fleet of foamy green Portuguese men-of-war, sailing purposefully and without being molested down the main...to me. By now, dozens of troops were on the bank, all realizing my dire predicament, and this time they weren't merely laughing. They were actually applauding, screaming encouragement as if the floating cholera epidemic could be motivated to do their will. Two feet from the bank, slipping on the muddy canal bottom, I tried desperately to get out of the water before this flotilla of excrement reached me and slathered my neck with enough *E. coli* to kill everybody in Chicago. To the breathless glee of every bystander, I failed to escape, and as I finally dragged myself from the canal, exhausted and defeated, I glanced at the old woman, who smiled toothlessly at me as she pulled up her pants.

CHAPTER SEVEN

WHEN I ARRIVED at the 2nd of the 16th Infantry, I was a first lieutenant, and I replaced a captain, the senior advisor who was on his way home. Since there was no senior advisor when he left, that responsibility fell immediately to me. There were two other Americans with the unit, a staff sergeant named Ray Ramirez from Raymondville, Texas, and a large, blustery, cigar-smoking master sergeant named John Killian, from Omaha, Nebraska.

Ramirez had a powerful build and a thick Mexican accent. Soft-spoken, genial, with a pleasing, homey sense of humor, Ray was the essence of valor, both brave and calm in difficult circumstances. He'd been in the Army for only about two years but during the war, soldiers who survived made a lot of rank quickly, much faster than today. Soldiers who lived left the Army. Soldiers who persished left, too. There was a very fast and frustrating turnover of personnel.

I never got to know Killian very well. Not too long after my arrival, he rotated home, too, which left just me and Ramirez, a young first lieutenant and an NCO, to handle all the advisory duties.

We didn't know it at the time, but we were on the verge of the bloodiest months of the Vietnam War, culminating in the Tet Offensive.

The battalion was very short of soldiers, although I wasn't as worried about it as I should have been, and there wasn't anything I could have done about it anyway. I learned quickly that advisors only advise, and they influence through suasion or, rarely, logic. My advice to Hong, the battalion commander, was usually ignored, not necessarily because it was bad advice but because there was some institutional risk in his doing what I suggested. Five years later, I would return to Vietnam, again as an advisor, and I was to discover that this dynamic had not changed. It is likely that advisors in Iraq and Afghanistan have a similar experience, and those who find the effort without such frustrations are probably rare—and very lucky indeed.

As for my tiny advisory team, Ray and I expected a captain to replace the one who went home, but by mid 1967, the Army was too short of combat captains, and for months I was left there as the acting senior advisor. To be sure, the emphasis was on the "acting," since I was enrolled in the world's most demanding on-the-job training course, and I was never a quick study. When a captain was finally assigned, he was definitely not combat ready.

LIVING WITH INDIGENOUS people gives an American a perspective impossible to acquire any other way. American units brought America with them to Vietnam, and although living in a U.S. infantry division base camp wasn't like taking up residence in the Plaza Hotel, it was nothing like living among the Vietnamese. The most important difference between Americans and their hosts revolved on the very nature of the war there. American soldiers went to Vietnam for a tour of duty, usually about a year, and if a soldier or marine survived the tour, he went home alive. Those grizzled and cynical troops we encountered in Bien Hoa, boarding our plane to go home, had served their time in the crucible and were on their way to the paradise of America. But Vietnamese soldiers were stuck there forever, and it didn't matter how often they got shot or ripped up with shrapnel. No matter what happened to them, they were still in the army, and when they became casualties they were repaired like old automobile tires and sent back into the fray until they became dead. Like our valiant American brothers who gave their lives there, the Vietnamese were lifers in Vietnam, but they also had their families with them and in danger, and so their perceptions of service were very much different from ours. No showers. No ice cream. No R&R in Bangkok. Just tough times and no end to them.

The level of training among the South Vietnamese varied widely from unit to unit. Some organizations were very well trained and highly motivated. These tended to be the all-volunteer units, the Ranger and Airborne battalions, although when the going was really tough, even the most elite units fell to pieces, stopped moving, ran away. The regular force infantry battalions were neither as well trained nor as highly motivated nor as well led as the elite organizations. But some of them, including my battalion, were at least adequate and could often perform exceptionally well. It was my luck, of course, that on a very difficult day in March 1968, my battalion was not at its best.

UNITED STATES ADVISORS in Vietnam performed a number of functions, but very few of them related to providing advice. Our most frequent and tactically significant contribution to the war effort was close air support. Responsible for directing air strikes on enemy positions, I was the interface between the South Vietnamese troops and the U.S. Air Force. Close air support could be a powerful weapon and would occasionally decide the outcome of a firefight. Having been accidentally bombed by a Vietnamese Air Force A1-E whose pilot had some difficulty reading a map, I can testify to the devastating effect of an exploding 250-pound bomb at close quarters. But we were in the open, the pilot could see us clearly, and we weren't shooting at him, although in retrospect no one would have faulted us if we had.

But in most cases, dropping bombs on enemy soldiers with precision was devilishly difficult to do in those days. Perhaps the hardest thing to do was to identify the exact location of the enemy soldiers, especially tough because the enemy was usually not sitting around having lunch but was instead unloading as much firepower at me as they could. Having some confidence that I knew approximately where they were located was not sufficient. I had to find both the enemy position and my location on a map and convert these tiny dots into six-digit grid coordinates. Map coordinates were the only way the attack aircraft could distinguish between the target and me, a very important distinction.

This was all complicated by a number of things. First, six-digit coordinates were only accurate to one hundred meters, and there was no technology at the time to make map reading any more precise. Second, dropping bombs from an aircraft that was flying at perhaps four hundred knots and getting shot at, too, was mostly art and valor, not science and sangfroid. The airborne forward air controller, an Air Force pilot circling in a slow Piper Cub or something similar, talked directly to the jet fighters and marked what he thought was the target with white phosphorus smoke rockets—while he was getting shot at as well. But even if the forward air controller had a high degree of certainty that he could see the target, the sheer inaccuracy of dropping dumb bombs required successive runs if we wanted *any* confidence that the tactic would be effective. Iron bombs just don't kill many enemy unless you drop lots of iron bombs and you don't much care about collateral damage.

The reliance on tactical air strikes had a deleterious effect. Doctrine said that any kind of massed fires—air, artillery, mortars—were a prelude to, and were supposed to support, a ground attack. Indeed, we had been taught to lean into supporting fires that kept the enemy's heads down and their rifles silent. At the last possible moment, the fires were lifted, but by that time you were supposed to be nearly inside the enemy's defensive positions. But in yet another demonstration of the disadvantage of relying on technology, even as crude as it was forty years ago, the air strikes became not a tool to support ground assault but instead a substitute for it. And instead of getting fixed in position while we attacked them, the enemy used the strikes as cover under which they routinely escaped. Few units were better at using air strikes to avoid attacking the enemy than Vietnamese infantry battalions, but one must be fair and note that it was we Americans who taught them to do this.

However removed this function was from the business of giving advice, it did give me considerable leverage with Hong and I could occasionally get him to do things that he was reluctant to do, because I controlled the close air support. If I felt strongly enough about a tactical or training issue, if he didn't at least meet me halfway, he may not get the air support he wanted because I may determine it was only marginally useful in the situation. So there was this delicate, interpersonal tango that evolved as I became more confident in my ability to assess what was needed to prevail in a firefight. A bit like a new parent, I was learning on the fly.

Ostensibly, my other job was to make sure that the battalion employed the key infantry principles all of us learned when we were nineteen years old: stay on the offensive, always employ sufficient resources to ensure success, and so on. In the real world, in the heat of battle and the rush to get something accomplished, we all tend to forget basic principles and often take the path of least resistance, to take the direct but dangerous route, to react without thinking, to employ air strikes rather than sound tactical principles. The legacy of this thinking can be seen in the decision to use insufficient forces in Iraq, to employ precision-guided munitions to the exclusion of almost all other tactics and to fail to exploit success.

Hong was a shrewd, honorable guy. Like most Asians, he was intensely concerned about "face," and consequently it was important to him that *I* not lose face in front of his subordinate officers and men. To an American mind, how things looked seemed far less important than the results of action, but understanding this important facet of Vietnamese life was critical to an advisor's influence. And Hong worked tirelessly to co-opt me into the planning process, even in those earliest weeks when I didn't have anything useful to tell him. At planning meetings, he would ask my opinion, but only after he had already told me he would do it. The worst thing for both of us would be his consulting me publicly and my response being some mumbled rubbish that demonstrated conclusively that I had no utility. So he gave me sufficient advance warning for me to think about the operation so that I could say something other than "I'm an idiot with nothing to contribute. Please shoot me so that I no longer must endure this embarrassment."

It was just as important that he not lose face either, and if he had done something that I thought was particularly dumb, I would be certain to tell him in private. I would go over to his little shack next door to mine, to tell him that I thought he was wrong, but only if he was alone. Most of the time, he would look at me in a slightly artificial manner, feigning interest in what I had to say, and then thank me politely. Until the combat operation was under way, I had no idea if he thought my idea was the greatest tactical innovation in history or the equivalent of attacking Moscow in winter. Enthusiastic acceptance and dismissive rejection generated the same expression.

However, the danger in becoming co-opted was the possibility of eroding independent thought. Finally getting the ear of the battalion commander and appearing to be his great pal carried with it the potential loss of objectivity. So the job of being an advisor had

its balletic qualities, and it was not unlike being a political candidate who needed to criticize his opponent without appearing to be
distastefully mean spirited. I had to seem twenty years older than I
actually was, thoroughly skilled in all aspects of armed combat, and
with the diplomatic skill of an ambassador. And I guess I could have
become a politician had I not developed an aversion to being nice to
people I can't stand.

WHEN I ARRIVED in Vietnam, the generals, well-meaning but quite
inept, were in the process of changing the nomenclature of our missions, and throughout my tour they never settled on what to call the
combat operations. Sometimes they were "movements to contact,"
other times "reconnaissance in force," still other times "search and
destroy." It didn't matter what they called them, since they were all
pretty much the same, with the same objective: locate the Vietcong
and then capture or kill them. The VC were not uniformed soldiers
like the NVA, the North Vietnamese Army. They were mostly farm-
ers who were recruited or, occasionally, forced into being VC, or else
they were disaffected youths, who in any society can be convinced to
do just about anything, no matter how insane.

The Vietcong looked like all the pictures I had seen: they generally didn't wear helmets, often wore black pajamas, and were armed
with AK-47s, SKS carbines, light machine guns, and once in a while
Chinese copies of Czech pistols, rare and valuable finds on the battlefield. B-40 rocket-propelled grenade launchers were ubiquitous, as
were the booby traps the Vietcong set. It was an unusual engagement
during which we did not encounter all these weapons.

The Vietcong lived among the civilians and were devilishly difficult to separate from them. As is the tragedy in all wars, the good guys
had guns and the bad guys had guns, but the civilians were caught

in the middle. They were farming, tending their cattle, and generally minding their own business, and suddenly they found themselves in the middle of a firefight, something that was impossible to avoid.

Because these people were not in a position to defend themselves, it didn't matter that many of them wanted to be on our side. In Vietnam, the rural population couldn't refuse to pay taxes or give rice to the Vietcong because when they did try that, they were slaughtered by the Vietcong. And then the survivors were taxed—and they paid. War is tough on soldiers and civilians alike.

In the late summer and early fall of 1967, the VC were still primarily composed of South Vietnamese, and it wasn't until slightly later, when the Vietcong began moving large numbers of fighters from elsewhere to our area of operations, in preparation for the Tet Offensive, that we started encountering other people, VC who were ethnic Cambodians, Vietnamese from other provinces, and even some North Vietnamese, most of whom had political or training functions. At the time, we didn't realize that they were reinforcing in preparation for a major offensive. We just noticed increasingly frequent contact with the enemy in larger formations and with more ammunition and greater endurance.

We tended to encounter the VC in units ranging from a squad, between five and ten men, to a couple of platoons, about fifty men. A massive firefight would ensue if we encountered them at company strength, say one hundred or more. Their tactical objectives reflected the antithesis of the fighting mentality of the Japanese my father had faced during World War II. The Japanese military culture had for centuries nurtured the notion that there was no honor in retreating. But the Vietcong, on the contrary, saw their mission as inflicting as many causalities as they possibly could on the South Vietnamese army, destroying as many men and as much materiel as possible, making life unendurable for the government troops and the Americans—and then vanishing into the night to fight another day.

No, they were decidedly *not* interested in dying for their country, but they had patience and a clear understanding of the Maoist concept of choosing to fight on their own terms.

If we cornered them they would almost always give up. During my first tour, we captured lots of VC, and they often switched sides and worked for us. In fact, my radio operators, ethnic Cambodians, were captured Vietcong.

"Look, we've got cigarettes and food," we said, and that was all it took to convert both of them from the enemy into reliable, hard-working comrades. They doubled as my drivers, which was quite startling, since neither of them had ever driven a vehicle, and for a few weeks there was some question whether Ray and I would die in combat or on the road. Ray never did trust their driving skill and would always be behind the wheel, with the Cambodians, in some-thing of a role reversal, riding comfortably as passengers. After living off the land in the swamps of the delta, having a steady supply of cigarettes and regular meals must have seemed like paradise to these boys. But no matter how difficult it would have been for them to envision the relative comfort of life on our side, nothing could have prepared them for having an American NCO as a chauffeur.

CHAPTER EIGHT

ONE MUGGY MIDMORNING, not long after I had joined the battalion, we were moving across rice paddies and heading toward a canal when I had my first face-to-face contact with the enemy. Rice paddy terrain was wide open—between five hundred and a thousand meters on a side—and bordered by low dikes. On the other side of a dike there was usually a canal. Most dikes were narrow, and some were quite wide, but along the sides, there were almost always some palm trees, often a few banana trees, and occasionally a bit of underbrush. It was in this cover along the canal lines that the Vietcong liked to establish ambushes.

The only weapon I was carrying that morning was the sidearm I'd been issued back in Saigon, the Colt M1911 .45-caliber pistol. This was the weapon developed during the Moro Rebellion of 1911, in Mindanao in the Philippines, where the Army found that its existing .38-caliber pistols were ineffective against the Muslim fighters—the rebels were crazed, rumored to have been taking dope, so they couldn't be incapacitated easily by .38 pistol rounds. The U.S. Army's response was to develop a large-caliber pistol, one that fired a bullet almost half an inch in diameter. Now, there are many benefits to being physically small in battle, but having to use a Colt .45 sidearm is not one of them. For a soldier my size it's a ridiculously heavy and unwieldy weapon, one with a devastating kick, a characteristic not enhanced by my proven poor marksmanship.

On this morning, we had begun moving after dawn, and at about ten, we were advancing quietly along the canal line when we encountered a squad of VC. With just a few small arms and automatic weapons, even a squad of enemy troops could generate a prodigious amount of firepower, and in no time they had us pinned down, hugging the ground.

I decided to attempt a flanking maneuver, taking four Vietnamese soldiers with me. As we scooted along in a half crawl, trying to get around to their flank, up popped a VC in black pajamas, his AK-47 at port arms. He was alone, manning the outpost protecting their flank position, and his startled eyes were open enormously wide, nearly popping out of their sockets.

In what Wyatt Earp would have envied, I yanked the .45 pistol from my holster, flicked the safety off, and then in one or two seconds proceeded to blast the entire magazine of rounds at this Vietcong standing no more than three yards away. And it was a verification of my inadequate performance on the firing range during training that I did not come within a mile of hitting this enemy soldier with any of my rounds. The young Vietcong fighter was so stunned by this shoddy spectacle of close-range ineptitude that he stood there dazed, frozen with fear or, more likely, disbelief. I would have had a better chance of hitting him had I *thrown* the pistol at him. It was my good fortune that the soldier next to me had a machine gun on a sling, and with a burst from the M60, he killed the VC instantly. I never took a pistol into the field again.

Every man should recognize his weaknesses, and chief among mine is being a lousy shot. I am definitely an area weapons man. Guns that deliver large volumes of fire are my forte, as are exploding projectiles. Given my ineptitude with aimed fire, an atomic hand grenade would be ideal. If you are looking for a sniper to nail some hapless boob at a range of one thousand meters, look elsewhere, but I am your choice if your combat tactics run to using thousands of rounds of automatic weapons fire to scare an enemy soldier to death.

———

I WAS A lieutenant filling a captain's slot, but for about four months the Military Assistance Command in Saigon didn't dispatch another American captain to our battalion. I tried to convince myself that it was because I was doing such a superb job as senior advisor, but the truth is they were short of captains. But by late 1967, I was notified that a captain was coming to take my place, and that I was going to be relegated to being his deputy.

I promptly told Hong, and he was mightily unhappy.

"No, no, no. I do not want another advisor. I already have you," the battalion commander said.

"I know, and I like being the senior advisor, but they've decided to send a captain to replace me anyway," I said.

"I do not want one," Hong said. "I'm going to call up and say I do not want him."

"Hong, you can do that, but they're just going to send him anyway. This is not the Vietnamese chain of command. It's the American chain of command, and it doesn't matter what you and I want."

Hong stood there, fuming. "All right, they can send him down here, but I will not feed him."

"No, please. You *must* feed him."

Hong walked away, back to his quarters, disgusted.

The next morning the captain arrived, and we could see immediately that Hong wouldn't have to feed him because he could have lived off his fat reserves for a year. He was slightly taller than I but must have outweighed me by one hundred pounds. I didn't know what assignment he had just left, but it must have had something to do with food. He seemed like a pleasant, genial guy but completely unfit for combat, and it was clear that this was not going to end satisfactorily. One of the first things he told me was that he'd been sent to the 2nd of the 16th because he needed to get some combat experience or else he wouldn't get promoted to major. I determined this to be a very poor criterion for the decision, but, then, who was I to judge? Four months earlier, I'd been sent there with no combat experience, too. On the other hand, I did not have the physique of a circus elephant.

The next morning at dawn, we departed our base camp to conduct a movement to contact. The terrain was still quite wet, and I explained to the captain that we would be wading in water up to our necks for the entire duration of the mission and that he shouldn't get agitated when he discovered himself covered in voracious leeches.

"Sir, let me brief you on the mission," I said, calling him over to a well-worn map of the operational zone. "Tomorrow we're going to be leaving at zero six hundred. This is the route we'll be taking." I traced on the map the various checkpoints we were required to clear before returning to our base camp. The circuit would be twelve and a half miles, a good hike in dry terrain, but it promised to be a genuine test of endurance in the mud and water of rice paddies and canals. The temperature would be more than ninety degrees, and the humidity would be unforgiving.

The poor guy was already drenched in sweat, just from standing there. "We've been through this area before, sir," I continued. "This is just my advice, and you can do what you want, because I'm working for you now. But I recommend very strongly you let me run the operation. If there's anything to do, I'll recommend what you should tell the battalion commander, and you can advise Hong. But please, sir, stick closely to me. Stick next to me, because I'm going to keep up with Hong, and you can't fall behind. If you fall behind, you'll lose face."

The captain stood there, smoking a cigarette, nodding like he could handle the mission, no problem. The next morning, we started our movement, and it was tough going, knees and thighs churning underwater, barely able to move. One thousand meters across a rice paddy, and then up a slippery berm onto a small dike, then across a deep canal, and then back up the other muddy bank and into another rice paddy. Over and over again.

We couldn't keep anything dry. We wrapped some items in the plastic bags in which our radio batteries were shipped, then tied them airtight with rubber bands, but the water leaked into the bags anyway. We kept our rifles high in the air, which was a hell of a workout for our arms and shoulders.

About a quarter of the way through the mission circuit, we surprised some VC in bunkers, and a short but stiff firefight ensued, a typical and familiar engagement. We had them outnumbered and outgunned, but before we got the better of them, they managed to kill and wound a few of our troops. While our soldiers were searching the enemy bodies, someone called for helicopters to evacuate our wounded and dead.

I secured the landing area with a couple of soldiers, and then the helicopters landed, delivering fresh water and more ammo. The choppers departed with our dead and wounded, a drenching spray of paddy water cascading from the helicopters' skids.

After the choppers were gone, we began to resume our movement to contact. I looked around for the heavyset captain, but I couldn't see him anywhere.

"Where's the captain?" I kept asking around. I asked the battalion commander. I asked Ray Ramirez. I asked the two radio telephone operators. Had *anyone* seen the captain?

Finally, a waterlogged, leech-bitten private told me in Vietnamese,

"Yes, Lieutenant, I saw him. The captain got on the helicopter and left with the wounded."

"He was wounded?"

"No, Lieutenant, he wasn't wounded. He said he was tired and needed to go home."

The captain never came back. His first day of combat was his last day of combat.

To be sure, the captain acted very unprofessionally, but he wasn't the only one to blame. It was the command's fault, too. This captain was demonstrably not prepared for combat, and he was sent to us with the sole purpose of improving his career prospects, not because he was the right man for the job. Personnel development is important, but enlightened leadership is required to ensure that the needs of the mission are not forsaken in achieving other, administrative objectives. In all organizations, leadership is the independent variable that determines success or failure. Ironically, the larger the organization, the more important is leadership because a burgeoning bureaucracy insulates narrow-minded decision makers from the results of their work. But leaders are often ignorant of this, forgetting the principles they learned decades before, and even ignoring their own experience and better judgment. It is easy to get complacent and lazy, to attend meetings rather than spending time with soldiers, to stop asking basic but important questions.

When that happens to commercial enterprises, they lose money. When that happens to governments and military organizations, people die.

———

WE WERE INVOLVED in many firefights in those early months—almost every day—but the first major engagement in which our unit took part came in early 1968, in the buildup to the Tet Offensive.

We had been out in the field for several days, moving to contact, but we didn't know that a company-sized VC force had dodged us and moved into position to attack the city of Cao Lanh, where many captured Vietcong were locked up in the main jail, not far from our base camp.

We got back to our base in the early evening, totally exhausted, and shriveled from having been up to our necks in water. Within moments of our return, most of the battalion was fast asleep. Around one thirty in the morning—when most of us were in the midst of the deepest REM cycle—our radio started crackling with word that the Vietcong were attacking Cao Lanh. The Vietcong had stormed the town and were focusing their attention on the jail. They wanted their prisoners out, while inflicting as many casualties as they possibly could on the Regional Force that was in control of the town.

The center of town was about a mile away, but the sounds of the battle were unmistakable. Tired as hell, still disoriented, we donned equipment, grabbed all the ammunition we could, and moved smartly up the road toward the continuous sound of automatic weapons fire and exploding grenades and mortar rounds, our route clear under the flickering orange glare of illumination rounds. The instant we crossed the bridge into the center of town, we found ourselves in the midst of a ferocious firefight. I was standing next to a V-100 light armored vehicle just as it was struck with a B-40 rocket-propelled grenade. Smoke and flames poured from the vehicle, and the wounded crew tried painfully to climb from the wreck and to safety. But about a squad of VC, in position in a ditch about thirty meters away, hosed the Vietnamese crew with a deadly burst of machine gun fire, killing them instantly, two wrecked bodies falling leadenly to the pavement.

Against the darkened buildings I could see the tracer rounds streaming in every direction. Looking down, I discovered my radio operator lying facedown in the middle of the street, the growing puddle of his blood glistening in the glow of the parachute flares.

This was my first experience in high-intensity night combat, and I didn't have a clue what to do. I was separated from the battalion commander and didn't know where he had gone, and I was very scared. Real-world combat is frightening and confusing at the best of times, but it is much more difficult and frightening at night, when it is impossible to determine the location of your men, and the intense sounds of exploding munitions and the sharp crack of rifle and machine gun bullets seem intensified and much more dangerous. Add to all of this the sharp relief of tracers against the night, and you have the perfect ingredients for a case of paralyzing fear.

It's a crucial question whose answer is incompletely delivered in the classroom: how is a man meant to lead during the incomprehensible confusion of war? It is easy enough to look at a battlefield map and move men and weaponry, as if playing a board game. It's much more difficult when you're lying flat on your belly in the dirt and mud or the middle of a gravel road, bullets and shrapnel whizzing over your head and smacking into your comrades nearby.

The most dangerous moment in battle is when the fear and disorientation make it impossible to think. I could still think clearly enough to know this: that I didn't know what to do. So I scrambled through the street, reached over the slumped body of the dead RTO, and grabbed the handset. I called my boss, the American who served as the province chief's senior advisor. He was a burly Airborne Ranger, probably in his early forties, though he looked and acted much older. With extensive experience in Vietnam and Korea, he was never overwrought—just the man you'd want next to you in a foxhole when times got tough. I figured at least he could offer me some guidance.

"Give me a SITREP," he said.

"It's a big mess. I don't know exactly where all the friendlies are, and the VC are everywhere, and the RTO is KIA, and I need some advice. I honestly don't know what to do."

"Well," he said calmly, "I'm not actually there on the ground, and so I can't give you any specific tactical guidance. But I'll give you a piece of advice: you'd better do *something*, even if it's wrong."

This didn't seem very helpful. I was desperate for clear direction, and I was not particularly happy with his insouciant suggestion. But in retrospect, that was the best advice anyone could have received. This was a crisis, and something had to be done. We overuse the term "crisis" all the time, and now everything has become a crisis. And if everything is a crisis, then nothing is. But when everything is going to pieces, when the cost of inaction is unimaginably bad, then something *must* be done, even if it is with less information than you'd like and insufficient time to consider alternatives. Do something, even if it won't work, because if you do nothing, regret will be your last living emotion.

Without the depth of thinking that characterizes most major decisions, we grabbed a couple of Vietnamese troops and attacked the closest enemy, just across the road in a ditch along the canal line. We reached the ditch, too, but on the enemy's exposed and vulnerable flank, and we dispatched the majority of them fairly quickly. The remainder of the VC were under pressure from our battalion's counterattack farther down the road, and the surviving enemy ended their assault and melted into the black night. They left their dead behind, and they left me with a combat lesson it would be impossible to forget.

WHEN I ARRIVED at the battalion, the unit had been using .30-caliber machine guns. They were very powerful and effective weapons, but they were old and heavy. First fielded in 1919, the guns were positively ancient by most standards, and with a tripod they weighed over forty pounds. Everyone was pleased when the battalion received brand-new M60 machine guns, relinquishing the old weapons. The new M60 was a splendid weapon, with a higher rate of fire than the old gun and about half the weight. And the M60 consumed modern 7.62-millimeter NATO ammunition.

But therein lay a problem. The battalion could not get 7.62-millimeter NATO ammunition, and so it had guns with no ammunition and ammunition with no guns. This sad predicament is what happens when well-meaning but inadequate people fail to think clearly about the ramifications of their narrow decisions. Because we couldn't go into combat without machine guns, this was a problem that required a very quick solution.

I set out on a day trip to Vinh Long, a city downriver and the location of the primary American helicopter air base for IV Corps. Although it was just forty miles away, the trip would take most of the day because of the poor and crowded roads and the necessity of ferrying across the river. I hopped in my jeep with my Cambodian Vietcong driver, followed by two two-and-a-half-ton trucks, and began that long trek down to Vinh Long. The Mekong is a vast river complex, and in places it can be miles wide, making the Mississippi almost look like a stream. The ferrying alone took over an hour.

When we got to the air base, I drove straight to the ammunition supply point, where I found a young American soldier, no more than nineteen, shirtless, operating a front-end loader amid mountains of pallets stacked with ammunition of all calibers.

I put my finger across my throat, telling him to cut the engine of the front-end loader.

"Yes, sir?" he said.

"I need some ammo," I said.

"What kind?"

"NATO 7.62 link four-and-one," I said, meaning machine gun link-belts with the standard cartridge mix of four ball cartridges and one tracer round.

"Okay. How much you want?"

I laughed, gesturing back to my trucks. "You see those two deuce-and-a-halves? Fill 'em up."

"Whaddaya got for me?" the kid asked.

I had come thoroughly prepared for the transaction. Reaching into the back of the jeep, I showed him a Vietcong flag with a suitable number of holes and bloodstains, some VC helmets and belt buckles, an SKS carbine, and a couple of AK-47s, all materiel we had captured in the previous weeks' fighting.

He flashed a grin and a thumbs-up and loaded my trucks with the ammo we needed. Over the next month, I made several trips to Vinh Long, until finally the battalion received its authorized ammunition for the new M60 machine guns, but in the interim the unassailable truth became clear: occasionally nonregulation but creative solutions are essential to success.

MOST OF THE time, life in the field was miserable. Invertebrates were always a problem in the delta, and even in the dry season, there were canals to cross. There seemed to be no minimum time of exposure to the water that would prevent leeches from securing to the skin and begin feasting voraciously. Because leech saliva contains a topical anesthetic, you often didn't discover you were a meal until the creatures were satiated and dropped off. You felt them falling down the escarpment of your skin to the top of your boot or to the bottom of your fatigue blouse. There they were: perhaps a dozen times bigger than they had been when they attached themselves, now engorged, menacing, and disgusting. And loaded with disease that they transmitted to you. Hepatitis mostly, whose prophylaxis required periodic injections of gamma globulin. The serum had the consistency of toothpaste and invariably left a knot under the skin of the buttocks that was enormously uncomfortable and took a week to dissolve. No fun. But better than hepatitis.

But the single most prevalent and successful life form was the mosquito. In base areas, sleeping cots were fitted with mosquito nets,

NEWARK PUBLIC LIBRARY
121 HI
NEWARK

and that served to keep them off, but in the field, which was where we spent most of our time, humans were at the mercy of their insatiable appetites.

One night, after prevailing in a huge firefight against a company of Vietcong whom we surprised in their base camp, I was so exhausted that I fell asleep sitting upright in a canal. Unconscious and snoring away in water up to my midchest, my weapon muzzle-up, supported above the soup with my left hand. At dawn I awoke with my head slumped and my eyes beholding my left hand, which had spent all night above the water. When a brain is only partially conscious, dreams have a surrealistic quality that make them particularly convincing, and I became quickly convinced that my hand was gone, replaced with a numb, smooth-skinned alabaster ball. My mind ran through the possible ramifications of having a ball instead of a hand and settled quickly on being thrown out of the Army because I was deformed and being forced to join a circus sideshow. And then just seconds later my brain cleared and it became obvious what had happened: my hand had served as a buffet for mosquitoes and was now the size of a knuckleball catcher's mitt. It took several days to return to normal, during which period the Vietnamese reacted to it with uncontrollable mirth.

I lost about twenty pounds in the first few weeks I was in Vietnam. This was not a catastrophe, as before deploying I spent my month of leave eating eight hundred meals a day. Fat and sugar composed my diet, and I was better prepared physically to endure a winter in Antarctica than a combat tour in Southeast Asia.

In the battalion, most of the time we ate dehydrated rice reconstituted with paddy water, which we rendered safe with iodine tablets. It was monumentally unpalatable, but it was life-saving nourishment. When it was available, embellishment was a few bits of chopped cucumber, and we always ate some hot peppers to keep intestinal parasites from hijacking our metabolisms. The protein component of our diet was very low, since we rarely had any meat. When we did, it was often sliced sow ears, which had the consistency and palatability of...sliced sow ears. From time to time we got our hands on a shipment of Vietnamese C rations, which consisted solely of canned sardines. The few thoughtful and patriotic Americans who kept us in mind sent care packages containing Spam, which we grilled in an aluminum mess kit over chunks of burning plastic explosive. The packages often contained Vienna sausages, which we devoured cold, and cookies that had been pulverized by the postal department's indifferent handling. If we got hungry enough, we went to the nearby Special Forces compound and essentially begged for food.

The SF troops were very accommodating and fed us exceptionally well. Relatively speaking, the food was so luxurious that I often had a difficult time adjusting to its high quality, and there was an astounding paradox in suffering from stomach upset after eating a proper steak but having no problem eating fish intestines.

There were times when even the meager food or the mail wouldn't arrive, and I'd have to go to division headquarters in Sa Dec and sort out the mess with the administration. It was a constant struggle, especially trying to keep our mail flowing steadily. And there was also the currency issue to deal with. We were being paid in military scrip, which we couldn't use in the Vietnamese economy. Even though we were in the U.S. Army, we weren't in an American unit and there was no PX where we could spend the fake money. One day I decided I needed to go to Sa Dec to get our mail and money problems repaired.

The American officer in charge of administration, a captain, dropped everything else to handle our problems, and he had things put right in very short order. He was quite a bit older and had spent a great deal of time as an enlisted soldier. He understood what life was like near the bottom rungs, and he dedicated himself to making sure that we were properly served.

It was then near dusk and thus inadvisable to attempt the long trek back to Cao Lanh alone, and so I elected to remain overnight at the division headquarters. But before calling it a night, I was enticed to the tiny club that served as the nexus of the social life of the headquarters advisors. They served cold beer and several colors of sandwiches, and everything was nearly free.

But, aside from the genuine and warming *camaraderie*, the principal attractiveness of the place was poker. And when one combines poker, beer, and Vietcong mortars, the result can be unpredictable.

IT IS ODD to meet people in person whom you've known only from their voices. For some months, I had spoken with many of these officers over the radio, and my mind had composed complete pictures of them, none of which was even close to being accurate. For example, I had envisioned Joe Ganger, the Air Force pilot who was our forward air controller, as a handsome, swashbuckling fighter jock, all slick, coiffed pompadour and windswept silk flight scarf. I was startled to see that he seemed twenty years older than I, with brush-cut grizzled hair and a smile at the ready. He had enlisted in the Air Force before the dawn of recorded history and had more flight time than I had hours on earth. He had saved our lives many times already, and so he was an old friend, but actually being in the same small room with him had an eerie feeling of dislocation, an out-of-body experience. There were others, too, including a helicopter pilot we called Joe Outlaw, an Army major.

Among the advisors at division headquarters, evidently, one of the staple foodstuffs was beer. Everyone knew that beer, when consumed with beef jerky and potato chips, formed the basis of a complete diet, providing all the nutrients required of combat soldiers. It should come as no shock that both the drinking and a serious game of dealer's-choice poker commenced simultaneously. Until then I'd only had a radio relationship with Ganger and Outlaw and the others, but we were making up for lost time, raising toast after toast, first to each other, then to the various armed services, fallen comrades, half-forgotten girlfriends. Eventually, the toasts were to nothing in particular, mumbled names, causes, and institutions.

We were in the middle of a roaring game, all of us really too incapacitated to play cards, when the whole club started to tremble and shake, accompanied by the loud boom and crack of rounds exploding nearby. It took us a few seconds to realize that we were under a mortar attack from the Vietcong, and as soon as we did, we headed for the bunkers, strategically situated around the tiny camp. Joe Ganger and a few others hustled me along to their assigned bunker, and I crashed in the darkness over unfamiliar terrain, dragged unceremoniously by the old friends I had just met. Ganger always parked his O-1 Bird Dog aircraft on a small airfield some distance from the division headquarters, and so his plane was not in any danger. But Outlaw's helicopter was parked as close as physically possible to the main headquarters buildings, right inside the wire of the camp. Standard operating procedure during an attack was for the helicopter pilot to take the aircraft off the ground and fly from the impact area, not returning until he received the all clear. And, dutiful soldier that he was, that's what he set out to do. So while I was being dragged to the safety of a bunker, Outlaw, after numerous adult beverages and hardly at the acme of aviating condition, was heading for the helipad. Through the sporadic explosions, I could hear the turbine whine of his chopper cranking up, and then I heard it lift off, the rotor's pounding sound receding into the distance.

Only a few people were wounded during the barrage, and when it was all over, we emerged from the bunkers and headed to the barracks for a little rest. It didn't occur to me until the following morning what an intuitively brilliant aviator Outlaw really was.

I awoke at dawn a few hours later, threw aside the mosquito netting, and slid off the cot's air mattress. On my way to the latrine, to my utter amazement, I saw Outlaw, still only partially recovered from the beer. Astoundingly, he swore that he did not remember taking off in the helicopter, landing it, or indeed anything else from the night before, no memory, he said, after the busted heart flush that lost him five dollars to a lousy pair of eights. Joe Outlaw: an aviator so intuitively good that he could fly in his sleep.

EVEN THOUGH WE were a regular army battalion, like almost all Vietnamese units we had soldiers' extended families living with us in base camp, making for a densely populated village. Although the minuscule camp was full of the invigorating sounds of family life, there was no proper sewage, and so it was also very, very smelly. Three hundred fifty soldiers, plus all the assorted wives, grandparents, and children, generated a raucous din and an endless supply of flies and other insects, absolute heaven for Margaret Mead and entomologists, but less than paradisial for a kid from New York City.

In any defensive position, it was important to plan for the eventuality of being attacked, and this task assumed a more significant importance because we were in a fixed position, and the presence of the dependents both complicated the defense of the camp and made it essential that it be seamless and successful. That entailed imagining being the attacker, to see the battlefield as he would see it. If I were attacking my base camp, how would I do it? Where would I assemble my forces prior to spreading out and assaulting? Along which route would I take my maneuver forces in order to attack?

Among the essential techniques was to position machine guns in such a way that they formed interlocking fields of fire, presenting attackers with an impenetrable wall of deadly bullets if they got to the perimeter wire. These were "final protective fires," FPFs, and calling for them implied the last opportunity to repel attackers before having to fight them hand-to-hand. Hand-to-hand fighting has been very popular in the movies, but it is to be avoided unless there is no alternative. Trust me.

Another important task was to plan for the employment of mortars and artillery, designating a number of the most likely targets in advance so that, in the midst of a battle, we wouldn't be mired in the painstaking and tedious business of adjusting fire, an especially difficult task at night. The nearby Special Forces B team had a section of 4.2-inch mortars, much larger than the 81-millimeter mortars that we carried and slightly larger in diameter than the 105-millimeter artillery round. It was a formidable weapon.

The NCO in charge of the 4.2-inch mortars was a huge, burly master sergeant named Marcou. He had a bullet-head he kept clean-shaven forty years before it became fashionable and a wry sense of humor honed during years dealing with the vagaries of unconventional warfare. He wasn't merely Marcou. He was "The Marvelous Marcou."

The frequency of enemy contact was increasing almost daily, and it seemed to all of us that it was only a matter of time before we were attacked. I drove the short distance to the SF compound and suggested to The Marvelous Marcou that he help me do a little fire planning.

"Good idea," he said, and we got right to the task of determining the most likely assembly areas and attack positions the enemy would use. This wasn't particularly difficult, since the avenues of approach to our base camp we limited in number, and the VC didn't have much imagination anyway. They possessed the stealth of a praying mantis and unlimited patience, but unless they had inside information their tactics were obvious and predictable.

And so The Marvelous Marcou and I planned some fires, selecting a number of targets, places where we thought the enemy was most likely to mass. There were a few clumps of trees, for example, right outside our wire, and obvious assembly areas several hundred meters across the fields to our front. The Marvelous Marcou calculated and recorded the firing data for his guns, and all I had to do was to call for fire on Target One, for example, if I saw the enemy establishing an aid station at the clump of trees.

And sure enough, about a week after meeting with The Marvelous Marcou and not long after the nighttime mortar attack on the division headquarters in Sa Dec, our base camp came under a ferocious assault.

We were all fast asleep when the enemy jolted us awake with an initial volley of rocket-propelled grenades, one of them hitting the corrugated tin roof of our hootch. Shrapnel blasted down, and my air mattress was instantly perforated at the edges, inches from my prone body. Miraculously, I scrambled off the cot without a scratch, although rifle and machine gun bullets were also already ripping through the thin wood of our quarters. Ray Ramirez and I ran and grabbed our weapons and sprinted outside and into our bunker just a few meters away, as the battalion took up defensive positions and returned fire. The enemy raked our compound with machine gun fire, and one tracer round ripped through the wooden walls of our shack, setting alight some of Ramirez's recently cleaned and starched jungle fatigues, just back from the local laundry. Against all logic, Ray poked his head out of the bunker, muttering about saving his uniforms.

And up he climbed, clambering from the bunker to recover his fatigues.

"Ray, are you nuts? Let 'em burn, let 'em burn!" I yelled as he heroically ran through the automatic gunfire and then returned to the bunker with his uniforms, smoldering, ventilated with bullet holes, and ruined.

A few minutes later, Ray and I scuttled with the battalion commander to the perimeter, illuminated with mortar flares that lit the battlefield with a golden, sunrise glow. Arriving at the perimeter, we could easily see a large number of enemy soldiers attacking our compound, and some had positioned themselves under the cluster of trees just outside the wire.

I hailed The Marvelous Marcou on the radio and told him we needed some of his four-deuce mortars on the trees. "Fire Target One," I said.

There was so much noise on the battlefield that I couldn't hear the report of the mortar round as it left the tube, but The Marvelous Marcou radioed that the first round was on the way.

I was hunkered down behind a bunker when, all of a sudden, I heard a sickening sound—*pfffffffffft...thunk*—and in the near daylight of the flickering parachute flares I could see a fresh, unexploded 4.2-inch mortar round only about a meter away. My heart shot up into my throat. Forgetting about having called The Marvelous Marcou for fire, my first conclusion was that the VC had somehow acquired four-deuce mortars. If so, we were really in trouble, for within the small confines of our base camp, they could kill dozens, if not hundreds, of people. Then, seconds later—*pfffffffffft...crash!*—another four-deuce mortar round smashed right into the hood of my jeep parked just a few meters away, a vehicle already riddled with bullets and looking like Bonnie and Clyde's 1934 Ford death sedan. The hit couldn't have been more perfectly placed, the unexploded warhead protruding vertically from the crumpled engine compartment.

And then it dawned on me: we were not going to be obliterated by exploding mortars after all because these were duds from The Marvelous Marcou. I yelled into the radio, calling for him to cease firing the mortars.

But it was too late for Corporal Mai.

Corporal Mai—ironically, *mai* meant "lucky" in Vietnamese—was not very fortunate. As Mai manned his position on the perimeter, defending against the onrushing VC, the last mortar round that Marcou sent our way slammed straight into his head, killing him instantly.

But none of the friendly fire had exploded. A 4.2-inch mortar has to travel at least nine hundred meters before the warhead arms, and the rounds had only traveled five to six hundred meters, almost undoubtedly because the propellant was wet or otherwise compromised.

By this point, the Vietcong had begun hosing the area down with small arms and automatic weapons. And they certainly had the element of surprise in their favor. But there were not enough of them to ensure success, to survive to reach the wire and breach it. We had an entire battalion on line, firing the FPF and mowing down the oncoming enemy. In addition, although the mortar support from Marcou's section proved an abject failure, not too far away were two guns of a South Vietnamese 105-millimeter artillery battery, from whom I asked for a few beehive rounds. The gunner cranked the tube down to zero elevation and fired an artillery shell filled with thousands of aluminum darts, much like a giant shotgun. Once again, the simple solution prevailed.

And so by the time the sun rose, we had carried the day, and we considered ourselves very lucky to be alive. All of us, of course, except for Corporal Lucky.

CHAPTER NINE

ON JANUARY 31, 1968, the start of Tet Mau Than, the New Year of the Monkey, the communists launched a massive and coordinated offensive, brainchild of North Vietnam's minister of defense, General Vo Nguyen Giap. Timed to begin in the early morning hours of the lunar new year holiday, the offensive was nationwide in scope, a well-coordinated attack of an estimated eighty-four thousand communist troops—both North Vietnamese Army soldiers and Vietcong insurgents—striking more than one hundred towns and cities in South Vietnam. It was the largest military operation yet conducted by either side up to that point, and it came as a radical shock to the generals in the Pentagon and Saigon because for years there had been a de facto truce observed around the celebration of the New Year holiday.

General Giap had embarked on an audacious military gamble. He later said the objective was, all at once, to destroy the majority of South Vietnamese and American units, to topple the government in Saigon, and to destroy American will to continue prosecuting the war. He surmised that when the Vietnamese government crumbled, tens of thousands of South Vietnamese troops would defect to the communist side. His targets included the ancient capital city of Hue, the American embassy in Saigon, and Tan Son Nhut Air Base—all high-profile sites and lightly defended. Most of the frontline forces of both the South Vietnamese army and the U.S. military were out in the bush chasing after the VC or going toe-to-toe with the North Vietnamese Army in battles near the DMZ line, so General Giap's strategy was, in effect, to go for the soft underbelly of rear-echelon targets that had yet to see combat.

Although the offensive was an enormous tactical failure, Tet is cited by many historians as a critical turning point, the moment after which the American people lost their will to support U.S. involvement in the war. Perhaps as many as forty thousand Vietcong and North Vietnamese soldiers were killed, and Giap could not maintain control of any of his tactical objectives, but none of that mattered. The American people watched television and saw that an enemy that had been pounded for years had still managed to infiltrate the heart of Vietnam and mount a vicious coordinated attack. Through the lens of television, viewers observed scenes convincing them that a war of attrition would not work in the asymmetrical environment of Vietnam. In a conflict that pits conventional armament against an unconventional force with less firepower but superior will, the guerillas win. The media, the electorate, and the politicians were losing their collective stomach. Perception had become reality.

ONE OF THE problems with our reliance on the media is that we get a stilted, binomial view of everything. Traditional media are particularly susceptible to episodic reportage. As long as events do not exceed some sliding threshold of either interest or importance, no one will know of them. Above the threshold, it's a deluge. And like an addiction, the threshold rises steadily. After years of stories from the battlefields of Vietnam, the daily fare on the network news became numbing and routine.

But for soldiers who were serving in Vietnam, this wasn't our perception at all. All hell had been breaking loose in our area of operations for some time, and the same thing was true elsewhere. Throughout late 1967 and early 1968, we had encountered increasing enemy contact, taking more casualties and killing more Vietcong. When the North actually launched the offensive, its ability to coordinate attacks across the country was certainly startling to journalists and to people at home—but not to us. It was shocking to the Americans at the embassy in Saigon and to all the rear-echelon troops in areas that had seen little enemy activity. To us the Tet Offensive was deadly and violent but not unexpected.

Moreover, those of us in the bush didn't know anything about Walter Cronkite's dismal conclusion that the war was a stalemate, the president's reaction to it, or the broader debate among the American public. There were no computers, no televisions, and no cell phones, and all we knew was this: we had to accomplish our mission and struggle to keep each other alive. In the middle of a war, a soldier's foci are getting the job done and taking care of each other. The subjective political issues—which way the war was going, what the political sentiment was, the hordes of protestors marching in the streets—were not transmitted to us. And it would have been of little interest anyway, since we spent every day trying to survive the deadly violence of combat.

WITH FORTY YEARS of hindsight, it seems a mistake to credit only the Tet Offensive with turning the tide of the war against the American cause. Single-factor analysis is almost never useful or accurate, and there were many independent variables that contributed to the malaise and recalcitrance of the American public after the Tet Offensive. The first is that even before Tet, the war was already overloading American sensibilities. We'd had significant numbers of Americans in Vietnam for three years—nineteen thousand American dead, ninety-four thousand wounded by the beginning of 1968—and worse, it didn't look like there was an objective end to it. And the South Vietnamese had no end game, either. Second, there was unstable volatility in the Vietnamese government, and the leadership had changed a number of times. The Kennedy administration was supportive of the military coup that toppled and executed South Vietnam's first president, Ngo Dinh Diem, but there appeared to be no subsequent Vietnamese government that was capable of seizing the day. Third, we had an unpopular military draft. People were being dragged into the service and it was selective rather than universal service, as it had been in my father's day. If you went to college you didn't have to serve. If you were married, you didn't have to serve. Young men like Dick Cheney and Bill Clinton could, and did, get a wide variety of deferments to avoid serving. And there are many true accounts—not urban legends, mind you—of judges who gave defendants the choice: "Thirty days in jail or three years in the Army. You pick." So the average quality of our soldiers, while their hearts were in the right place, was not especially high. There was not an equitable distribution of obligation, and that contributed immeasurably to dissention and to a dysfunction that persists to this day. Military service is an uplifting experience, it appears, but only if others do it instead of you.

One of the important lessons of Tet was that, as in any human endeavor, especially warfare, strong leadership is essential, and one of the principal duties of a leader is to pay attention to trends. Serving as a private or a sergeant or a captain, trying to fight a war day to day, one has the attention span of an invertebrate. But if you're a very high-ranking officer, you'd better pay attention to tomorrow, not to today. So, if the national command authority had been doing anything that justified the trust handed to it, it would have come to the conclusion that the enemy was building for something big in

January 1968. But our leaders failed us, as they would fail us again and again.

Even if they had possessed crucial intelligence information, there is no convincing evidence that our general officers were smart enough to react to it. Believing ignorantly that an unconventional conflict was all tactics and no strategy, the majority of high-ranking people were focused on details, mired in statistics, and inured to the comforts that did not afford themselves to the warriors at the point of decision.

The failure of the American adventure in Vietnam occurred mostly by omission, not by commission. We searched for years to find the right way to beat the Vietcong in a counterinsurgency and we never did, but not because we were inherently without the knowledge to do so. We *knew* how to do it, but we didn't have people in charge who understood that being a bureaucrat does not convey leadership ability. President Johnson had no idea of how to use the military instrument of power in any way, even in a conventional context. Alas, despite his superb political instincts, the president didn't understand much about war, and Secretary of Defense Robert McNamara did not seem to understand a lot more. McNamara surrounded himself with a very talented, academically tested cadre, but they were no help in an intellectual process in which assumptions had no basis in fact and the conclusions, perforce, were flawed. About the military, they were just ignorant.

And the truly tragic aspect of the debacle was that many experienced military officers at the pinnacle of the chain of command failed this country because they didn't offer their best advice. Oddly, many of them were browbeaten, letting themselves get overwhelmed by McNamara and his staff to the point that they were too intimidated to speak frankly. This was nothing new. Even Napoleon despaired of such creatures: "The people to fear are not those who disagree with you," he said, "but those who disagree with you and are too cowardly to let you know."

To our great sadness, we would see these officers again in 2003.

Although prepared for martyrdom,
I preferred that it be postponed.

—WINSTON CHURCHILL

In one respect I am extremely lucky, hit in the least significant part of anatomy—my head.

Pieces of shrapnel pierce my skull, ripping through the bone in a number of places, and my head is squirting blood like a fire hose. Reaching around with my fingers, I find a hole and put my first aid pack over it. I find out later that it isn't the biggest hole, but it's the first one I discover. I continue to bleed, everything a red-tinted blur. The firefight is raging, and the terrain is open and unforgiving. All around are unobstructed rice paddies, bordered by low dikes, but there is a nearby tree line that offers some minimal but blessed cover.

I am bent over a wounded soldier when another mortar round explodes nearby. I duck, wince, and grimace reflexively, then glance furtively to where the shell landed, as if looking there will invite more explosions. One of the young soldiers, alive just a second ago, is now heavy-lidded, rheumy-eyed, and already gray with death, an empty husk.

Bullets tear through our little refuge. We are stunned and stalled, and if the VC launch an assault from their bunkers we shall all perish, shot, bayoneted, twisted mannequins for our comrades to discover, no longer compatriots but memories. They will look at us with shock, then sadness, then resignation, and then, merely a logistical problem, we will be hauled away in helicopters. Combat at the level of small units is not a grand, strategic ballet. It's the swift and violent theater of death.

We are pinned down, and every second adds to the danger of being overrun by the VC. One of the battalion's staff officers is with us, wounded by mortar shrapnel, thrown by the explosion into the shallow canal a few meters away. I scamper to the lip of the canal and peer down, staring at his outstretched arm and his wide, imploring eyes. I jump into the water and struggle to haul him out, muscling his limp, lanky frame out of the canal as others pull him onto the bank.

He is bleeding from many small holes in his long legs. I lie on my side next to him, cradling his head, telling myself, He's lucky, has no arterial bleeding, no major wound, and he'll make it. Just a couple of days before, someone took a picture of the two of us back in the battalion's base camp, and we looked exactly like what we were: a couple of war buddies, one American, one Vietnamese. Now we are both seriously wounded. A few seconds later I am staring into his sad, brown eyes as they roll smoothly upward, the irises disappearing forever. A brief tremble and he is gone.

Life is something of a con game. We all have expectations and hopes. Life is worth living as long as we can convince ourselves that our paths may be difficult but our objectives are reachable. Even the most ardent skeptic harbors a tiny seed of optimism that he nourishes in his own, secret con game. But when things collapse in the extremity of armed combat, often hope does, too, and the only salvation is the stark realization that something must be done and you must do it.

I check on Ray and rush back into the chaos. I grab a South Vietnamese machine gunner and two riflemen, telling them to keep firing while I move across the open area toward the closest enemy positions and throw myself against the camouflaged earthworks. I throw a hand grenade into the bunker and scramble back across the open area, chased by snapping bullets until the grenade explodes, and I drag a wounded soldier with me. We do this over and over— inching forward, rifles spitting, hauling wounded friends back. Some are still alive, bleeding and in pain, but others have stopped bleeding, at peace and no longer overcome with the fear that strikes us all.

In combat, there is a huge benefit that comes with being a very small person. I can survive on very little food and even less water. I can curl up and sleep anywhere, crawl anywhere, hide anywhere. Small people are not much of a target, and so I don't understand how large, slow people survive the rigors and dangers of war. If I were two inches taller, I'd be dead. Fueled by fear and the adrenaline it produces. I run, shoot, carry, drag, bleed. I don't reload but instead snatch abandoned weapons from the battlefield.

Einstein was right: time slows down. In battle, three minutes seems like a lifetime.

I am not weighing the alternative missions and making some rational choice. My mission is simple: get as many of the wounded out of the open as I can and prevent the enemy from swarming our little position. Good luck never lasts, though, and the gunner and one of the riflemen are running forward with me when they are felled by automatic weapons fire, and then the other rifleman is shot in the leg. I watch him bleed to death in seconds.

Now I feel alone with my wounded and with the enemy soldiers who are trying to kill us. I am tired and weak and ill, but an odd, calm feeling begins to wash over me. Convinced that I won't survive, I am now relaxed and ready to accept the end, and it is this inevitability of mortality that helps me overcome my fear.

My field of vision collapses to the width of a knife. Blood stream-ing into my eyes, I am a functioning blind man. My head is oscillat-ing frantically to absorb things outside the narrow beam of sight. I think about my comrades, most of whom are already dead or dying or otherwise badly wounded. My brothers in arms are all watching me, so I know I must manufacture courage I do not possess to do what my brothers would do if they could. They are depending on me and I can't let them down. The only thing I know is that something must be done and I must do it.

It's almost funny how the realization hits me. For some reason, in the midst of the death and screaming and chaos, I remember a famous anecdote, probably apocryphal, that I was taught years before, an aphorism of the first-century Jewish sage Hillel the Elder. The story goes like this: A rich man has come to consult Hillel, say-ing, "Rabbi, I pay for everything in my dirt-poor Judean town, and now the people come to me and they say they need even more money. What am I supposed to do?" And Rabbi Hillel answers the rich man's question with a series of his own questions:

"If I am not for myself, who will be for me?

"And if I am only for myself, then what am I?

"And if not now, when?"

Being exposed in the middle of a firefight is not the healthiest place to be. There is a high volume of continuous fire from auto-matic weapons, from a large number of enemy soldiers, and it is ripping the air and ground everywhere. I'm scared, but now I don't focus on the danger. I am thinking only of the voice of a man already dead, reaching across two thousand years:

Jacobs, if not you, then who?

And if not now, then when?

THE RECOGNITION OF valor is an arbitrary intellectual construct. In the heat of battle, soldiers do not think of valor, do not rate acts of brotherhood or compassion or soldierly virtue. Gallantry in the midst of almost certain death is not an act of physical courage, either. To be sure, physical courage can be encountered often in all walks of life, but in strenuous circumstances, it is *moral* courage that makes the difference. It is moral courage that drives the great events of our lives. Starved and weak, the valiant defenders of the Warsaw Ghetto had few weapons and very little physical strength. But they still possessed the courage to hold the Wehrmacht at bay longer than did the entire French army. Moral courage was the only weapon tiny Rosa Parks had, and she used it to change the face of America. Moral courage is not a complicated concept, really, for in its undistilled form it is merely the act of doing the right thing when it is much easier to do otherwise.

What is it that motivates soldiers to keep fighting when the situation is difficult or even hopeless? Why would anyone persist in moving forward to destroy enemy positions when the chances of success and survival are vanishingly small? An action like this is almost never the result of brilliant tactical analysis. In a crisis, thoughts are processed slowly, incompletely, or not at all. When the will triumphs, there is no physical reason for it, really, no explanation that makes sense to those who have not experienced abject fear, sickening horror, and incalculable loss.

The freedom that we enjoy today has been purchased with the blood and sacrifice of countless men and women who were simply doing the right thing, what they were supposed to do, when they needed to do it. Valor is the common currency of war, and this is the reality of combat: for every decorated warrior, there are thousands who receive no recognition for their gallantry and their selfless sacrifice. For every person who has been recognized, there are countless others who have not, legions who performed extraordinary acts under fire with nobody surviving to witness them. Soldiers act not for the accolade but for the lives of their comrades, and every action that is cited for its extraordinary heroism is merely a proxy for all those forever lost in the mist of the battlefield. Medals worn by the living are testaments to the beloved fallen.

So the great irony is that individual effort in battle is not the act of logic but an act of love. You follow your instincts and your training, to be sure, but mostly you follow your heart. Soldiers fight for each other, safe in the conviction that the love of comrades trumps the fear of death, that the pain of one's wound is nothing compared to the unendurable agony of failing one's friends.

"I understand you've got wounded Americans down there," says a disembodied voice, the pilot of a Navy gunship trying to keep the enemy's heads down.

"Roger, we do," I say into the radio handset.

"What's your location?"

I encode the six-digit grid coordinates.

"Can you pop smoke?" The Voice asks, and I fumble for a smoke grenade and muster the strength to throw the canister. It pops in the open fireswept field, foaming a perfect plum color, and almost instantly The Voice comes back on the net. "I identify purple smoke."

"Roger," I say. "Purple smoke."

"Where are the bad guys in relation to the purple smoke?" asks the pilot.

"In the smoke. They're right here," I yell through the intolerable noise of the firefight. It is only now that I understand how difficult things are, that they are likely to get much worse.

There is a pause, and the Navy pilot says calmly, "Oh, that's not very good." The Voice. It is so relaxed and matter-of-fact. It is not the frantic, barking, truncated fragments of panic but instead the mellifluous, compelling Voice of Logic and Reason, the Voice of Salvation, even if the message is not encouraging.

The Voice says, "Look, I see an open area maybe fifty, a hundred meters to the south. Can you get your wounded there? My wingman is coming in."

Can I get them back there? Yes, of course I can.

No, I can't.

I really don't know the answer, do I? The lumbering gray helicopter swoops down, flares its tail boom, and is immediately engaged by ferocious enemy fire. Driven off or destroyed, I can't tell. My vision is failing, my heart racing, my strength fading.

I think I am very sick. I must be coming down with the flu. I'm tired, cold, my hair is on end. I have the flu and need to rest. I have the flu and need to lie down and sleep.

On my back, I look up and see my boss, Major Nolan. I am sick at home with the flu and don't understand what he's doing here. I'm flat on my back and trying to lurch up but can't. He isn't smiling, and so I must have a pretty bad case of it.

And then I hear the gunfire and the explosions, the crack of bullets and the whizzing of hot shrapnel, and I am briefly back where I started, in the midst of combat. What is the reality? I hope for the best, just a bad case of the flu, but I fear the worst, perforated and leaking and fading away.

The first reaction to crisis is denial. This seems real, but it is not happening to me. This is a movie. It's a dream. It's a figment of my imagination, a small fragment of some long-forgotten fear that has quietly grown and now overwhelms my consciousness. I am not wounded. I'm okay.

It's a deep-seated defense mechanism, some hardwiring in my reptilian brain that assures me that nothing bad will happen. To be an infantry soldier in combat you have to delude yourself—to believe in your own invincibility. Getting hurt is something that is going to happen to somebody else, to the enemy, to the guy standing next to me, to Corporal Lucky.

The Voice is silent, but his rockets and machine guns are not.

I am walking or I am running or crawling or being carried to an open area, and I dream I see the old B-model Huey, the insignia of its previous owner, the U.S. Army, in sharp bas-relief under the streaky, faded battleship gray. I must be alive because I can see the remaining helicopter on the ground, a grossly underpowered hunk of junk that can barely get into the air even without all the rockets and ammunition, manned by a crew with more valor than sense.

I don't realize it at the time, but this rickety old crate is flown by The Voice, and as Ray and I and some badly wounded Vietnamese are loaded into the thing, I can hear the crack of bullets through the air and the petrifying bang as enemy rounds slam into the thin skin of the aircraft. I am dizzy and sick—bang—but as I am slid into the helicopter—bang—I think I see the comforting smile of Major Nolan, and then the ship struggles to rise into the bullet-riddled air—bang—I glance to my right and there, inches from me, is Ray's pained face. He is a child at a party, blowing red bubbles, red juice dribbling from his mouth. And I can see beyond Ray, to the vague, inert forms of my Vietnamese comrades.

I know now that it is over and, resigned to it, I fade.

CHAPTER TEN

WE WERE PROBABLY deposited not very far away, at the medical battalion of the American 9th Infantry Division, which was not far from the Vietnamese 9th Division, but it may have been at the surgical hospital nearby. Or it could have been some other place altogether, for all I know.

My first recollection was coming to half consciousness on a gurney, with Ray faceup on a table next to me. At his head was a nurse, it seemed, and as if she were calling bingo numbers, she announced to everyone that Ray's blood pressure was forty over zero. A medical degree was not required to conclude that his blood pressure was a bit too low.

Seconds later, right next to me, two masked men put Ray under and were rummaging among his innards.

"I can't find anything," one said. "How about you?"

A grunt. Neither one of them can find anything inside Ray. But I had seen the holes and the blood, and I knew conclusively that there were things inside Ray that there shouldn't have been. They weren't looking hard enough. Look harder. Lift that intestine a bit higher and you'll find the pieces. Move his liver around, you inept, lazy bastards.

"Let's go look at the films," the first one said, and they marched across the tent and switched on the light behind some X-rays. A minute later, they returned, one of them saying, "So, fragments in his chest." They materialized a huge pair of bolt cutters, and with a noisy crunch proceed to crack Ray open. *Crunch!* From four feet away, someone was being disassembled, as if he were a balky automobile engine undergoing a complete rebuild. New rings and valves and a high-performance camshaft, and Ray would be as good as new. It is a tribute to Ray's indomitable spirit and to the skill of these lovely masked men that Ray survived.

And then off to my left, I noticed a team was noisily working on a U.S. soldier, a mummy swathed in bandages and looking like Joseph Heller's soldier in white, the victim of an artillery round rigged as a mine. There were two doctors and a nurse, valiantly but vainly trying to keep him alive. The nurse was working his chest as if he were a heavy bag, pounding away, right left right, again and again. And she was a big girl, tall and muscular, with Popeye forearms.

He was dead, and the doctors gave up, but the determined nurse was still pounding away on this kid's chest, driven by what? Hope that he may live? Anger that she had lost another young soldier? He was gone, beyond her efforts and love, and she could no longer help him. So, with no rest for weeks, both angry and sad about the steady stream of her broken young men, she came striding purposefully toward me, ham hands at the ends of swinging Popeye arms. She stopped at my side, a female shot-putter with the size, build, and strength of a yeti, angry tears streaming down her round face. And she glared at me with the vituperation reserved only for her worst enemies and for slackers.

"Well, what the hell's wrong with you?"

My head was a mess, with blood everywhere, and I was sick and weak and I thought I was going to die. And if I didn't die from my wounds, it was clear that she was going to do the job. I was convinced that it wasn't the explosion that killed the bandaged soldier. It was this nurse's hydraulic press chest-pounding. Her relentless drive to keep her boys alive had done him in, and I didn't want it to happen to me.

She repeated, "What the hell's wrong with you, young man?"

"There's nothing wrong with me," I blurted out excitedly. "Just give me a couple of aspirins and I'll be on my way. But please don't pound my chest like you did that other guy."

And that's the last thing I remember.

DAYS LATER, I was in a ward of an evacuation hospital, in something that appeared to be a long half-cylindrical tent. Very early every morning, the doctors and nurses started their rounds at one end of the ward, working down, bed by bed, to the other end. As the medics replaced bandages and debrided wounds, cutting away dead and dying flesh, the pained groans and screams and then the long, exhaled sighs of relief moved closer. I was in the very last bed, and the anticipation of pain was painful. Finally, one young doctor looked down at me.

"Whoa," he said. "That's interesting. I've never seen *that* before."

"What?" I said. "What haven't you seen before?"

"Hold on. I've got to get some other people to take a look at this."

"What, what, what?"

He returned shortly with other doctors and nurses. Somebody had a camera and was snapping pictures of me up close with a flash. The medics thrust their faces into mine, and they looked hideously, fish-eye distorted, all giant, crater-pored noses. Trembling with a fear that I had known only in combat, I assumed that they were about to decide to amputate my head, to preserve it for research purposes. Whatever

was wrong with me presented a unique chance almost never encountered. A clinical opportunity like this occurred but once in a lifetime.

"What's this all about?" I said.

"Your face is collapsing," the doctor said.

My face is collapsing? "Well, I don't *want* my face to collapse."

"Don't worry. We'll fix it."

He said that the air pressure needed to be equalized between the
inside and outside, or some similar mumbo jumbo, that they'd have
to inflate my sinus so that the bones could properly knit. Otherwise
my face was going to heal up in this grotesquely collapsed mask.

"Okay," I said, with great suspicion. "I don't want my face to
collapse."

The doc returned a few minutes later with a length of surgical
tubing, and dangling from one end appeared to be a used condom.

"Okay, now," he said. "We're going to snake this up into the sinus
above your right eye, but you have to cooperate. We'll let you drink
some water during the procedure and that'll make it a little bit easier."

"Alright, but I don't want my face to collapse."

"It's not going to be very comfortable, I'm warning you."

He commenced to stuffing this damn thing up my nose. I said,
"Whoa! Ouch! That hurts!"

"Just bear with us—we'll get it up there." And after what seemed
like two or three hours of the worst discomfort this side of a cystos-
copy—it was probably only about fifteen seconds—he managed to
get this rubber apparatus in place.

"That was just about the worst thing I've ever felt in my life," I
said.

"Yeah, it's not going to feel a whole lot better when we blow up
the balloon."

And then he literally blew it up. He put the free end of the tube
into his mouth and blew up the condom inside my head, just as if he
were inflating a balloon. Then he folded the surgical tubing to tie off
the air and taped it to my forehead.

"Now, don't fool with that. We have to leave that in there for a few days."

When he came back some days later, he just grabbed the tubing taped to my forehead, deflated the balloon, and, with one sharp yank, pulled the whole thing out.

The intense discomfort notwithstanding, I was grateful, and I thanked him profusely for preventing my having to join the circus as The Amazing Concave-Face Boy. I suggested that when he left the Army he'd be a hugely successful plastic surgeon.

He chuckled. "I'm not a plastic surgeon," he said, failing to suppress a wry chuckle. "I was drafted six months ago. I'm a gynecologist."

IT WAS THE kind of dream that seizes you when you are most vulnerable: waking from a deep sleep, eyes open—or perhaps not. Days after being wounded, I was inured to believing anything, and an apparition appeared at the foot of my bunk, a man in vivid white, laundry-clean, a ghost. I closed my eyes for a long second, and when I opened them, he was still there, the archetype of corporeal persistence.

Blink. Still there.

So, maybe not a dream.

I was at another evacuation hospital, and as I carefully regarded the ghost, he came into sharp focus. He was a Navy officer, nattily turned out in his vanilla uniform, starched cotton and white bucks, misplaced in a world dominated by brown mud, ocher dust, and red, red blood. With the irredeemably bad manners perfected by staff officers and elected officials, he began to grill me about what had occurred on the morning of March ninth.

"What's this all about?" I said.

"I'm conducting an Article 32 investigation."

What had I done? An Article 32 investigation is the military equivalent of a grand jury procedure, but the accused enjoys protections not afforded in civilian jurisdictions and can be represented by counsel and can cross-examine witnesses. What had I done, and where was my lawyer?

"Article 32?" I asked. "Why are you doing an Article 32?"

"You know the pilot who picked you up? The skipper thinks he endangered his crew and government equipment."

"*What?* For picking up *wounded* people? Are you nuts?"

The entire hospital could hear me screaming in indignation, threatening to remove my drains and IV lines, to lunge at him and strangle him to death. And I would have done so, too, if the staff hadn't rushed over to the commotion I was causing and dragged the startled rear-echelon drone away from the certain ignominy of being throttled by an incapacitated soldier the size of a twelve-year-old.

The name and fate of the Voice, the pilot who saved my life, would have remained a mystery to me but for a chance encounter I had thirty-five years later in New York City. By a complete fluke, and in a demonstration of the inexorable law that things happen for a reason, I ran across a man who knew the Voice. At the invitation of a good friend, I was attending the annual meeting of the Naval Aviation Commandery at the old Seventh Regiment Armory on Park Avenue, a soldier floating in a sea of naval aviators. As befits an event like this, the predinner cocktail hour was sufficiently long to encourage the consumption of numerous adult beverages and the recounting of many war stories, some of them true.

At one point, a well-lubricated former Navy flier suggested that traditional interservice rivalry precluded my having warm feelings toward the Navy.

"No, I love the Navy. I *love* the Navy," and I told him the story of the old B-model Huey rescue, and the crazed hospital scene, and the naval officer in the ice-cream whites and his ludicrous Article 32 investigation and how the doctors and the nurses had to keep me from killing him.

"Wait a minute," he said. "I know the pilot you're talking about."

"You're kidding."

"No, his name is Wes Weseleskey, and he's a friend of mine. He's a retired Navy captain, and he received the Navy Cross for that action." He went on to say that Wes's skipper didn't like him very much and looked for any opportunity to give him a hard time, but that cooler heads prevailed, and the result was his Navy Cross.

A year or two later, Wes was given the organization's annual award, and I attended the dinner and met him for the first time—all over again. Wes was a bear of a man, with a thick white Hemingway beard. With the calm demeanor characteristic only of those who can operate coolly in a catastrophe, his smiling eyes betrayed the warmth inside. And I should have imagined that he would be like this, a man I knew in my darkest hour but never really met. He was my brother, and Ray's brother as well. Wes said that when he set the helicopter down at the hospital, he had to hose out the aircraft because the deck was completely covered with blood. Wes Weseleskey lived the code of the warrior. He came for us even though he didn't have to.

And he knew that we would have come for him, too.

*If Columbus had an advisory committee,
he would probably still be at the dock.*

—ARTHUR J. GOLDBERG

CHAPTER ELEVEN

OUT OF THE hospital, but only temporarily. The nature of a combat wound is that it often necessitates continuous medical care, subsequent surgeries, occasional tune-ups and replacement parts. And aging doesn't help much, either. But I healed relatively quickly in 1968, and, now a captain, I returned to the States with orders to report to Fort Benning, Georgia, where I was given command of a company in the infantry Officer Candidate School. I was not particularly pleased with the idea of commanding what was essentially an administrative organization, but my demands to be assigned instead to a proper infantry unit were first ignored and then vociferously rejected. Evidently, I had failed to scream loudly enough. Perhaps I had lost my edge as an *enfant terrible*.

The OCS program of instruction was six months long and turned enlisted men into officers. Many of the candidates had already been in combat, and they all returned to Vietnam after graduation. With more than half a million troops in Vietnam, there were numerous opportunities to become a casualty, and the Army had a nearly insatiable appetite for new lieutenants. The Infantry School graduated a new crop of about two hundred officers nearly every week of the year.

I reported to Fort Benning, then to my brigade, and then to my battalion commander, moving inexorably down the food chain, down to the level that is intentionally designed to combine a surfeit of responsibility and a paucity of authority. My battalion commander was a pleasant lieutenant colonel who tried hard, not always with success, to conceal his own disappointment with being in charge of an organization without a direct tactical mission. Indeed, considering the fact that almost everybody would have preferred to be elsewhere, it was a tribute to the overriding professionalism of the cadre that we recognized the importance of what we were doing and turned out some very good officers.

The battalion commander told me that I was going to command 65th Company, and I asked him where it was.

"Just turn right out of the headquarters, then left at the next street, and it's on your right-hand side." Now dismissed, I rose, saluted smartly, and left. Following his directions, I encountered a series of large cinder-block buildings, each three stories high and containing an OCS company. But no 65th Company. Indeed, I passed every numbered company in my battalion *except* 65th Company. Cautiously approaching the one building without an identifying shingle, I was gripped with a feeling of increasing disappointment. The grass was overgrown, and in a sure sign that no soldiers were assigned to the unit, the rocks were a natural rock color and not painted white.

An officer's assumption of command is almost always accompanied by a standard ceremony, with the previous commander's passing the company guidon to the new boss, followed by a few brief remarks. As the size of the unit increases, the pomp is multiplied way out of proportion to the utility of the exercise. A division of fifteen thousand soldiers is commanded by a major general, and when it changes hands, the ceremony is a sight to behold, rank after rank of troops with little interest in the actual proceedings or in the general officers involved but still striving mightily to perform as professionally as possible. Their interest in doing an admirable job for people they don't know is even more remarkable in light of the interminable, repetitive, and stultifying practice that such a ceremony requires. But as disagreeable as it sounds, it is still an important ceremony in the life of a military unit, as this is when the new commander makes his first, and lasting, impression on the troops, especially important at the low level of an infantry company, a unit with fewer than two hundred men.

Well, I should have been pleased, for there would be no change-of-command ceremony for me. But I'd been made the commander of a company that did not yet exist, except on paper. Entering my building, I was met by a number of second lieutenants, all recent graduates of OCS. I had a supply sergeant who was irascible, short-tempered, and sullen, all desirable qualities for the job. I had a company clerk, a refugee from Cuba with an impenetrable accent. And that was it.

My executive officer was the senior lieutenant, Dick Berls, and I asked him about a first sergeant. He told me that the first sergeant was on order, as if he were a replacement fuel pump. Alas, Berls was pretty sure that the first sergeant wouldn't get to the company for some time, that we'd have to activate the company without him. This was very bad news, because a first shirt solves all problems and causes everything of importance to occur in a company of soldiers, and the absence of one is an incalculable stroke of rotten luck, especially during the process of activation. With officer candidates arriving in a matter of a week or two, many tasks would have to be accomplished on the fly. It was a bit like performing open-heart surgery on a sprinter while he's competing in the one-hundred-meter Olympic finals.

But it was a huge success, wholly the result of having the world's best lieutenants and noncommissioned officers. I believe that my company clerk, Cresencio Alvarez, had earned one or more advanced degrees in Cuba before he emigrated, just after Castro's ascendancy, and that he had an IQ of about two hundred. One of my lieutenants was an entomologist, and this proved useful in Georgia, where many arthropods are larger than humans and prey on them. Dick Berls, my executive officer, was from California and looked then—and still looks today—like the quintessential surfer dude. For all I know, he was a distant relative of one or more of the Beach Boys.

Realizing that he was working for someone with a short memory and a shorter attention span, Dick planned for every important task and enlisted the resources among the officers and NCOs to accomplish them efficiently. From time to time, he would ask me my opinion, but those instances were almost certainly only for the purposes of co-opting me and ensuring that I didn't begin to think that I had wandered into the company area by mistake.

ABOUT SIXTEEN MONTHS after I had returned from Vietnam, I received a bizarre phone call from somebody who identified himself as a colonel at the Department of the Army.

"Are you Captain Jack H. Jacobs, Infantry, OF108672?"

"Yes, sir," I replied, sounding very tentative, as if I weren't quite sure who I was. Whoever this colonel was, he knew my service number and sounded authentically, and suspiciously, official. I don't recall his name, but it was something preposterous, Colonel Schmedlap, perhaps, or Colonel Smith, in either case an unnatural name and something that had to have been manufactured at a meeting of conspirators.

He continued, "Were you in an action on the ninth of March 1968 as a member of the advisory team attached to 2nd Battalion, 16th Regiment, 9th Vietnamese Infantry Division?"

The old Article 32 investigation? I thought I had scared away the Navy apparatchiks more than a year ago. But maybe this was a new investigation, something involving me directly. I searched the discontinuous strands of my recollection and found nothing. My memory was poor at best, usually incomplete, and most often nonexistent. Typically, I had a hard time remembering what I had for breakfast, let alone something that had happened in 1968.

"Yes, sir, I was."

"Okay, thank you very much."

Now I was nervous. "Sir, what is this all about?"

"I'm just trying to identify who you are and where we can find you. You'll be hearing from us." And then, unceremoniously, he hung up the phone.

Colonels in Washington do not call captains at Fort Benning. What was this all about? I remember staring at the telephone receiver, as if it were an animate object, in possession of secrets I could wring from it if I just stared at it long enough. I firmly gripped the telephone for quite some time, silently imploring it to divulge what the call was all about. If I held the receiver long enough, I could *will* it to tell me the truth. The telephone knew what was up, and I didn't. But the stubborn instrument revealed nothing, and slowly, almost deliberately, I placed the receiver back in its cradle. I was staring sightlessly at the wall.

I was in trouble. This phone call stemmed from my tendency to speak extemporaneously, from the capacity of my mouth to move far in advance of my brain, the same thing that in school had gotten me sent to the principal's office and occasionally disciplined. I concluded that this was the result of my scrounging machine gun ammo from Vinh Long, or maybe from my vituperative radio exchange with the duty officer at the corps tactical operations center, when I threatened to track him down and kill him if he didn't send me ammunition during a firefight. If I had been the duty officer at the other end of that radio conversation, I'd have me investigated, too. Then all too briefly, I believed that the call was actually good news. I hadn't been paid during my first four months in Vietnam. The Army owed me money, and I was finally going to receive it.

But no—I wasn't that lucky, and I remained thoroughly perplexed until several months later, when I received another phone call from the Department of the Army. This time a different colonel called, saying that he was from the Army's Awards Branch.

"Is this Captain Jack Jacobs, OF108672?"

"Yes, sir."

"Congratulations. The secretary of defense is pleased to announce that you will receive the Medal of Honor for your action on nine March 1968." And he continued to describe how some major would call me to arrange the logistics of travel for me and my family to come to the White House for the ceremony, as well as dozens of other details, none of which penetrated the impervious membrane of my surprise and confusion. Because I wasn't giving the attention to the call that it deserved, everything from my end consisted of illiterate grunts and other subhuman noises. It undoubtedly sounded to Colonel Whatshisname as if I were either insubordinately brusque or certifiably deranged or, since they are not mutually exclusive, perhaps both.

Briefly, it occurred to me that this was a crank call, but long-distance telephone service was prohibitively expensive. Any gag call would have to be local, and I didn't know anyone with the talent to disguise his voice sufficiently to remain unknown to me.

The creativity, yes. The chutzpah, yes.

The talent, no.

But as promised, an Army Major called me some days later, and, in the same halting, mumbling inarticulateness, I managed to converse at a very low level of sophistication with him, but just enough to learn how to get everybody to and from Washington and to bring with me adequate socks, underwear, and uniforms. And having dealt with others who had been shocked into insensibility by the news, the Department of the Army gave me sufficient time, about a month, I recall, to compose myself. This, they had learned, was adequate to preclude people like me from embarrassing themselves during the ceremony at the White House.

———————

A FEW YEARS ago, somebody asked Senator Bob Kerrey how one becomes a Medal of Honor recipient. Formerly the governor of Nebraska and now the president of the New School in Manhattan, Kerrey had been a Navy SEAL in Vietnam, lost a leg in fierce combat, and received the award himself for action at Nha Trang in 1969. He may have been quoting someone else, but he said there were four crucial factors:

"You have to do something.

"People have to see it.

"They have to be able to write.

"And they can't hate you."

More than being merely clever, this deft observation cuts straight to the notion of sacrifice, and even to the essence of merit generally. Sacrifice is the essence of military service, even in peacetime. Relinquishing the benefits of doing what you *want* to do and instead doing what you *must* do is at the crux of service to the community. To be sure, there is a measure of self-aggrandizement in every human endeavor, and no matter why they join in the first place, members of the armed forces extract from their service an intense satisfaction from having done something important and useful. Moreover, sacrifice for the whole is not a triviality, especially in an age in which the vagaries of a complex, changing, and dangerous world put a premium on the quality of our security and the patriotism of the very small number of Americans who provide it for the rest of us.

Every aspect of military service, particularly the personal sacrifice inherent in it, is intensified during armed combat against a hostile enemy. For every person cited for performing a valorous act there are many more who were brave and received no accolade. The actions of patriots do not lose their value because they are not observed, and those who are lauded for having performed meritoriously bask not in the brief sunshine of public gratitude but in the eternal pride of representing all those who cannot.

———————

THE CEREMONY WAS scheduled for October 9, 1969, and my family and I arrived in Washington from disparate places a few days before that. The Army ensconced us all in the Madison Hotel, which was the height of luxury at the time, and it seemed especially so to someone like me, whose previous standards of excellence were warm Spam and a tent that didn't leak. It was easy to get inured to posh accommodation, room service, and being able to call on other human beings to perform inconsequential services, and after only a few hours of civilized doting by genuflecting staff, I found the entire arrangement to be quite agreeable. I thought it curious, however, that the Defense Department would risk exposing soldiers to this classy treatment, risk my concluding that I would never again enjoy this kind of life on three hundred dollars a month and that I should resign right after the ceremony, earn a proper salary, and live permanently in the Madison. The staff would come to know my name, anticipate every luxury I might arbitrarily desire, and free me from the tyranny and ennui of mundane tasks. Never again would I have to drive a car without a gas gauge or worry that the washing machine's wringer would run amok and devour someone's arm. On my behalf, others would battle balky carburetors, feisty cockroaches, and third-hand appliances with minds of their own. In winter, looking outside would not entail first scraping the ice from the *inside* of the window. So, in a matter of hours or even minutes, I had concluded that a life of luxury was for me, and that it would be much easier for a pedestrian soldier to become accustomed to ease than for a well-to-do, parasitic layabout or a smug academician to become enchanted with the demands of military service.

Three other soldiers were to be decorated during the same ceremony, cited for action in different battles, and early that morning, we were all driven to the White House in a variety of Cadillacs, Lincolns, and other vehicles with functioning speedometers and genuine vinyl upholstery. Prior to the ceremony, we received a tour of the White House, and in the East Room we met several people who had been familiar faces on news programs: Secretary of Defense Melvin Laird and Secretary of the Army Stanley Resor, for example. In the center of the room, there was a large table displaying delicious-looking pastries, all of which were either gooey or dusted with powdered sugar and could not be eaten without decorating my uniform with the stuff. I settled for a cup of coffee, only adequate even by standards in the Army, where the beverage was routinely prepared by boiling the grounds until the liquid had acquired the chemical properties of nitric acid, then strained through a sock or a pillowcase. I have been to White House receptions since then and can report that things have improved dramatically, with most pastries now bite-size and easy to consume even by someone as sloppy as I am. The coffee is still pretty awful.

We were ushered into the Oval Office, and we four recipients received a short briefing from the president's military aide, an Army colonel. He described how we would form two lines and then on cue march outside and mount a platform constructed on the South Lawn. Our instructions were not complicated: find our taped marks on the platform, salute when appropriate, and shake President Nixon's hand after he presented the award. There was no guidance on smiling, however, and although I believed that I had kept my face appropriately stony, as befitted the solemn occasion, photographs show me grinning quite broadly while shaking hands with the president.

We milled around for a minute or two, and then Nixon approached me and whispered, "Are you nervous, son?"

"No, sir, I'm not," I said.

"Well, I am," Nixon said, smiling weakly. And as I looked at him, it occurred to me that he appeared exactly as he did in the media: overly large head, prominent ski-jump nose, small beads of perspiration collecting on his upper lip over the pancake makeup. He was his own double, the one who appeared in photographs and cartoons, and it was shocking how accurately life could imitate art.

When we marched outside, the sight was startling, even shocking. The day had been designed by Providence and was brilliant, the sky a shining, cloudless light blue, and there was a faint, comfortable breeze. But what was most arresting was the size of the crowd.

Since the attacks in 2001, security is now very much different from what it was in 1969. Back then, it was possible to drive down Pennsylvania Avenue, and before that, Harry Truman made it a habit of taking a regular walk around Washington. Now, of course, travel by air has all the convenience of a stagecoach ride but without the comfort, and it includes the inspection of shoes and the confiscation of toothpaste and water. It now takes less time to drive to many destinations than it does to fly, and a one-hundred-year-old woman is just as likely as a bona fide terrorist to be patted down. In fear of being accused of profiling, of being arbitrary, the government has opted instead to be nonjudgmentally ecumenical by inconveniencing everyone and in the process becoming grossly inefficient, making it more difficult to detect a threat.

But on October 9, 1969, when life was simpler and perhaps more logical as well, the gates to the White House lawn had been opened, and anyone in Washington who wanted to stroll onto the grounds and watch the ceremony was free to do so. Government workers had been given the morning off, and thousands flooded the grounds. There was a throng, a solid wall of people really, all the way to the wrought-iron fence hundreds of yards away.

It wasn't until the ceremony had ended that it occurred to me that I was now a very different person. No longer just a soldier, I was now a representative of the 3,400 recipients who'd come before me, of the 450 recipients still surviving at the time, and, most important, of all the soldiers who died defending the nation. From that day on, how I comported myself would have to be wholly a function of being entrusted with a responsibility that I hadn't had the day before.

CHAPTER TWELVE

ABOUT A YEAR after activating my OCS company, the unit was preparing to graduate its second class of about two hundred new lieutenants, and I had almost come to grips with my disappointment at not having command of a proper tactical organization. Since I had had two assignments in a row that were nontraditional, it was easy to come to the conclusion that the Army viewed me as something of an oddball and a second-class citizen, marked by an indefinable characteristic that suggested I be kept at some distance. In reality, it was nothing of the sort, and if I had been more intellectually mature, I would have seized on a more valid reason for being out of the career mainstream: the Army was quite impervious to reason and logic, and my assignments were the result not of any personal animosity but of the arbitrariness that characterizes most large, cumbersome organizations. Being at the bottom of any ladder and watching the antics of senior officials can easily convince novices that the basic principles they learned on entry are not worth remembering, that luck is the currency of success, or perhaps it is the rapacity and unctuousness of the more unappealing climbers that are worth emulating. In our own minds, it is the failure not the success that we often remember, and the lesson it teaches is rarely a good one.

Just before graduating my second cycle of new officers, my battalion commander reported that the demand for lieutenants was waning and that my new mission was to shut down 65th Company. A year earlier, I had suffered through the administrative nightmare of activating it, and now I was stuck with shutting it down. Less daunted by embarking on another complicated task than I was saddened by the prospect of disassembling what I had built, I was still shocked by the confirmation that it is much simpler to take something apart than to create it in the first place. So, although the result is almost never attractive, one of the world's irrefutable laws is that building something is difficult. Destroying it is easy.

———————

NOT LONG AFTER I was told to deactivate my company, I received orders to attend the Infantry Officer Advanced Course, designed to reinforce knowledge of company tactics and to teach captains how to be staff officers at the levels of battalion and brigade. Unlike the basic course, almost all the instruction was in the classroom, and this precluded the inexpert administrative fumbling that accompanied student-run activities in the field. The course had the added advantage of being at Fort Benning, and so I would not have to move my family again. By the end of the course, I would have been in one place for two years, a lifetime by Army standards in 1969. Frequent deployments and changes of station are a part of the fabric of military life, and families usually grow to be experts at relocating, ameliorating one of the many stresses inherent in service. But it is never any fun, and most stressful were those years in which we were required to move more than once. In 1967, for example, we moved three times, and the only salvation was that we had so few possessions that everything we owned could be packed into the first five feet of a moving van.

WITH HUNDREDS OF officers in my advanced class, almost everyone a combat soldier, there was a solidarity rare in other professions. We had common experiences and thus common stories—about great troops, disastrous mistakes, world-class meatheads. Everyone had been in units with moronic commanders, conniving supply sergeants, heroic private soldiers. Not uncommon were dart games played through mortar attacks, flights of helicopters delivering soldiers to the wrong landing zones, and misplaced air strikes. In any other circumstances, diverse personalities like ours would have had nothing in common, but the bond of soldiering was strong, and it was combat experience that we shared. That, and the certainty of being sent back to Vietnam when the course was over. With the administration's possessing no clear objective measurement of success in Vietnam, the large majority of captains would head back to Southeast Asia for their second or third combat tours.

And poker. The bonding strength of poker cannot be exaggerated. There was a small group of about half a dozen of us who became long-term friends, a friendship that solidified through the gelling agent of dealer's-choice poker. It was something of a floating game, with each player in turn hosting a session in his quarters. These meetings began just after dinner on Friday and usually didn't finish until the beginning of morning nautical twilight on Saturday, leaving the host's kitchen a soggy, smoky mess and his wife resolved to file for divorce the following Monday. These began as penny-ante games, but we soon concluded that bluffing was impossible if the cost of doing so was not prohibitive, a lesson about human nature clearly lost on contemporary American officials. So, stakes were raised, and then raised again, until we reached the level at which the loss of a significant hand would prevent the purchase of food for a week, and those were exactly the right stakes. Of course, there's an exception to every rule, and one of our number was nothing if not an eternal optimist. He stayed in every hand until the very end, and his luck was such that he frequently drove us to exasperation by drawing an inside straight, or drawing the case ace for a winning two pair, or—the worst—refusing to be bluffed and so raking in the pot with a ten high.

In the class many of my closest friends were graduates of the U.S. Military Academy at West Point, mostly members of the classes of 1964 and 1965. Among my peers, they were the most adept at culling amusing anecdotes from the horror of combat, commanded both the best and the worst soldiers, and played cards with the most verve and stamina. They were dedicated and irreverent, literate and vulgar, brash and maudlin. They were versions of *me*, actually, except that they had gone to West Point, which conferred on them an air of professionalism that I had not possessed when I had come on active duty four years before. My original plan of completing my service and then going to law school had faded, dissipated, and had finally vanished. In those increasingly infrequent times I contemplated leaving the Army, I quickly rejected doing it. I loved the mission and I loved the people, and neither the danger nor the insecurity nor even the prospect of having to serve on a mind-numbing staff was sufficient to deter me from staying.

About halfway through the course, many of my West Point friends received unsolicited letters from the Army, asking if they would like to attend graduate school and then serve on the West Point faculty in one academic department or another, and I can't recall anyone who didn't jump at the chance. Not having gone to West Point myself, I got no letter. But although I wasn't a world-class intellect, I thought that if the Army was paying soldiers to engage in graduate study, I wanted to be one of them. If anyone needed additional schooling, it was I, and I convinced myself that ultimately the service would benefit from my acquiring a more substantial liberal education.

Some might argue that there was another motivation. With a general aversion to returning Medal of Honor recipients to combat, the

Army was not going to send me back to Vietnam. This meant that, in all likelihood, I would be assigned to some ghastly staff at a superfluous headquarters performing insipid, pointless tasks for superior officers of inferior quality. And so I called my assignment officer in Infantry Branch and begged to go to graduate school.

It is possible that, by then, Infantry Branch was so fed up with me that it would have assigned me to be a lifeguard in a car wash if I had asked for it, just to get rid of me. But in any case, after being accepted by Rutgers, I received orders for two years to earn an MA in political science when the advanced course was over, in a few months.

Meanwhile, from time to time at the Infantry Officer Advanced Course we would be subjected to distinguished guest speakers. The typical guest speaker is a friend of the course director or else his brother-in-law, to whom he owes some enormous favor or a moderate sum of money. In the alternative, the guest speaker is someone whose speech is so incomprehensibly abstruse that the course director, not understanding a word of it, thinks that it must be deep and incisive. One encounters these people, these distinguished guest speakers, at academic institutions everywhere. They are often hired to deliver commencement addresses, for which they are paid sums equivalent to the gross domestic product of South America, but they also turn up at social clubs and on cable news channels, where they receive far less, although, regrettably, the lack of remuneration does not seem to deter them. No matter where they are encountered, the effect of these distinguished people is pretty much the same: a sudden feeling of relaxation and well-being, followed by unconsciousness. Polite applause signaling the end of the session is usually sufficient stimulus to emerge from the coma.

The exception was Dr. Fritz G. A. Kraemer, something of a permanent fixture in Washington and a legend.

Born in Germany, Kraemer was a Lutheran who had no stomach for Hitler, and he escaped to America in 1939. He became a citizen and was inducted into the U.S. Army four years later, becoming an infantryman in the 84th Infantry Division, and he fought in the Battle of the Bulge. Kraemer was a sharp-eyed scout for national security talent, a mentor of Henry Kissinger, Alexander Haig, and Herman Kahn. For many years, he was the Senior Civilian Advisor to the U.S. Army Chief of Staff, and there he was a major influence on American strategy during the Cold War. When Kraemer died, at the age of ninety-five, everybody who was anybody attended the military funeral.

One afternoon in early 1970, Dr. Kraemer came from Washington to speak to our course at Fort Benning. And he was very, very good. Everyone, even those with little interest in anything more sophisticated than the characteristics of weapons, were impressed by his depth of knowledge and the ease with which he talked about so many important national security issues. After the speech, the head of the leadership department at the infantry school, Colonel Hoefling, invited me and a few other students to attend a cocktail party at his quarters for Dr. Kraemer. At some point, quite late into the evening, Colonel Hoefling buttonholed me.

"Listen," he whispered, "Dr. Kraemer is completely bombed. Do me a favor. You have your car here, don't you?"

"Yes, sir, I do."

"And you know where the VOQ is, right?"

He meant the visiting officers' quarters, where big shots stayed the night. These were spartan facilities, each just a wood-paneled bedroom with a minuscule sitting room, but at least it had a private toilet, and it passed for elegance at Fort Benning, Georgia, in 1970.

"Get Dr. Kraemer, put him in your car, drive him back to the VOQ, and make sure he gets to bed. He's really in the tank."

I collected Dr. Kraemer and steered him into my rusting Chevy station wagon. Even in his condition, I was embarrassed to give him a lift in the thing. It had three speed on the steering column, a pathetic and balky engine, an exhaust pipe belching smoke, and cancer, a truly sad piece of junk. During the short drive we started chatting and, in retrospect, it's astounding how lucid he was, given how much he'd had to drink. Yet his intellect was such that he could carry on a proper conversation, although his words were slurred and with each passing minute sounded more like Erich von Stroheim.

"So, what do you do, my boy?" he asked. He seemed actually quite chipper.

"I'm a student at the Infantry Officer Advanced Course," I said.

"What are you going to do when you're finished?"

"Actually, I just got word. The Army is sending me to graduate school." I was very proud of myself.

"Oh, that's excellent. What field?"

"Political science."

"Wonderful. And what's your utilization assignment?"

"Uh. Actually, sir, I don't have one yet."

There was a long pause, and I thought that Kraemer had passed out. "Hmmm," he said, finally. "That's not good at all."

"Not good? Why not, sir?"

"For one thing, it means that you'll be coming to the Pentagon."

"The Pentagon? My God, I don't want to go to the Pentagon."

I thought, I would rather have a colostomy than go to the Pentagon. It is endless suffering in a heartless bureaucracy, manned by zombies and sloths. The place is a purgatory, and perhaps even hell itself.

"Well," said Dr. Kraemer quite matter-of-factly, "you *are* going to the Pentagon, because you do not have a specific utilization assignment."

Fumbling with the key while struggling to prop him upright, I got Dr. Kraemer into his quarters. I poured him into bed, and he was asleep before I reached for the doorknob seconds later.

I had been so pleased with myself that I was going to graduate school that I hadn't thought about a utilization assignment. Of course I needed one. The Army was prepared to spend lots of money sending me to school, and it wanted something in return. And this was going to be more costly for the government than one would think, since for everyone going to school there had to be someone else taking his place in the ranks of the operational Army. Oh, yes, the Army was going to extract from me its retribution. I was going to be reimbursed, with interest, for all the snide remarks and hyperbolic criticisms, for following only those orders from superiors I thought worthy, for being most comfortable in irreverence. The soldier who regarded bureaucracy lower than all other things was going to be a bureaucrat.

I ARRIVED AT Rutgers for the fall semester of 1970, at the peak of the antiwar movement, a year after Woodstock, and four months after the Kent State shootings. I was clearly a member of the establishment: short hair, clean clothes, blemish-free skin. I often spoke in complete sentences, rarely said "like" and "you know," and wore shoes with uppers. In something of a reversal, I didn't wear a uniform, but all the other students did: denim, a vest, a surfeit of facial and body hair. Overnight my compatriots had changed from people who had faced the abyss to those who occasionally thought about stuff. Had I given it much consideration, I would have anticipated mean-spiritedness, vituperation, hypocrisy, and the other uncivilized behavior that is characteristic of those gripped by high emotion but without a clear understanding of facts.

Alas, none of this occurred, which was unfortunate because it would have provided considerable grist for recounting scenes that resembled those in the film *Born on the Fourth of July*. Those things surely happened to others but not to me. But although there was no lack of civil discourse, a pleasant surprise, the depth of my classmates' grasp of national security was merely the veneer provided by television news. More laughable was their citing the difference between just and unjust wars but not having any understanding of the concept or, more pathetic, any knowledge of who Aquinas and Augustine even were. But the conversations that were the most entertaining for me were those that required disabusing them of common but erroneous wisdom.

There was—and perhaps still is—a widespread notion that putting a uniform on anyone, no matter how well adjusted, would instantly transform one into a psychopath. The conventional understanding was that if you wanted to destroy a lifetime of good moral development and rectitude, merely send a young man to war, and he will return unfit for society. War is no uplifting experience, but neither is it the catalyst that will transform the majority of its participants into demented, antisocial malcontents. I was once asked by a reporter if I had recurrent flashbacks. I replied that I did, but they were of a girl I had known in high school.

———

MEANWHILE, I STILL didn't have a utilization assignment. Since I would owe the Army four years of my future—two for each year in graduate school—the prospect of spending it in the Pentagon was more demoralizing than almost anything else, including the daily routine of having to disassemble and reassemble my car's ignition system. This entailed removing the steering wheel so I could get to the ignition switch circuitry, and I bought a tool designed expressly for that purpose, a purchase normally made only by car thieves. Having very little money was no fun, but it did engender a certain measure of ingenuity and self-reliance.

I had moved my family into a rented house about ten miles east of the campus, in a working-class subdivision of modest homes that were heroically but inexpertly maintained. The children in the neighborhood were shaggy louts, lank hair obscuring the vision from bloodshot eyes, and they were only infrequently in attendance at school. On Halloween, offering treats to these budding delinquents did not preclude the minor vandalism that inevitably followed, and there appeared to be no negative correlation between giving them candy and having the front door spray-painted. I decided to save the money.

It had been about two years since I had last seen Dr. Fritz Kraemer lying unconscious in the narrow bed at Fort Benning. In four months I would receive my graduate degree, but I still had no utilization assignment. I had forgotten completely about our conversation. Evidently, he had not.

My irreverent creativity had deserted me, and I was having trouble concocting a workable plan to avoid Pentagon service at the same time I was polishing my thesis, keeping my car glued together, and repainting the front door. One morning, I received a call from a colonel who identified himself as Amos Jordan, head of the Department of Social Sciences at West Point.

"Fritz Kraemer called and said you ought to come up here and be on the faculty."

He invited me for a visit, to meet him and others on the faculty and see if I liked the place. I found it remarkable that Kraemer had remembered our conversation or anything from that evening, let alone had remembered our talk faithfully enough to act on it more than a year later. My own memory is such that I recall very little about things that I've promised to do, and when I *do* remember, the recollection contains very few details. I am startled when I get a phone call from someone reporting that everyone is assembled at the meeting in Los Angeles and asking me if I'll be a little late. It's very painful for me to reply that I am in London and will be a bit later than they expect. Most of the time I merely have a vague feeling of disquiet, a sense that I am required to do something or to call someone, but that's hardly enough information to act. Writing things down helps occasionally, but I misplace the notes.

Despite never having been to West Point, and with an incomplete sense of where it actually was located, I was nevertheless inclined to accept the assignment without delay. But Colonel Jordan wanted to meet me, and sounding too enthusiastic on the phone might give him the impression that I was bereft of other opportunities, or that maybe I had just committed a felony and was looking for somewhere to hide until things blew over.

My father had never been to West Point either, but he had some idea how to get there. So a few days later, we drove the hundred miles north, and I instantly fell in love with the place. It is a national treasure, a spectacularly picturesque campus perched on an escarpment over the Hudson River and steeped in history stretching back to a time before the formation of the Union. It is unlike any other military installation, the equivalent of an Ivy League campus swarming with smart young people, but the air is filled with the intoxicating perfume of tradition, dedication, and service. The buildings are of native granite, and the views are breathtaking. Monuments and statues are everywhere, strategically sited so that neither cadets nor faculty forget the contributions of Washington and Patton, or the sacrifice of soldiers during the Civil War. The flagpole is the mainmast of the battleship *Maine*.

I tried hard to appear businesslike, to avoid drooling noticeably, grinning like a moron, or telling Colonel Jordan that I would be so overjoyed to join the faculty that if he told me the address of one of his enemies I would be honored to send a few of the boys to pay him a visit or at least surreptitiously remove his steering wheel and dump it in a landfill on Staten Island.

No need for favors. I was in.

More important, the Pentagon was out.

A few short weeks later, Infantry Branch called me to confirm that my utilization assignment would be service on the faculty of the U.S. Military Academy. For the first time since I joined the Army, I was pleased enough to thank my assignment officer. And I very nearly did. Until he delivered the bad news.

"There's one hitch," he said. Have you ever noticed that there's always *one* hitch? There are rarely more, because Natural Law Number Seven (b) dictates that one hitch is all that is required to destroy plans and success. Why go overboard erecting many impediments to happiness when only one will do? It makes sense that the default condition should be the smallest number of hitches required to ruin things. So there are rarely lots of hitches. But alas, the number of hitches, at least for me, is never zero.

"West Point doesn't need you until 1973," he said. This faceless assignment officer, this Nemesis for whom the name was invented, was almost certainly grinning broadly, euphoric in the knowledge that he had disappointed me and was about to make my life miserable. I pictured his casually taking a bite of a liverwurst sandwich, perhaps pointing at his telephone and smiling conspiratorially at the officer next to him, sharing the fun of delivering bad news. I had come to the conclusion that Infantry Branch was composed solely of officers who had to pass special psychological tests, examinations devised to distinguish between people who enjoyed torturing small animals and the truly sadistic. Assignments officers were the latter.

"But '73 is next year," I deduced brilliantly.

"Right," said Nemesis. "Until then, we're sending you on a short tour."

A short tour is the assignment officer's ultimate weapon. It is served with no family accompaniment in one of the world's numerous undesirable locations. It would be one thing to be stuck alone in Paris, Rome, or Rio for a year—most hard-nosed patriots would be able to make the best of such a bad situation and survive the experience with limited permanent damage. But locations for short tours were selected precisely because they were *not* Paris, Rome, or Rio.

"Where?" I asked.

"Korea."

"*Korea?* No, sir, I don't want to go to Korea. It's almost on the Arctic Circle—it's freezing in Korea. No, sir, Korea's definitely not for me."

The truth is that Korea is *not* almost on the Arctic Circle and it's usually not much colder in the winter than New Jersey, but it still wasn't for me. An assignment there would have all the worst characteristics of stateside duty—equipment shortages, maintenance headaches, and insufficient training funds—except that it is 6,800 miles from home.

Well, the conversation continued for quite some time, with my complaining about going to Korea and his insisting that I was going. My voice was trembling with unhappiness, but his betrayed a glee, actually a schadenfreude that is the special, secret pleasure of serial killers and assignment officers.

After some time, he had grown quite tired of my resistance. There was a long silence on the phone.

"What about Vietnam?" I asked finally.

"No, no, no," he said, as if he were admonishing a six-year-old he had just caught doing something irreparably damaging to his moral development. "No, you can't go to Vietnam," the major said.

"Why not?"

"Well, you can't. Recipients can't serve in a combat area."

As for Medal of Honor recipients' not being allowed to return to a combat zone, I knew that was complete nonsense. There was no codified rule, no regulation. In theory, of course, the Defense Department would prefer not to lose a Medal of Honor recipient to enemy fire, but it had occurred in the Second World War, and Keith Ware, decorated for action in World War II, was killed in action in Vietnam. Even today, Gordon Roberts, a recipient who earned his award as a young medic in Vietnam, is still on active duty and has served multiple tours in Iraq.

But in 1972, the Army was adamant. We argued strenuously for quite some time and eventually reached something of a compromise.

"Okay, you can go to Vietnam, but you must serve in the headquarters of the Military Assistance Command in Saigon," I was told. "You may not go to a combat unit." Nemesis, the divine goddess of retribution, had assumed the form of my assignment officer, I had faced her in a close encounter, and I had vanquished her.

"No, sir. No combat."

A ship in harbor is safe,
but that is not what ships are built for.

—WILLIAM SHEDD

NEWARK PUBLIC LIBRARY
121 HIGH ST
NEWARK

CHAPTER THIRTEEN

I ARRIVED IN Saigon on the Fourth of July in 1972 and was shipped to Camp Alpha, not far away. The minute I could find a telephone, I rang up the Airborne Advisory Team, and after what seemed like twenty rings, someone answered, identifying himself as Sergeant First Class Biondo.

"I need to speak to the Senior Advisor," I said in my most officious tone of voice. I suspect I sounded like a radio announcer advertising a new antacid.

"Not here," said Biondo.

"How about the deputy?"

"Not here."

"The admin officer?"

"Nope."

"Where is everybody?"

"Up north," he explained. "The division just came out of An Loc and is near Quang Tri right now."

"Timing is everything," Mark Twain once opined, and he may have had me in mind when he coined it. Few people have had worse timing than I. As if Nemesis had decided to concede the game but not without winning a set, I had returned to Vietnam just in time for more hell breaking loose, to that time in the war of the most ambitious conventional invasion by the North Vietnamese, and the largest military operation since three hundred thousand Chinese had stormed across the Yalu River during the Korean War. Archives show that the American leadership had been expecting a major attack sometime during 1972, but the size and ferocity of the assault was almost as big a surprise as Tet had been more than four years earlier. With the bulk of his army, General Giap had struck at South Vietnam simultaneously on three fronts.

In the I Corps Tactical Zone, North Vietnamese forces overran South Vietnamese defensive positions in a battle that lasted weeks and captured the provincial capital of Quang Tri before moving south in an attempt to seize the ancient capital city of Hue. The Vietnamese Airborne Division had held the line in the highlands south of Da Nang, but they would now be tested in the north, charged with the mission of recapturing the city of Quang Tri.

"What's this all about? What do you need?" Biondo asked. Military people are inherently suspicious, and nobody is more suspicious than a noncommissioned officer, especially one like Biondo, who, I would later learn, had been promoted and busted so many times that he said he was the original Elevator Man: up a few ranks, and then right down again, time after time.

"Well, I want to come to the Airborne Advisory Team."

"Where are you?"

"I am over at Camp Alpha."

"Give me your name, rank, and service number, and I'll see what I can do. I have a friend in the orders section at MACV headquarters. I can be there in about two hours."

And sure enough, two hours later, Sergeant First Class Rick Biondo, from Aliquippa, Pennsylvania, showed up with orders for me to join the Airborne Advisory Team. As simple as that. Nemesis must have been asleep or, more likely, busy torturing someone else.

Memory is a wonderfully selective evolutionary adaptation. Like a mother whose recollection of the pain of childbirth has been erased by the subsequent joy of having a child, five years after being wounded I wasn't focused on the dangers of combat. I had lived among my friends and family, in a civilized country that had suffered almost nobody killed by artillery, as near as I could remember, and my memory of the misery of combat had faded. In addition, I was running the financial calculations in my head: $3.50 a day for being assigned to an airborne unit, family-separation allowance of a dollar a day, hostile-fire pay of two dollars a day. That was not quite $6.50 a day, an extra fifty dollars per week, and barely of interest to a laborer, but to a soldier with three other mouths to feed, it seemed like a fortune.

Biondo took me in a jeep through uncompromisingly aggressive traffic to a small shop on a narrow, crowded street in downtown Saigon, to buy a red beret and several camouflage pattern uniforms unique to the Vietnamese Airborne Division. One front pocket was emblazoned with the winged sword of Saint Michael, patron saint of paratroopers and the field commander of the Army of God mentioned in the Book of Daniel. Alas, Michael is also the patron saint of grocers and, less encouraging, of sickness.

Now smartly outfitted and fully kitted out, we drove to Tan Son Nhut Air Base and boarded a small cargo plane, a C-123 flown by Vietnamese pilots who took us north several hours to Phu Bai Airport. The strip was located just to the southwest of Hue, the old imperial city that had been under siege for months during the Tet Offensive, the citadel penetrated and captured by the North Vietnamese Army but finally retaken in a long, deadly battle.

The war had changed dramatically since 1968. In 1972, the NVA had invaded in force, a large conventional army fighting conventional tactics. This was now a war of armor and heavy artillery, of massed fire, attack and counterattack. Almost five years earlier, the battle-field dangers were direct-fire weapons like small arms and machine guns. Now the enemy had augmented his arsenal with devastating artillery, 122-millimeter and 130-millimeter pieces, and tanks.

We landed at Phu Bai, and with the engines still cranking, the crew threw an odd assortment of equipment and numerous crates of ammu-nition onto the pierced-steel planking of the tactical runway, and then the C-123 promptly took off and disappeared into the low, dark clouds, leaving Biondo, a few Vietnamese paratroopers, and me on the deserted strip. When I had served in Vietnam years earlier, Phu Bai had been a very busy military airport, but now it was an eerie, empty ghost.

We stood around for a while, waiting for someone to meet us, but after about ten or fifteen minutes we were still by ourselves. I was not so naïve as to expect to be met by a band, children with floral offerings, and a large, boisterous contingent of well-wishers, but nei-ther did I anticipate nobody. This did not augur well.

"There should be a helicopter meeting us," said Biondo. "Let me get on the horn and find out what's going on."

He made a call on a battered PRC-25 radio, and within a few minutes a U.S. Army UH-1H helicopter came in for a landing. The crew chief waved to us, and we threw the gear, ammo, and then our-selves on board and took off.

We were flying north to Firebase Sally, the headquarters of the Vietnamese Airborne Division, and landed there amid an impenetra-ble wall of swirling dust. The pilot feathered the blade, the dust tried to settle and then cleared a bit, and we hopped from the aircraft.

The place was not what I expected and surely not the same Fire-base Sally that years earlier had served a succession of units. American military organizations tend to construct meticulous approximations of stateside installations: latrines, showers, theaters, painted rocks. In 1968, and even as late as 1970, Sally had been a relatively com-fortable place to live. Everything had been temporary and makeshift, but it had also looked appealingly neat and tidy, kept that way by legions of soldiers and by contingents of local hires, some of whom had undoubtedly been Vietcong. Whatever else one could say about the enemy infiltrators, it is my understanding that they had been admirably diligent about keeping troops' boots shined, uniforms pressed, and barracks cleaned. They were the enemy, but they took excellent pride in their housekeeping work.

By the time I got there, things were not quite the same. Firebase Sally resembled nothing so much as the ruins of a field defensive position in the Dark Ages or the remnants of captured earthworks at the Somme. Defensive positions were mostly unmanned and had collapsed. Disintegrating sandbags were everywhere. I nearly tripped over a large chunk of spent shrapnel. As I hopped out, somebody pointed me in the direction of a line of bombed-out bunkers, where I found the sergeant major of the American advisory team, and he led me inside a small, crumbling fortification. Behind a rickety plywood field desk sat a white-haired American colonel, the senior advisor of the Airborne Advisory Team.

"Sir, Captain Jacobs reports," I said, saluting.

The colonel returned my salute and shook my hand. "Captain Jacobs, how are you?"

"Fine, sir."

"Great," he said. This was nearly the end of a very, very short interview, as if he were late for an appointment or suffering from the runs. He gestured vaguely behind me toward the sergeant major. "He'll give you some ammo and grenades. Your helicopter is already cranking. You're replacing the senior advisor to First Battalion. Good luck."

I saluted smartly and exited the bunker, but I was not entirely pleased with the "good luck" bit. Everyone wants good luck, and nobody wants bad luck, except for trial lawyers who advertise on television and people owed money. So, under normal conditions—at a wedding or a bar mitzvah or even at the end of a divorce proceeding—wishing someone "good luck" is good manners. But in the middle of a place that looked like it had been ground zero of an atomic blast, and delivered with an abruptness that telegraphed a fear that

Firebase Sally would soon be overrun by the entire People's Liberation Army, "good luck" sounded as if the colonel didn't have the heart to append "...and you'll need it, pal."

The helicopter was loaded haphazardly with boxes of bandages, ammunition, hand grenades, and Vietnamese C ration cans of sardines. Set indifferently atop this pile of boxes and crates was a portable generator with a hand-crank motor. And perched atop *that* was Captain Jack Jacobs, fully combat ready, weapon loaded, and now suspicious that he had perhaps made a small error in judgment, that maybe Korea would have been a slightly better way to kill a year, that if Korea was really too cold, he could have just worn gloves and an extra sweater.

Escorted by Cobra gunships and a light observation helicopter, my chopper flew west and north from Firebase Sally, and the terrain soon started to look rugged, cross-compartmented, and remote. I looked out the open door and down. Below I saw a small, denuded hilltop, and from the way we were circling, it was clear that this was our landing zone. But it did not look like a very hospitable place at all. For one thing, small figures were crawling on the ground, and the tails of bandages trailed behind them. More ominously, every few seconds an explosion could be seen detonating among the troops on the hill. We started corkscrewing down, spiraling into the maelstrom. The helicopter doors were already rolled open, and the crew chief manned an M60 machine gun that he began firing steadily, almost indiscriminately. Either this man had never learned fire discipline, which was not good, or the surrounding terrain was crawling with enemy soldiers, which was worse yet. Dismayingly, it was the latter. The long-forgotten crack of incoming rifle and machine gun fire penetrated the infernal noise of the chopper's jet engine and whirling blade.

After years in the United States, luxuriating in the comfort of relatively civilized society, relaxing in the intellectual comfort of graduate school, in fear only of forming indefensible arguments about esoteric minutiae, I had almost forgotten the ugly reality of combat. It is never any fun to confront a large number of people who are try-

Jacobs's Greek great-grandfather "Papoo" in Williamsburg, Brooklyn.

Jacobs's mother's parents, either at their wedding or shortly thereafter. He was from Poland, probably Czestochowa, and she was from what is now Moldova or some place nearby.

Jacobs's father's parents' wedding picture, very risqué for the early years of the twentieth century. They were both from Ioannina, Greece. She was originally Rebecca, and his name was Jacob. Like many Romaniote Jews, he had no surname, so the family name became "Jacobs" by default at Ellis Island.

Unless otherwise noted, photos are from the author's private collection.

Jacobs's father, most likely age four in 1923. The sailor suit notwithstanding, he served in the U.S. Army in World War II.

Jacobs's aunt Adele on left, now ninety-one, and Jacobs's mother, Marsha, who died three years ago at eighty-four.

Three-two Charlie and
Three-two Alfa in base camp,
Cao Lanh, 1967.

Cao Lanh, 1967.

Jacobs on radio, left, and the
Commander, 2nd Battalion 16th
Infantry, 9th Vietnamese Infan-
try Division, Cao Lanh, 1967.

Staff Sergeant Ainsley Waiwaiole and Jacobs, early 1968.

War buddies, early 1968. Jacobs's friend did not survive.

The Commander, 2nd Battalion, 16th Infantry and Jacobs, the morning after a massive enemy attack on base camp, early 1968.

The White House, October 9, 1969.

Author's private collection
Source: White House Photo

The White House, October 9, 1969.

Author's private collection
Source: White House Photo

Officers of the 65th Company, Officer Candidate School, Fort Benning, Georgia, 1969.

Too small for a helmet liner,
Fort Benning OCS, 1969.

Official photo, just after White House ceremony, October 9, 1969.
Author's private collection
Source: Department of Defense photo.

Before and after: above about 1952, below fifteen years later.

Author's private collection
Source: Cub Scouts of America (top)

ing to kill you, but with the distance of a few years, the mind elevates to prominent position the noble things that occurred and the service that was performed, filing the unpleasantness in a folder deep in the recesses of the subconscious.

Watching hell looming closer to me with each second, all the misery suddenly came back to me. In combat there was too much time and never enough time. Days were boring and frantic. They raced past and dragged on forever. The situation was obvious and totally lacking in clarity. Too hungry, too thirsty, too painful.

I was not even officially *here*, and I was already in contact with the enemy. But as I was about to learn, such was the state of affairs in Vietnam in 1972 that we were constantly in contact with the enemy. We were locked in a deadly dance with them, and we couldn't shake loose of each other.

As the helicopter flared close to the ground, I could see that the hilltop was really a hill*side*, sloping irregularly and so pockmarked with mortar and artillery craters that a proper landing wasn't possible. In as professional a demonstration of aviation skill as I could recall, the helicopter hovered inches from the ground, while the crew chief started throwing the crates and equipment—ammunition, weapons, cases of sardines—from the chopper onto the hill. Meanwhile, some of the troops who were wounded but ambulatory, and panic-stricken with the prospect of eventually dying on the hillside, tried desperately to clamber aboard the helicopter, several soldiers hanging from the skids and trying unsuccessfully to escape. I looked down at their faces, their mouths agape and eyes popping with fear.

"Don't get off, don't get off, don't get off!" the crew chief yelled at me, and just as the pilot made the decision to gain altitude and get out of there, there was a deafening roar, the engine groaned, and then the helicopter shuddered and smashed into the hillside.

The impact threw me from the chopper, and from the ground nearby, I could see that the aircraft had landed on its side, right on some of the soldiers, the tail boom destroyed by an exploding projectile, by the impact, or, most likely, by both. The main rotor blade had shattered into dozens, perhaps even hundreds, of pieces, becoming deadly shrapnel that killed and maimed troops on the ground. Body parts, most of them disconcertingly recognizable, littered the scarred earth. Lying next to me was one soldier with a bandage on his arm covering a previous wound, and he showed me that his lower leg had been nearly lopped off, hanging by a bit of torn flesh, the sharp ends of bones protruding grotesquely. Disengaged from the load of the transmission and the rotor, the ungoverned turbine engine screamed, spewing a dense cloud of kerosene smoke and threatening to explode.

The three crew members had survived, and I could see the crew chief scrambling from the cargo area and the pilots lowering themselves from the wreckage. The tree line just below the hilltop was now teeming with enemy soldiers who increased their rate of fire. In something of a reprise of my medical evacuation in 1968, I heard rounds banging into the dead helicopter airframe, a beached olive-green whale. Gunships blasted the enemy positions, and under this covering fire the observation helicopter attempted a landing just a few yards away to rescue the crew. Incoming mortar rounds continued to explode on the tiny hill, and I saw one of the pilots, clear of the smoke, wave at me to join the crew in their escape.

Uncharacteristically, my thought process was clear. Perhaps it's true that combat focuses the mind to a beam of infinitely small width and almost limitless power, and everything can be seen with a clarity encountered in no other environment. I found most of my time under fire to be periods of fear and confusion and debilitating indecision. But at that moment, with the opportunity to escape only meters away and a decision to stay behind almost certain to result in painful injury or worse, my powers of logic were not to be denied or browbeaten by emotion. If I stayed, I would face death or dismemberment. But if I left in the rescue helicopter with the crew, when I returned to Firebase Sally I would be loaded onto another chopper and brought right back here, where I would face death or dismemberment. I was already here. Why make *two* trips?

"Go on! Go on!" I yelled and, from my position on my side, assuming that they couldn't hear me over the burning chopper, cracking machine gun fire, and exploding mortar rounds, I waved at them to leave. I must have looked a complete fool, a supine homeless inebriate, waving feebly at passersby. Almost recklessly but certainly bravely, the helicopter swooped down, and in seconds it had snatched the crew and was on its way, the gunships hosing the area down to cover the escape. Neatly done.

Mortar rounds were still detonating, and I crawled around the hillside, looking for a weapon and a radio. My M16 was gone, thrown down the hill by the crash, or perhaps it was under the chopper, but I found another in only moments. There were lots of weapons lying about, discarded by the wounded or legacies of the dead, and neither would need rifles where they were going. Soldiers had taken cover among the shell holes and against rocks, and it was near a larger rock that I found a PRC-25. There was no radio operator to be found, and because the place was a very unpleasant impact area, I seemed to be the only person on the hillside interested in the thing. My task was to find the man I was replacing, and he was definitely not on the hill. With no idea of the frequencies we were using or the call signs in operation that day, the chances seemed slim that I would raise anybody.

But I did have a few things in my favor. First, the radio's tuner could be adjusted in discrete steps and was not continuously variable, like old radios. There was a finite number of frequencies, not an infinite number. Second, all American ground combat units, except for us advisors, had already been withdrawn from Vietnam, and in this isolated area, there were only a very few. And an FM radio is a short-range, line-of-sight instrument. If I found an American voice, its owner couldn't be very far away.

So I began clicking through the detents, and after a few minutes, I heard American voices. I waited until there was a break in the conversation and I called in.

"Any station this frequency, please respond, over," I said.

A voice asked, "Is this my Turtle?"

I was. The reason why a replacement is known as a Turtle is understood only by people with greater historical acuity and more time on their hands than I. Perhaps a new arrival is naïve, scared, withdrawn into his shell. Recalling that day, the appellation seems accurate.

"Roger that," I said. "What's your location?"

"Hey, Turtle, were you in the chopper that went down?"

"Roger."

"Well, I know where *you* are. I'll come police you up in a few minutes," he said confidently, and not much later he appeared over the rise and took me to the battalion headquarters not far away, dug into the side of a hill overlooking a dirt road that wound its way toward the Ia Drang valley. We had an excellent, distant view of two old American bases, Barbara and Ann, both fallen to the North Vietnamese, and I had little doubt that we would eventually attack these strongholds. It was a race, really. Would we rout the North Vietnamese before the politicians, who were tired of it all, declared that they had had enough? A more interesting competition involved me: could I cheat the Angel of Death again?

NOT LONG AFTER I settled into the side of the hill—perhaps it was just a few days after my arrival—I was sitting next to my counterpart, the South Vietnamese battalion commander, when without warning a North Vietnamese tank emerged from behind the two hills of Firebases Barbara and Ann and lurched to a stop in the middle of the road. It was quite some distance away, but it was impossible to miss.

The battalion commander and I were having a meal of boiled rice and hot peppers, and if he noticed the tank he didn't divulge any evidence.

I cleared my throat, subconsciously figuring that if I made any more obvious gesture, the tank crew would notice us immediately. I whispered, "Sir, do you see that tank out there?" Why whisper? Maybe I thought that the enemy had superhearing.

He looked up, with the casualness of Fred Astaire. "I do," he said, quite unperturbed, and continued on his rice. Maybe this happened all the time. Perhaps this tank's appearance was a regular, benign occurrence, and every day the North Vietnamese tank commander drove down the road, stopped just like today, and brought tea and biscuits to the First Airborne Battalion's forward observation posts.

I gently, very gently, elbowed the battalion commander. "Why don't we kill it? Let's call in some artillery and kill it."

"No, no. That tank doesn't know we are here. If we shoot at it, they will know that we are here."

"They don't know where we are?"

"If we shoot, they will know they are being observed," he said. "We shouldn't shoot."

"Yes, okay," I said. It would be an understatement to say that I was skeptical, that I found this reasoning to be the nadir of logic.

The turret of the tank began cranking around, and in a short while, the tank's main gun was pointing directly at us.

I elbowed the battalion commander. "Sir," I said, "now the tube is pointed directly at us."

"No, no. He doesn't know we're here. It's just a coincidence."

"I still think we ought to take the tank out."

"Don't worry about it. Come on, eat your rice."

A tank round is just a very, very large exploding rifle bullet, faster than the speed of sound, and if one survives its impact, the explosion is experienced *before* the report of the gun is heard. And that is exactly what happened. Like a long-dormant volcano releasing the retained energy of millennia, the side of the hill next to us erupted, and we were thrown to the ground.

"Sir," I said, "do you think he knows we are here *now*?"

He personally called back to the Vietnamese artillery battery in direct support, gave it a six-digit grid coordinate, and within a few rounds had adjusted fire onto the tank. It began to smoke, and then it burned quite furiously, exploding much of the ordnance inside. It was quite a sight.

The next morning, as if nothing had happened the previous day, as if the charred hulk of the tank were not really sitting in the middle of the road, an enemy truck appeared from behind the hills, towing a 122-millimeter howitzer. The gun's crew climbed from the vehicle and busily began to unhitch the piece from the truck and move it into position to fire. From this distance, they looked like ants trying to get control of a grasshopper's carcass. There was a great deal of backing and filling, and through binoculars I could see what appeared to be the section leader giving a series of instructions, accompanied by wild gesticulatory arm movements that either were not followed or were lousy instructions in the first place. Like an inexperienced driver trying to parallel-park for the first time, there were a lot of K-turns.

"Look, we're not going to wait until they start shooting at us again, are we?"

"Oh, no, Captain. I will take care of them right now," he said, and in a moment or two, half a dozen friendly artillery rounds rained on the enemy location, destroying it.

I was thankful that he didn't have to be convinced twice, but I thought it was curious that I should have to twist his arm to do something so basic, something so intuitively obvious to any professional soldier. The lessons I had learned in training and in combat were not very complicated. If you have the chance, kill or capture the enemy and don't give him the opportunity to survive to kill more of your own troops. Use overwhelming might, for there is no such thing as too much firepower. However, this was not the thinking of the Vietnamese commanders, and ignoring basics made it difficult for them to prevail against a determined enemy that did follow the known routes to military success. Perhaps after all the years we had been in Vietnam, we Americans forgot what we had learned in victory and instead taught the Vietnamese the wrong lessons: use air strikes rather than maneuver, employ only the resources you have rather than those you need, attack but then leave so that the enemy can move back.

A generation later, we were to forget again.

ALTHOUGH MOSTLY BUDDHIST and animist, Vietnam had a large minority of Roman Catholics, originally converted by Portuguese missionaries. Subsequently, the French, anticlerical but staunchly Catholic, strengthened the hand of the minority, and many became influential military and government functionaries. A large percentage of the Airborne Division was Catholic.

By the late fall of 1972, we had been engaged with the NVA almost continuously since I had joined the Vietnamese Airborne Division. We had taken back all but the northernmost sliver of Quang Tri Province, were moving slowly to the west, and found ourselves near La Vang Church, one of the most important Catholic shrines in Southeast Asia. The NVA had gained control of the church, perhaps five or six hundred meters to our west, with two or more companies of soldiers, perhaps even the best part of a battalion, and we had the mission to destroy this impediment to our move westward. At each other's throats for months, both we and the NVA were tired and extremely hungry.

At a very early age, a soldier is taught the time-proven method of taking an objective. On paper, it is simplicity itself: with a portion of your unit, lay down a withering base of supporting fire and use the rest of the unit to assault the enemy defensive position while his soldiers are fixed by the supporting fire. So central is this technique to overall success on the battlefield that units in training spend a great deal of time practicing it. Different terrain, different enemy dispositions, different scenarios, but the method of assault is pretty much the same. And the technique is the mainstay of armies around the world. North Koreans, Russians, Americans, and just about everybody else with a fully developed army has a similar conventional tactical doctrine.

But at La Vang, neither we nor the North Vietnamese were doing what we had been trained to do. With a large open area between the two units, neither side seemed to have much interest in following doctrine. Soldiers on both sides were trying not to expose themselves and instead fired blindly at each other in massive volleys of small arms and automatic weapons. No fire and maneuver. Only fire. And most of it was unaimed. After hours of this, we had collectively fired hundreds of thousands of rounds of ammunition at each other, and had suffered dead and wounded, but we had not advanced an inch against the NVA, and they had made no progress against us. Like Sisyphus, we looked doomed to continue this numbing exercise forever—or at least until one side had expended all of its ammunition.

All of a sudden, from our left and precisely halfway between the two warring armies appeared a hapless cow, just loping casually along. It was meandering from left to right just as carefree as could be, evidently oblivious to being in the middle of World War III. This picture was a priceless, previously undiscovered Dalí: a thousand troops, death all around, tracers streaming, and a cow ignoring it all. One could almost hear the professor addressing the assembly of Art History 101, stentorian voice dripping certainty, explaining the metaphors on the canvas: the two warring sides are modern politics and the cow is the universal hope for peace. The church is attempting to help, to mediate, salvation for all. Except that in real life, the two warring sides were merely scared troops trying inexpertly to kill each other, the church was full of communists, and the cow was just a cow—meat, real, fresh, red meat.

In an instant, the tracers signaled the shifting of thousands of rounds from both sides—to the cow.

And it is a testament to the poor marksmanship and inadequate training of both sides, and probably an explanation of why the war lasted so long, that the cow almost made it across the kill zone alive.

Finally, to our far right, the cow collapsed in an ungainly heap. And now, the objective was no longer for the enemy to drive us back across Route 1 and then into the sea, or for us to destroy the enemy and take back La Vang Church.

The mission was to get the cow.

And there it was, sprawled in the open, free for the taking. There it was, hundreds of pounds of fresh, delicious nourishment, and all we had to do was just go out there and get it. And all the North Vietnamese had to do was just go out there and get it.

There was only one way to acquire the cow: mount a classic military assault, the kind we had been trained to conduct but had avoided all day. And so spontaneously, with almost no instructions from my battalion's leadership, two companies began pouring accurate, aimed supporting fire at the enemy to keep their heads down, and one company maneuvered professionally to the cow, achieving the objective, and brought the cow back to our lines.

Had we only used the same technique in assaulting the enemy at La Vang Church five hours earlier, we'd have taken both the cow and the church. Evidently, we simply weren't sufficiently motivated to seize the church, but we were certainly motivated to get the cow.

By the way, friendly casualties sustained during the intense combat to seize the meat: *zero*.

HAVING RETAKEN THE city of Quang Tri from the North Vietnamese, the Airborne Division had struck southwest toward the Ia Drang valley, where the remaining NVA forces, several divisions strong, had gone to evade destruction. We moved inland, across Route 1—Bernard Fall's *Street Without Joy*—to the hills west of the road. Previous American units had used each hill as a firebase, so that enemy infiltration could be observed and neutralized. And all the bases had women's names: daughters, wives, and girlfriends of the commanders. Gone forever were the strong, dominating operational names from World War II, like Overlord and Torch. In Vietnam we had Sharon and Sally.

More recently, by the 1990s it appeared that we had either run out of ideas or instead thought that the public was too ignorant for subtlety and had to be reminded of what the government was trying to do. Names were clumsy cognates, like Operation Iraqi Freedom and Operation Deny Flight. One is almost shocked that the Defense Department didn't call our move into Iraq Operation Eliminate Saddam, His Sons, and Their Henchmen. One can expect that when we leave Iraq, some genius in the Pentagon will dub it Operation Withdraw Under Political Pressure.

Firebase Sharon's most striking feature was a tall, rickety observation tower, and it was a lousy place to position a battalion of paratroopers. In a combat environment dominated by indirect fire, an enemy artillery battery would use the tower as a registration point and take almost no time to destroy anything and anybody on this hill. Not far away, perhaps six hundred meters to the west of Sharon, there was an equally small hill, denuded of vegetation and blocking the route toward Firebases Barbara and Ann and the strategic valley farther southwest. And it was a splendid location from which the NVA could observe Sharon and adjust artillery fire on it. They had recently put a 130-millimeter artillery round with a delay fuse right through the tower, and it finally detonated inside the bunker at the base, killing half a dozen Vietnamese paratroopers in the process.

To alleviate the pressure and pave the way for future operations, my battalion, the 1st Airborne Battalion, received orders to seize the naked hill to our front. The estimate was that there was about a reinforced company on the hill. When we finally got there, we found more than a battalion, as well as a regimental headquarters, perhaps five times the number of enemy expected.

Because there was no safe way to get there from Sharon, it almost didn't matter how many enemy troops were on the hill, because success was going to be very difficult to achieve anyway. We would have to descend into the valley and then climb the hill, all without any cover or concealment. And for some inexplicable reason, we were to conduct this operation not at night, when we would have had a chance to get somewhere near the objective without being detected, but in broad daylight. Go figure.

A frontal assault was sheer suicide. The only way to have some chance of surviving this was to have two companies support by direct fire from Sharon, while the other two companies maneuvered to the left and tried to take the objective from the flank. The artillery pre-strike planned on the objective was massive by any standard. There were to be five thousand rounds of 105-millimeter artillery, one thousand rounds of 155-millimeter, and one hundred rounds of 175-millimeter, the latter terribly inaccurate but psychologically overpowering and destructive if the rounds got anywhere near the target.

Nevertheless, almost everything else was against us, and I said that we were going to lose a lot of men going up the hill, maybe as many as forty or fifty. The commander looked at the hill, then down at the map, and then he stared straight into my eyes.

"I think you're right," he said calmly. "But we're doing it anyway."

As for direct fire support, we had limited access to a few new, cutting-edge weapons. It has since been replaced by more modern and sophisticated equipment, but thirty-five years ago the TOW anti-tank wire-guided missile was state-of-the-art. The missile was fired from a short-barreled fiberglass tube about ten inches in diameter, and the guidance system was essentially a primitive computer that had less memory than today's cell phone, but was strikingly accurate and effective. The gunner placed the sight's crosshairs over the target, and the missile would do the rest. It had a very substantial warhead, and if there were no enemy tanks, the TOW would do a splendid job on enemy bunkers.

I told the battalion commander that we should emplace the TOW forward, with the two companies providing fire support and use it to destroy bunkers and to chase from their positions those who survived.

"No, no," my commander said, sternly shaking his head. "I don't want to do that."

"Why not?"

"If we bring the TOW up here, we'll put it at risk. If the enemy destroys it, I'm going to get fired. No, I can't risk using the missile."

My brain immediately processed his response into the only logical conclusion: *This guy is nuts.* But uncharacteristically, I restrained myself, and I tried logic and my most soothing tone of voice. I sounded so relaxed and soporific, I nearly put myself to sleep explaining that the huge contribution of the weapon to the mission's success was going to be worth the marginal additional risk. Finally, probably owing more to my persistence than his acceptance of my logic, he agreed, and the TOW performed exactly as advertised. He wouldn't risk it even one more time, though. Later, when the battle was over and we had seized the hill, attributable in large part to his using the TOW, he said that one gamble was quite enough for him, and he never employed it again.

We did lose dozens of troops going up the hill. As planned, we poured fire from everything we had on Sharon, routing enemy soldiers who then became easier targets for our riflemen and machine gunners. Our two companies that maneuvered up the hill to assault the enemy flank had a very tough time of it, and I saw paratroopers cut down by raking enemy fire. One unfortunate soldier took a direct hit from a mortar, and another was shot in the head and might have survived but died days later because we couldn't evacuate him. In extremely close and violent fighting we managed to capture the crest, and we quickly established a hasty defense against a counterattack, almost certain to be launched as soon as the NVA could muster the men and artillery to do it. A day or two later, the North Vietnamese Army did counterattack, and although they lost a large number of soldiers, the counterattack was successful, and they threw us off the hill. It was then that I learned one of the most important lessons in the use of any instrument of power, indeed in any human endeavor on or off the battlefield: it always takes more resources than you think. *Always.*

There is no such thing as too many resources, and anyone who believes he has too many assets has certainly miscalculated and needs to check his math. A commander who avers that he has been given enough troops is either lying or an idiot. If the question is, "How many soldiers do you want?" the correct answer is, "All of them. And while you're at it, go find some more, too." General Colin Powell, as perceptive a leader as this nation has recently produced, got it right when he articulated his famous principle: always use overwhelming combat power. Failing to do so adds further risk to an already risky enterprise. When there is a great deal at stake, when the result of failure is unacceptably unpleasant, don't skimp on resources.

Because nobody can predict the future, and because all of our conclusions are functions of our assumptions, there is no way to view any outcome with certainty. There is risk in every human endeavor. Some activities involve very little risk, and so, for example, there is not much danger in brushing your teeth. Certainly, there must have been cases in which oafish or inattentive people have slipped on wet bathroom tiles, fallen facedown, and driven the toothbrush into some vital cranial structure. But the chances of that happening are probably very low, even among those of us with poor hand-and-eye coordination, and brushing teeth carries with it a commensurately low risk. Other activities are not as benign. If you wanted to watch yourself on the evening news, I suppose you could leap from a tall building on the remote chance that hitting the sidewalk at almost two hundred miles an hour would *not* splatter you all over the concrete, but perhaps the risk is unacceptably high. And no one would bet his entire net worth, if he had any, on an investment that had almost no chance of success. But these are at the extremes of normal distribution, and most decisions aren't that simple. They involve some combination of moderate risk and moderate reward, and the path to success is harder to determine with a high degree of certainty.

But when it comes to national security, risk is too high to skimp on the commitment of resources. If leaders decide that an objective is so important that achieving it requires the use of the military instrument, then they must ensure that they employ a surfeit of it, and deciding to use less is a reprehensible abrogation of the public trust. In a less forgiving political system, such ineptitude is punishable, occasionally with a one-way trip to a public event. In the United States, the result is usually a presidential medal and a lucrative book deal.

Furthermore, my experience in attacking the hill opposite Firebase Sharon was instructive of a second inviolate law of human endeavor: it always takes more resources to hold an objective than to take it in the first place. *Always.*

We sustained significant losses going up the hill, but we lost it because we had inadequate resources to hold it. The D-day attack on Normandy's beaches to seize Europe from the grip of the Nazis entailed the use of about nine divisions. At the end of the war, there were 119 division equivalents in Europe. We didn't start with 119 divisions, only to withdraw and leave a small force behind. The sole purpose of the first ten divisions was to make room for the other 110. It's relatively easy to start up a business, but most businesses fail in the first year because they planned for insufficient resources to sustain the enterprise. And marriage is pretty much the same thing. It's easy to get married, but it's considerably tougher to stay married. I should know.

Now, I have taken lots of objectives, sometimes by myself and sometimes with some nearby reluctant riflemen or machine gunners, but I have been chased from about half of them for lack of resources. Although many have searched, and some fools have actually concluded that they have found them, there are no shortcuts here. Technology provides important leverage, but it is no substitute for intelligent planning, massive resources, and the will to persevere. Whether by design or happenstance, miracles do occur, but one should be ever mindful of Damon Runyon's trenchant observation that the race may not always go to the swift or the battle to the strong, but that's the way you should bet.

BY DECEMBER OF 1972, those of us still in combat had a strange and disquieting feeling of abandonment. American tactical air strikes were hard to get, even in engagements in which they could clearly be used to huge advantage. There were fewer American voices on the tactical radio, and most frequencies in range of our reception had fallen silent. Even the faces and attitudes of the Vietnamese officers and men reflected an inevitability of loss, a fatalistic sadness.

Combat remained nearly continuous and as violent as it ever had been, but we were making no progress on our campaign. My battalion had stalled completely, and I was situated with one of our companies as far forward as one could be without actually sharing a bowl of rice with the NVA. We had routed a North Vietnamese battalion and were occupying their old bunkers, but the NVA had retreated only one or two hundred meters, to previously prepared positions. The weather was miserable, windy and wet, and in many places the water table had risen above ground level. Bunkers became impossible to keep dry.

And it was cold. During one period of a week, I lay in the open in about four inches of cold, fetid water, while it rained without stop and the NVA persisted in trying to kill us with 122- and 130-millimeter artillery, augmented with an occasional tank round fired our way if the crew saw us clearly or were themselves bored or frustrated. So, it was raining continuously, and I was getting shot at all day long and half the night. There was hardly any food, and it was impossible to cook rice, anyway. Scared to death, starving to death, and freezing to death. The combination of water, wind, and low temperatures produced the daily threat of hypothermia, an ironic gift to the soldier who had come to Vietnam to avoid being cold in Korea.

The weather had slowed us to a stop, but so had malaise. There was little interest among the leadership in ordering an advance when it was likely that the few yards gained would be lost soon afterward. And no attack was possible without fire support. We lacked air strikes, but there was also a dearth of artillery fire, with the majority of fire missions dedicated to striking NVA positions deep in their zone or to supporting units that were actually on the offensive. Friendly gun crews had little interest in being outside their bunkers any more than they had to, and it was rare that we conned them into a fire mission in our direct support.

But in what may have been one of the last fire missions in support of Americans in contact, late in the year I was very lucky to receive assistance from an unexpected source. One night, I saw what looked like a convoy of enemy trucks wending its way on a road in the enemy zone. There was no moon, and it was drizzling and overcast anyway, but I could see the trucks clearly because some of them were running illuminated headlights, a boneheaded thing to do for which I was much obliged. Exercising light discipline is always important but nowhere more than in this kind of environment, in which large formations of soldiers are opposing one another, sensitive to the smallest tactical advantage, and will deliver massive punishment to those who relax their vigilance.

The convoy was moving quite slowly, and I waited almost breathlessly for a few minutes. When it had reached a portion of the road that ran parallel to the front lines, I saw with amazement that the convoy contained hundreds of vehicles, a target of opportunity so rich that few are ever fortunate enough to see one. Excitedly, I radioed for artillery, but none was to be had, and my excited and repeated requests must have sounded like the frantic but comical bleat of a lost sheep.

Then I heard an unfamiliar call sign on my frequency. "Understand you need fire support," he said. The voice was American, but it was nobody I recognized.

"What's the target?"

"Large convoy," I said excitedly. "Vehicles in the open, hundreds of them." I could hardly contain myself. I had no clue who this was, since we had almost no American units left in Vietnam and certainly none but advisors in Quang Tri. Maybe this was a gag. War pushes people to extremes, and I and the other American advisors were a pretty raucous bunch, given to dangerous stunts, practical jokes, and similar childish behavior. Since I had never really escaped adolescence, I fit right in. Yes, maybe this was some stunt by Furrow or Howard or Lawrie, all of whom were creative, energetic, and as easily amused by simple foolishness as I.

Then again, maybe not.

"Coordinates?" he asked, and I encoded the center of mass of the convoy and told him it was moving from southwest to northeast at about five miles an hour. He asked for a bit more information, like the observer-target azimuth, which we typically did not have to provide, but I gave him whatever he wanted. This was all terribly confusing, but if there was an outside chance of engaging a target as large as this, I intended to play along.

He said that he would fire one white phosphorus round, to mark the target, and that I was to give him corrections from that round. A few seconds later, he said, "Shot, over," indicating that the round was on the way. I waited for the marking round to impact.

And waited.

Nothing.

I radioed, "Round lost. Repeat."

"What do you mean, 'Round lost, repeat'?" He was very put out, this joker.

"I didn't see the impact," I replied, as if he were an imbecile who had never fired artillery before. "It must have been a dud or else lost. Fire another one."

The Joker: "What the hell are you talking about? The time of flight is sixty-five seconds. The round isn't there yet."

Ridiculous. There wasn't anything in the artillery arsenal that fired a round so far that its time of flight was as long as sixty-five seconds. I was cold and in the open and tired. This had been a diverting entertainment, but the fun was over, and it was time to ask the Joker to identify himself. "Okay, who *is* this?"

And in the clear, eschewing his protective call sign, he yelled, "This is *Newport News*, you moron."

USS *Newport News* was a heavy cruiser, with a displacement of more than twenty thousand tons, a crew of some sixteen hundred officers and sailors, and a battery of devastating 8-inch guns. With no access to any information other than that which arrived by mail from home weeks after the fact, I had no idea that the ship was anywhere near Vietnam, let alone in range to fire for me. Indeed, I had had no news about anything. Being in combat was a very crude form of selective sensory deprivation. There was plenty of rain, cold, misery, pain, and sadness—but very little news. I had thought that we were all alone, and yet here was a thin thread of hope, an offshore breeze straight from America thousands of miles away.

Just then, the marking round screamed into the area and detonated right in the middle of the convoy, lofting burning particles of white phosphorus into beautiful, deadly arcs around the impact point, a giant, opening white rose of death.

"Fire for effect!" I yelled into the radio. "Fire for effect!"

"Firing *battery one* for effect," he said. Only one round from each gun?

"Battery one?" I was used to artillery gunners firing thousands of rounds of 105-millimeter shells. "That's nowhere near enough. This is a huge target."

"Trust me," he said, "that's enough."

And he was right. A few minutes later, three rounds of 8-inch naval gunfire landed amid the convoy and exploded with such breathtaking force that much of the convoy was utterly destroyed immediately, and the secondary explosions lasted for hours. I forgot the penetrating drizzle and the biting cold, and instead I stood there and watched the spectacle. It was an awesome and fearsome sight, and I thought that there are few things as comforting as being far from home and meeting a new friend just when you need one.

STILL FORWARD WITH the lead companies of the battalion and making no progress against an enemy who evidently had no intention of going home, I usually accompanied Vietnamese officers who made regular forays to inspect the frontline bunkers. With little else to do except wait for an artillery round or a rocket to make life difficult, and because the days seemed years long, almost anything was preferable to lying in water, waiting to become a casualty. Inspecting the line was dangerous duty because the enemy was ensconced only a short distance away and they had little to do but wait for us so that they could pick us off. Occasional rifle shots and short bursts of machine gun fire shattered the eerie silence from time to time, usually attempts to kill soldiers on both sides who ventured outside their bunkers to relieve themselves. Since urinating inside a bunker that was shared with others absolutely *guaranteed* getting shot, the odds were much better outside. Incoming mortar rounds were a constant problem, as were artillery barrages. Occasionally, a seeing-eye 122-millimeter round would find its way into a bunker and kill the occupants, convincing everyone else that luck was everything. Not surprisingly, praying for deliverance was a paratrooper's most time-consuming passion, and survival was proof that the practice worked. The dead were obviously either unworthy or insufficiently pious.

In the second week of January 1973, President Nixon ordered the complete withdrawal of all American forces, including our little band of airborne advisors. Two years later the North Vietnamese swarmed into the South, and the Republic of Vietnam ceased to exist. Our involvement in Vietnam ended with a bang in 1975, but two years earlier, when I and the remaining tiny contingent of combat troops shipped home, our departure was but an ineffectual whimper.

Chapter Fourteen

By agreeing that I would stay out of combat when I had no intention of doing so, I had cheated, of course. The Army leadership couldn't fail to discover my subterfuge and was not pleased, but they got over it. When I returned to the States, I received a few unpleasant, even rude, telephone calls from Washington, but I acted contrite, which was all they wanted. Indeed, most people who occupy small, inconsequential offices are happy to do little more than establish who's in charge. Bureaucrats begin by *wanting* to do good things but quickly find themselves co-opted by the inertia-ridden structure and subsequently find it perfectly sufficient to mark territory, verify their positions in the pecking order, and attempt to exert a modicum of influence on those who can't defend themselves.

But such large, Weberian considerations were of less immediate consequence to me than the tyranny of simple mathematics. I had been in Vietnam for about six months, and my assignment at West Point was not due to begin for another six months. That meant that I was the perfect candidate for a temporary assignment to—the Pentagon. My first few days at home consisted almost entirely of frustrating telephone conversations with my latest assignment officer. The previous one had likely sent himself to some choice slot like the airborne battalion in Vicenza, Italy, and I am not surprised that assignment officers almost never get stuck with less desirable posts like recruiting duty in International Falls, Minnesota, or in the Pentagon's Office of the Acting Principal Deputy Assistant Undersecretary of the Army (Interim).

Neither entreaties nor threats seemed to have the desired effect on the Army, and Pentagon service was looming dangerously. I called the Department of Social Sciences and spoke to Major Howard D. Graves, the department's executive officer, to plead my case, but there was no room for me until the summer. Graves was appropriately named, all business and very stern. There would be no quarter given from West Point.

But a few days later, in a convincing demonstration that Fate is fickle and possessed of a well-developed sense of humor, Major Graves called to report that I was coming to the department after all, that I wouldn't have to wait until the summer, and that—hosannas, everyone—I would escape the Pentagon again. And the reason? Well, my unbridled joy was the result of another's misfortune: one of the instructors, a senior officer on loan from the State Department, had conveniently suffered a mild heart attack and would be out of service for the rest of the spring semester. Unless you consider the fact that the heart attack may have shortened his life by five years, we both won. I avoided the Pentagon, and he got a six-month vacation at full pay.

———————

EIGHTEEN THOUSAND YEARS sounds like forever, but consider that the Earth is about five billion years old. So in geologic time, eighteen thousand years is a fleeting nanosecond, and it was that recently that New York was covered by an enormous glacier. As the ice age ended, the glacier melted and revealed the violence it had done to the landscape in the hundred thousand years since its most recent, relentless advance and retreat.

As the glacier marched southward, it had acted like a giant sheet of rough sandpaper, carrying enormous blocks of granite that mercilessly scoured the thin crust of the Earth and gouged a wide, deep channel that subsequently filled with water as the glacier melted, draining the high ground and dumping the liquid into the ocean.

Today we call this glacial scar the Hudson River. At the southern end sits New York City, where, like the Mekong half a world away, the river is about a mile wide. It is a formidable barrier to movement, even today: just ask any commuter who struggles into the city from New Jersey.

The strategic importance of West Point is immediately evident to the casual observer the instant he looks north over the widening Hudson from Trophy Point, at a constricted narrows guarding the approach to New York City to the south. During the Revolutionary War, both British and American generals realized the value of controlling the plateau on the west bank of the river. George Washington, who considered West Point the most important strategic position in America, personally commissioned the fortifications in 1777 and transferred his military headquarters there in 1779. His ragtag Continental soldiers built forts and gun batteries and even draped a 150-ton iron chain across the Hudson to control river traffic. The fortifications worked, and the redcoats never managed to capture West Point, in spite of the best efforts of Benedict Arnold, Fortress West Point's original commander.

The grounds of the place, the oldest continuously occupied military post in America, are suffused with a kind of quiet grandeur, but in its earliest days, it was hardly the elite institution it is today. In fact, it was more of a repository to which some wealthy Americans sent their laggard sons for a few bracing and character-building years of eating gruel and marching in the snow.

The U.S. Military Academy was created in 1802 by the pen of Thomas Jefferson, but it was Colonel Sylvanus Thayer, who served as Superintendent from 1817 to 1833, who was the real father of the Military Academy. He upgraded academic standards, instilled discipline, and emphasized the Honor Code, and the system he created has produced a steady stream of military, government, and business leaders since then. It is a unique place indeed.

The Department of Social Sciences has always been very special, and its genesis was the vision of Brigadier General George Lincoln, fourth in his class at West Point, a Rhodes scholar and a principal strategist for George Marshall during the Second World War. His experience at the nexus of power during that war had instilled in him a deep understanding for the intelligence and expertise required of those charged with the responsibility of maintaining the nation's security, and when the war was over, he embarked on a tireless quest to assemble the best minds he possibly could and place them in his department at the U.S. Military Academy. Unappreciated at the time, and still not universally employed even among civilian universities, Lincoln's notion that institutions of higher learning should be genuine academies, homes for first-class intellectual development and inquiry, was something of an alien concept.

The service academies comprise the University of the United States of America. West Point is a place that transforms good minds into excellent ones, and although all institutions aspire to do this, almost none of them have the luxury of being able to structure an environment in which, to succeed, people must rely on each other as well as themselves. The notion that we either hang together or hang separately, the idea born of the realities of armed combat, the notion of a community of peers, is embodied in West Point.

For me this was a radical change of physical atmosphere, going from the uncomfortable accommodation of a flooded bunker in Vietnam and trying to dodge artillery rounds to the magnificent campus of West Point, from deciding between two pairs of socks, both wet, to contemplating the complexities of strategic arms limitation. But the lack of discomfort at West Point was accompanied by a bit of nostalgia for my time in the middle of a profound, though fatally flawed, enterprise, and I was still young enough to have a hormonal proclivity for excitement. Deer hunting was a seasonal but adequate palliative.

Like most military installations, the majority of West Point's acreage consisted of large open fields or thick woods, undeveloped tracts of land employed as artillery impact areas, firing ranges, and places in which cadets practiced small-unit tactics. The post was crawling with deer, and due to a lack of predators, the deer population was growing ever larger. Statistically, there would eventually be more deer than disease-infected ticks to feed on them. Even thirty-five years ago, deer were vying with humans for control of suburban areas, and a major insurance company—which ought to know because it processes claims for these things—estimates that every year 1.5 million cars collide with deer. This is excellent for car manufacturers and auto repair shops, but it is unwelcome news to everyone else. Introducing packs of hungry wolves into housing developments is one way to shrink deer herds, but the insalubrious effect on school populations is not to be ignored.

The typical solution to the deer problem is hunting, and at West Point culling the herd kept its numbers manageable and had the additional advantage of giving the staff an annual opportunity to roam around the woods, shoot guns, and eat venison. Purchasing a New York State hunting license made one eligible for the deer area lottery, in which a random drawing gave the best hunting areas to those whose numbers were drawn first. Understanding that they were dealing with people whose field experience consisted almost exclusively of hosing large swaths of terrain with millions of bullets in the hope of killing a few enemy soldiers, the management cleverly drew the hunting areas in such a way as to minimize the likelihood of contact among hunters in the field. My friends knew that I had worked in a slaughterhouse years before, and so I quickly became the first choice to butcher deer, in exchange, of course, for a small hunk of venison.

One year, toward the end of the final week of hunting season, nearly all of us had nailed a deer, except Barry McCaffrey, good friend of mine in the department. McCaffrey eventually retired as a general, but at the time he was an infantry major of consummate professional skill. Three times wounded in combat, and twice decorated with the Distinguished Service Cross, he was fearless and brilliant. One of his wounds was particularly severe. A forearm had been struck by two or three machine gun rounds and nearly blew the thing off. Doctors were planning on amputating, but he talked them out of it, and they pieced it together with screws and a stainless-steel spar. They saved the arm, but it didn't work very well. Among the things his bionic arm couldn't do was to operate a bolt-action or lever-action rifle, but he wanted to hunt deer, and so he bought a Browning semiautomatic that loaded a fresh cartridge after each squeeze of the trigger. Awesome firepower was now at his disposal.

On the very last day of the season, in the afternoon, he called to report proudly that he had bagged a buck. He lived just across the street, and I walked over there, ready to skin and butcher the thing, but what I saw hanging from the tree in front of his quarters was basically a deer hide filled with blood and assorted bits of deer. It was a complete wreck, and there wasn't much meat to save.

"I don't think there's any salvageable meat here at all," I said. "What the heck happened?"

Evidently, when he arrived at his assigned area, he saw a deer only seconds after getting out of the car, and he opened his trunk to extract his new rifle. With a bit of difficulty, he loaded the weapon and squeezed off a few rounds. One or more bullets hit the deer, and the animal fell to its front knees, but it quickly scrambled to its feet and made a valiant effort to trot away. Running down the dirt road after the deer, he chased it, snapping off a hasty shot from time to time, some of the rounds inflicting more nonfatal wounds. Finally, the deer collapsed to the ground, alive but weighed down with lead. A few more inexpertly placed rounds finished the job.

I was saddened by the suffering of the poor deer and by the waste of otherwise perfectly good venison, but my disappointment was alleviated by the knowledge that, although he had an excuse and I did not, here was someone who was as lousy a shot as I was.

THE MID-1970S WAS a very difficult period for the Army. Training was a shambles, troops served reluctantly, money and equipment were in short supply, and the organization and its leadership had been thoroughly discredited by the debacle in Vietnam. And it wasn't just the Army. Those who did not believe that the entire nation was in a stupor only had to listen to President Carter, who worked hard to convince us that the country was suffering from a chronic malaise, although there is persuasive evidence that Carter himself was one of its causes. In this regard, there is something to be said for electing to both the presidency and the vice presidency only those who are old and infirm, because it gives us a high degree of confidence that after leaving office they will not survive for long and thus will not become pestilential, public nuisances. If we were so enthralled about hearing more from presidents who have retired, there would be a serious effort to repeal the Twenty-second Amendment to the Constitution.

Even if it was an unpleasant time to be in the Army, it was a good time to be at West Point. Protected from many of the harsh realities of the active Army, the intelligent, motivated, and idealistic cadets developed and thrived under the tutelage of a faculty that had survived the folly of the previous decade and were the wiser for it. And what a faculty it was. Exceptions to both Gresham's Law and the Peter Principle, many of these talented patriots rose to high and influential rank in both the Army and in business. One explanation for this phenomenon is that these officers were inherently good people, dedicated to the principles of the nation and serious about the importance of educating young soldiers. But another is that there was a certain magnifying leverage that resulted from being together in such a rich environment, where an unfettered and often irreverent exchange of ideas among talented people could forge a new and formidable alloy of intellectual strength. Perhaps these men became better soldiers and more accomplished intellects simply because they were all together in one place. One is thus driven to conclude that qualitative change results from quantitative change not among the proletariat but among the bourgeoisie. Marx would be apoplectic.

I TAUGHT COMPARATIVE politics and international relations and had a magnificent time doing it, but there was some disutility in being one of the five hundred students who came through my classes in the three and a half years I was on the faculty. Among other shortcomings, I had a very disordered mind, and as I grow older my brain seems to be increasingly reluctant to organize itself. Perhaps it is the result of my head wound, or maybe I am genetically programmed to be a scatterbrain—most likely it is both—but as a result the lessons in my classroom tended to be a bit digressive. The good news was that they were at least superficially entertaining. The bad news was that the cadets had no way of knowing that they had learned the course material until they were examined. I worried about it, too, but I had unconsciously embedded teaching points in the rest of the verbiage.

But I did not restrict myself to comments about subjects closely related to the course material, or even to things that were even peripherally related to the course material. Since I had an opinion on everything, I shared with cadets nearly any thought that occurred to me, including the intellectual bankruptcy of both civilian academia and the military hierarchy; the fact that *Rocky* was the worst picture ever to win an Academy Award; the disgraceful inability of cadets to write properly, which I ascribed to their parents, their grade school teachers, and the Department of English at West Point; and what an idiot Billy Martin was. Since none of this seemed at first inspection to have anything to do with the subject matter, it is not surprising that the whole performance was disconcerting to everyone, and I would not have been surprised if a cadet had sued, alleging that he did not get the education to which he was entitled. However, I had planned my defense carefully: the education was free and the cadet got a small stipend as well.

But there was one subject extraneous to the course material on which I spent some time by design: leadership. West Point is a proper college but it is also a refinery in which this nation catalyzes its military leadership. Considering the large number of graduates of the service academies and of the ROTC program who have risen to extremely high office or have shouldered responsibility of historic significance in times of crisis, spending a few minutes discussing leadership is not an idle pursuit. It's not that cadets didn't receive instruction on this topic, for there were entire courses of study devoted to it. But there is a tendency among all educators to compartmentalize inquiry and thus to compartmentalize knowledge. Bad idea. At least in the business of defending the United States, all capabilities must be employed, and consideration of leadership principles belongs nearly everywhere anyway, including in courses on comparative political systems, the reign of the Tudors, and pediatric cardiology.

Concepts I learned as a young soldier are catholic, but basic precepts are often easy to ignore, especially when times are tough. But it is precisely at those times that one must consider the principles that transcend time. Many things in life are intuitively obvious, and yet some of us forget them. For example, most people grasp that you shouldn't drink twelve beers in three hours and then drive a Mustang at a speed of 125 miles per hour the wrong way on an interstate, but we know from televised police tapes that the practice is more widespread than we would have thought. Clearly, the miscreants were absent from class on the day this principle was discussed. It goes without saying, too, that you should not put beans up your nose. There really should be no reason to explain why it's *not* a good idea to put beans up your nose, and yet the number of people who put beans up their noses is not zero. Because this is a publication that aspires to wide distribution, there will be no further discussion that combines orifices of any kind and foreign objects of any kind, but you get the idea: left to their own devices, human beings will ignore basic principles.

And so, although I spent some considerable classroom time enlightening the cadets about the vagaries of the British parliamentary system and the prescience of John von Neumann, I spent almost as much time discussing leadership principles, first-order considerations that would serve them well long after the general formula of a quadratic equation had been forgotten.

And most of them are obvious, so obvious that they are easily ignored. For example, it sounds unnecessary to insist on articulating an objective, but it is something that is often elided and so can't be emphasized often enough. Don't start doing anything unless you know precisely what it is you're trying to accomplish. This sounds simple and impossible to avoid doing, and yet people of all stations ignore it all the time, frequently with disastrous results. In the beginning, it is easy to expend resources in pursuit of an objective that is unclear, poorly considered, or half-baked, but that is often what people and governments do.

To be sure, there have been some successes like penicillin and Teflon that were the results of accidents, but even in those instances, the discoverers recognized what they had found, and in any case I cannot recommend basing the success of business or national security on sheer chance. By its very nature, an objective is a measurable state. That's why it's called an "objective." And you will know when you get there because you specified it at the very beginning, when you set out to achieve it in the first place. Probably the only person who ever ran a marathon without knowing that it was slightly more than twenty-six miles was Pheidippides, and he died when he hit the tape. In the Second World War, the Allies' objective was clear, unequivocal, and measurable: the unconditional surrender of the Axis. So unshakable was this objective, so obvious was the end state, that the Allies were prepared to do anything to achieve it. We firebombed Tokyo and Dresden, dropped two nuclear weapons on Japanese cities, and were prepared to take a million American casualties invading and subduing Japan. There is no substitute for deciding what you want to do *before* you start.

So I regaled my students with an excessive number of war stories, anecdotes about the unpleasant aspects of marriage, and sundry apocrypha solely with the purpose of convincing them that overwhelming resources are the keys to success; that simpler plans are invariably bound to be more successful than more complicated concoctions; that if you ask someone to be responsible to more than one boss, you're asking for trouble.

Among the most important considerations, and one that few people consider, is the potential for failure. Once leaders become convinced about the utility of a course of action, there is often an insidious sanguinity that mesmerizes them. Swallowing implicit assumptions—there are no barriers to entry; we have a monopoly in this niche; the natives will welcome us—they are driven into a rarified and totally illogical state in which alternative outcomes are not even considered. But in any human enterprise, risks cannot be appreciated until they are explicitly articulated, and that includes asking, "What can go wrong?" Ready to make an attractive investment in a portfolio of subprime loans? Better ask what can go wrong first. Ditto for booking passage on a hydrogen-filled dirigible, signing a nonaggression pact with Hitler, bombing Pearl Harbor, crossing the Yalu River, invading Iraq.

And then there's the truth. Discussing lying at West Point is like preaching to the converted, because one aspect of life at the Military Academy that attracts cadets in the first place is its Honor Code, which includes a prohibition against lying and tolerating those who do. But it's worth reminding even the cadets, because life offers an almost unlimited number of opportunities to quibble, to equivocate, and to deliver outright lies. The first lie is a bit like the first puff, the first snort, the first pill. You can't stop. It's easy to start lying, but nobody has a memory good enough to keep it up indefinitely with success. In the highest-profile cases people get into big trouble less for committing illegal or immoral acts than for lying and covering up. From Richard Nixon to Scooter Libby to a professional athlete whose ideal body type is that of the Incredible Hulk, it's rarely the proximate act that gets them in legal hot water. It's the cover-up, the lie concocted to cover for the previous lie, and Martha Stewart would surely report that if she had the chance to do it again, she would leave the insider trading to those who find prison an uplifting experience.

CHAPTER FIFTEEN

HOWARD D. GRAVES, the department's executive officer, was reassigned a few months after I arrived, and just before he left, he called me into his tiny office and closed the door. Howard was as strict as a married man can be without actually ditching his family and becoming a Trappist, and he took his duties very seriously, even those for which he had no responsibility. He had been a Rhodes scholar, and eventually he became a three-star general and superintendent of the Military Academy. His purpose in calling me to his office was to offer me counseling, for which one should be grateful, since constructive criticism almost always has some measure of benefit.

He said that he had been impressed with my performance, but that if I persisted in being irreverent, cavalier, and sarcastic, none of them characteristics valuable to advancement in the Army, I would not get promoted to major. Ostensibly, Howard, already a major, knew what he was talking about. I thanked him for his concern and insight and expressed to him my determination to stop being irreverent, cavalier, and sarcastic.

I tried, of course, and who wouldn't? But I had no capability to be anything other than irreverent, cavalier, and sarcastic, and I soon concluded that Howard D. Graves, Major, Rhodes Scholar, and all-around very bright guy, was right. I thought that I was one of those odd people who are not well suited to the Army in peacetime and are useful only in combat. I pictured myself encased in a glass niche that would be broken in a crisis, releasing me to do my duty. "Break glass for Jacobs!" would say a prominent sign below. Not getting promoted had some potential advantages, too. These days, one must continue to perform and thus to get promoted, or else face separation from the Army. The closest analogies are a rat on a treadmill and a U.S. representative running for reelection, although one could argue that they are the same thing and should not both be cited. But in those days, and before the current practice of eliminating substandard performers, one could be marginally productive at some low level of sophistication and still make a contribution until retirement. After Howard's frank guidance, I envisioned remaining at West Point and continuing to teach until very old age, a wizened prune regaling generation after generation of cadets about the good old days in Vietnam, when we slaughtered our own beef.

And I actually would have been delighted to remain on the faculty at West Point, except that, despite Howard Graves's dire prediction, I was indeed promoted to Major. And no sooner had I been bumped up in rank than I received orders to go to the Command and General Staff College at Fort Leavenworth, Kansas, indicating that the Army believed I still had some redeeming value—or at least potential for rehabilitation.

The Command and General Staff College is essentially the Army's school for midlevel managers, where majors are taught how to operate on generals' staffs. Perhaps the most useless of all Army ranks is that of Major, since it guarantees staff assignments for the duration the officer holds it. A captain can command a company, and a lieutenant colonel can command a battalion, but in the infantry the only thing a major can command is a slightly higher salary than a captain.

The course of study, a year long, included examinations of major battles in some depth, and we focused on the staff considerations that rendered them successes or failures. We learned the operation, care, and feeding of administrative and logistical systems, the things that permit the Army to shoot, move, and communicate. In most wars, these are the things in which the public has no interest but which occupy almost all the consciousness of commanders and private soldiers alike. Armchair generals, the old saying goes, talk strategy, but real generals talk logistics.

Although some majors were never asked to attend Command and General Staff College, the selection process for this school was not particularly selective, and being chosen was not necessarily a sign of fast-track promotion, but it *was* an indication that an insufficient number of superiors had been irritated enough to throw you out of the Army. An interesting hypothetical example is a lesson for any promotion system. Let's say an officer was an excellent, even outstanding, divisional brigade commander as a colonel in Operation Desert Storm, the First Gulf War in 1991. Because he had performed so admirably, he was promoted again and again, until he became a genuinely awful and incompetent general officer. An organization is smartest when it promotes people not for what they've *done* but for what they *will* do. Even after the passage of more than three decades, one hopes that my promotion to Major was less a function of what I had done as a lieutenant than of what the Army thought I could accomplish at much higher rank. But we'll never know.

As soon as it dawned on me that I was leaving, I already started missing West Point. It was one of those rare assignments of which I hadn't had enough, and I was fortunate that thirty years later I was asked to teach there again. Some of the cadets have been the children of my students from three decades earlier, and it is distressing to see some of my former cadets now grizzled, arthritic, and drawing retirement checks.

Moving is always a chore, made only slightly easier by not having much to move, but the planning for it takes diligence. Some things go in the moving van, and other things are taken on the trip. In the car, the junk underneath are those things not required until the destination, where initially there is no place to live, and the items in the next layer are what will be needed during the journey. The children are stuffed anywhere they fit. They complain about being jammed against the combat boots or having to sit on the toaster, but they get over it, especially when their discomfort is ameliorated by the prospect of ice cream at the next rest stop.

An unobservant person at the best of times, I was preoccupied by the details of moving a household, and my attention was diverted from almost everything else. Then, shortly before we were scheduled to leave for Fort Leavenworth, my wife announced that she wasn't coming with me. For the first minute or two, I honestly didn't understand what she was talking about. We were being reassigned to Fort Leavenworth, Kansas, and of *course* she was coming with me. And then, to ensure that I understood precisely what she was saying, she stated quite matter-of-factly that she didn't want to be married anymore. That this was a complete surprise to me is some indication of a number of things, including the superficial quality of the communication between us and the low intensity of the relationship generally.

We had been married when we were very young, much too young by any civilized standard, and the struggles to make a living, go to school, raise children, and go to war had cumulatively been too heavy a burden to be borne by an immature relationship engineered by immature people. Military service is particularly hard on marriages with weak foundations, and it is surprising that any survive the extended multiple deployments, long hours, and frequent relocations. Ours didn't.

I recovered quickly from the shock and asked her if she was sure about leaving. She said she was quite sure. Heather was twelve years old and David was nine, and I told her that I couldn't prevent her from leaving, but she wasn't taking the children with her.

I was more astounded by her reply than by her decision to leave in the first place: she no longer wanted the responsibility of a husband *or* children. "You're a much better father than I am a mother," she told me; all she wanted was some time to decide what clothes she would take with her and what she would leave behind. No shouting, no foot stomping, no histrionics. And characteristic of the entire marriage, no emotion either. And just before we stopped conversing altogether, I asked her when she had decided on this drastic, shattering course of action.

"A long time ago," she said. "I've been totally unhappy for two years."

———

MY EX-WIFE DISAPPEARED into whatever new world she had decided to fashion for herself, vanished from the children's lives, and didn't surface again until they were grown. Surprisingly resilient, and mindful that they now had responsibilities unlike those of other children their age, Heather and David threw themselves into being as mature as they possibly could be. They were reliable about doing their homework, performing occasional light housework, and chastising me when I didn't behave properly myself. I received a stern lecture one winter morning from Heather, who gave me a hard time for not staying ahead of the ice accumulating on the heater's outside ventilation louvers. They had crusted over with a thick rime, and the furnace had quit. Scraping and then coaxing the heater to life took an inordinately long time, it seemed, and she continued to remind me about it for the rest of the winter, ensuring that it didn't happen again.

At Fort Leavenworth, I was one of about nine hundred majors in the course, and because I had dependent children, even without a wife I was authorized to occupy government quarters. I was Mr. Mom before there was such a term. When I wasn't in class, I washed dishes, did the laundry, darned socks, and exchanged banana-nut loaf recipes with the women in the neighborhood. I have a magnificent recipe for pound cake from that era, but some others I received from my well-meaning neighbors were not as successful and the only ones that did not contain a can of condensed mushroom soup: okra and sausage in cheese sauce, sour tuna roll-ups, and beef liver with wheat berries and bananas.

CLASSES AT THE college fell into the normal distribution one finds among many phenomena in nature. Many were boring in the extreme, poorly presented, or of interest only to fans of arcana such as operations research or systems analysis. I could not envision ever being required to write computer code, but in one course that was all we did, an infuriating waste of resources when one considers that a brief survey would have been sufficient to give us an appreciation of the process. However, some course material was exceptionally fine, professionally important, and engagingly presented. Maybe because I was interested in the subject matter, I found discussions of strategy and tactics to be unusually well done, even by the relatively high standards of Army professional schools. I was transfixed by the lessons of Gettysburg, Waterloo, and the Battle of the Bulge, which we dissected and reassembled with the care of a vascular surgeon. Even more fascinating were the engagements that were less well-known but brimming with strategic import: the Battle of the Pripet Marshes, and the closing of the Kursk Pocket, in which six hundred thousand German troops were surrounded and captured by the Red Army.

To me, the most striking lesson of most of the cases was how easily the lessons themselves slipped from the grasp of those who should have learned from them. In 1941, Hitler committed to attacking Russia in the middle of a miserable winter. One hundred thirty years earlier, Napoleon—despite being an undisputed strategic and tactical genius—had tried the same march on Moscow, and it didn't work then, either. Why we are doomed to learn the same lessons over and over again is a mystery. Certainly one part of this insoluble equation is the nature of large, hierarchical organizations, which are poorly equipped to handle the vagaries of crises. Alas, this shortcoming is amplified by the low level of skill and professionalism among many of those who populate these structures.

There are as many behaviors as there are people, but the sharp-eyed Napoleon, who made plenty of his own mistakes, was superb at identifying strengths and weaknesses among his subordinates. I believe that both the circumstances and the observation are likely to be apocryphal, but they are instructive nonetheless. At the beginning of the modern media age, in an interview conducted by a number of reporters, Napoleon wittily collapsed his subordinates into four categories.

"The first are the dumb and lazy," he said, "and these I make my infantrymen.

"The second are the smart and energetic. These I make my field commanders.

"The third are the smart and lazy. These I make my generals."

Laughter.

Then one of the reporters asked, "But that's just three. What about the stupid and energetic?"

Without missing a beat, Napoleon replied, "I have them shot."

If it only were that easy. We have been plagued by the energetic but stupid, the indomitable nincompoops, the enthused extremists with all the answers or, worse, with the *one* answer for everything.

The only certainty is that we must be ever vigilant, for they still walk among us.

———————

BECAUSE IT WAS an engagement of immense historical importance, and because almost 150 years later it is still an event suffused with emotion, the Battle of Gettysburg received much attention at Leavenworth. Although it was truly the turning point of the Civil War, Gettysburg was not the decisive engagement it could have been, and that was a lesson in itself. The victorious Union forces failed to chase after General Lee, perhaps because wholesale destruction of the enemy was not a strategic objective. General Meade let Lee's forces get away, and the war and its suffering lasted another two years. It wasn't until later, when President Lincoln put Ulysses S. Grant in charge, that the strategic objective became the destruction of the Confederate force. The selection of Grant, a fighter but a man who liked his pint, was a matter of some consternation. But Lincoln wanted an aggressive commander who would win the war, and the lesson—that one of any leader's most important tasks is to surround himself with able people—was quite clear to those who were paying attention.

And there were few cases we studied that were better examples of leadership failure than that of the Dardanelles campaign in 1915. A truly loathsome and repellent British commander, Sir Ian Hamilton, with no appreciation for the tenacious enemy, the impossible terrain, or indeed his own forces' valiant but limited capabilities, presided over the deaths of forty-four thousand of his own men and the wounding of one hundred thousand more in only nine months. On finally coming ashore, after more than three hundred thousand casualties on both sides, Hamilton was reported to have remarked that the place looked far different up close than it did from his ship.

So the events that left the most indelible pedagogical marks were those of extremes. The stupidity of ordering Pickett's charge over open terrain raked by gunfire from a firmly emplaced defense. The failure of the Germans to mass their overwhelming resources at Bastogne in a coordinated fashion. The commanding leadership of General Patton, who turned an entire army of soldiers on a dime and led his men to victory at the Battle of the Bulge simply because it had to be done.

But Hamilton's reprehensible callousness has stuck in my mind as much as almost anything else, a ringing tocsin of disgrace I can still hear a century later. The notion that private soldiers are a commodity is shared by inept leaders everywhere, and only those who have been under fire with magnificent young warriors can truly appreciate their value and their sacrifice. One of the combatants in the Dardanelles campaign was a young Turkish lieutenant colonel named Mustafa Kemal, who eventually renamed himself "Ataturk." There are many things that can be said about Ataturk, and some of them are quite pejorative, but in 1934, above the landing beach at ANZAC Cove, he erected a memorial dedicated to the memory not of his own soldiers who died in the campaign but to the Allied troops who were sacrificed there.

ABOUT HALFWAY THROUGH CGSC, the tension among the students at Fort Leavenworth began to rise. It started as a slow murmur and rose to audibility by late winter, when the officers and their families, now sick of the penetrating cold of the place but faced with several more months of winter and the probability of one more snowstorm, began to fret about their next assignments. Although the course was named the "Command and General Staff College," almost none of the students would be heading to assignments in which they would command anything more animate than a mechanical pencil. This was really a staff college, and to staffs most of us would be going.

There is nothing inherently wrong with a staff. Derived from the Old English word meaning a stick used for walking, it has always been used in the sense of an object that is employed for support, and in fact a commander's staff has precisely that function. A small unit is uncomplicated and has a limited range of capabilities, but once it contains more than a few hundred soldiers, it isn't small anymore, and the commander can't run it by himself. He needs subordinate commanders, and because the unit has to be able to support itself, even for a limited amount of time, he needs still others to organize administration, intelligence, transportation, medical care, communications, and supplies, and he needs help to develop and execute plans. The business of war fighting gets very complicated very quickly.

All Army organizations larger than a company have staffs. It makes sense that the larger the unit, the larger the staff. A brigade contains about twenty-five hundred soldiers, and so its staff is larger than that of a battalion, which has only a third as many. The major general who commands a division of fifteen thousand people has an even bigger staff, and so on. The Army Headquarters has a truly huge contingent, and the Pentagon has a population larger than most small countries. A staff's constituency is the commander, but it must serve the commander's subordinates, too, but when staffs get very large, as they are in high-level headquarters, the constituency becomes the staff itself. Left alone, and with nothing governing their growth, their size will approach infinity.

Luckily, we can rely on the Congress to refuse to fund such a large enterprise in the executive branch, although that's mostly because Congress needs money for its own bloated staff. And although you might think that having a very large number of people on staff would make work easier and more efficient, you would be wrong. And you could also be excused if you thought that a large staff would enable organizations to identify potential difficulties and fix them before they became big problems. You would be wrong about that, too. The staff of the Senate Banking Committee doesn't pay any attention to the nation's banking system until it collapses, and then its modus operandi is to call banking officials to appear before the committee so that they can be given a proper public flogging. What was the staff doing about the banking system *before* it collapsed?

And there are few better examples of staff inaction than congressional handling of professional baseball. The sport is a business enterprise that is permitted by Congress to operate as a monopoly, and you would think that this arrangement would include a little congressional oversight. But you would be mistaken yet again. After years of doing nothing, amid accusations, news stories, books, articles about steroid abuse, and almost as much exposure on television as baseball itself, Congress finally performed exactly as it has done on most other issues: it called players and officials to testify and, as if our elected officials were all played by Claude Rains, announced it was shocked, *shocked,* that players may have been using steroids.

Perhaps the best advice about staffs is to have extremely low expectations of them, so that they deliver a pleasant surprise on the rare occasions when they actually perform some useful service.

And to avoid duty on them. Except for my brief stint as my battalion's air operations officer when I was a lieutenant in the 82nd Airborne Division, I had successfully avoided a staff assignment. As the Command and General Staff course was nearing its end, my assignment officer called to report that there was now no way I could avoid a tour on staff in the Pentagon. I insisted that the right place for me was back with troops, that if I had to serve on staff it should be at the lowest level. I thought I could make my biggest contribution to the Army as the executive officer of an infantry battalion.

On the other end of the telephone, my suggestion was met with silence, and for a long second I thought that the connection had gone dead.

"Sir?" I said tentatively into the receiver.

He was saying nothing, just for the effect.

"Sir?"

"You're going to the Department of the Army staff," he stated flatly, "and that's all there is to it."

I suggested that there were undoubtedly hundreds of infantry majors who would love to serve as staff officers, who already had spent plenty of time avoiding troop duty and were expert at being on staff. And his response was exactly what one would expect in an organization whose first principle of career development was careerism rather than what was good for mission accomplishment. He reported that he intended to send to troop assignments those who had assiduously avoided troop assignments in the past, and that this was for the purpose of making them competitive for promotion. My observation, that these officers should have thought about this years ago, fell on his deaf ears, and it looked like the fight was over.

Desperate times call for desperate measures, and when all else has failed, it's time for the Hail Mary pass, the Inchon landing. If there was ever a time to draw to an inside straight flush, this was it.

"Well, I'm not going."

"What do you mean you're not going?"

"I'm serious. I won't follow the orders to go to the Pentagon. I want to be with soldiers. I'm already here at Leavenworth and can just present myself to the commander of the Disciplinary Barracks when the course is over if that's what you prefer."

A few weeks later, Infantry Branch cut orders for me to go to the 7th Infantry Division at Fort Ord, California. I have been told that when I was three years old, holding my breath and turning blue made no impression on my parents, but at the age of thirty-one, acting like a three-year-old seemed to work remarkably well.

CHAPTER SIXTEEN

.

FORT ORD WAS perched on a high bluff looming over northern California's Monterey Bay. For a soldier who had spent his formative military years in the Deep South, it seemed out of place, a typical downscale enclave plopped incongruously into an area of geographical splendor and affluence. Established after the Civil War to keep the old rebels in line, many Army camps and posts have training areas carved from pine and cypress forests and are overgrown with kudzu, and just outside their gates are gaudy, neon highways of used car lots, pawnshops, strip joints, and trailer parks. Monterey, on the other hand, is the home of the Pebble Beach Golf Club and the annual Concours d'Elegance, where aficionados display hundreds of automobiles, each with a value equivalent to the cumulative annual salary of an infantry brigade. Of course, there *are* used car lots, pawnshops, strip joints, and trailer parks, but they are somewhere out of sight, removed from the tender sensibilities of sniffy, well-heeled residents and of tourists who visit the quaint and expensive tea shops of Carmel-by-the-Sea.

Although I had threatened my way to the 7th Infantry Division, my battle to get assigned to a tactical battalion was not yet over, because the Evil Spirit of The Bureaucracy follows potential victims relentlessly, looking for opportunities to snatch the unwary and press them into servitude. The division had two infantry brigades of three battalions each, and thus six slots for a major to serve as an executive officer, the second in command.

But before I had a chance to ask which of those precious slots now belonged to me, the division's personnel officer announced that I would become the executive officer of Headquarters Command. You may be forgiven for not knowing what Headquarters Command was, and indeed I didn't know either, for it was a military organization not found in nature and may have been created solely for the purpose of having a unit called Headquarters Command. It does have the sound of a high-level think tank, perhaps a semisecret group of select officers and enlisted men with the mission to devise critical plans or exciting and important clandestine operations essential to the survival of our nation.

In fact it was nothing of the sort. This was a merely brigade-sized unit that had been cobbled together from odds and ends, organizations that did not quite fit into the rest of the division and that no one else wanted: a military police unit of no particular pedigree; people who ran the stockade; a company with no specific unit mission and composed solely of women; and administrative, logistical, and communications units of one type or another. The troops were not smartly turned out, even by the revoltingly low standards of 1977. It appeared to me that there were intra-Command competitions to determine who could grow the longest hair and the bushiest beard, but the contest for "Scruffiest, Dirtiest, and Most Ill-Fitting Uniform" was something of a dead heat among hundreds of soldiers. All these disparate units had one thing in common with each other and with their parent, Headquarters Command: they were not the infantry.

I began a litany of logical reasons why I shouldn't be assigned to Headquarters Command, and I was not surprised that none made any impression on the personnel officer. That each of these reasons relied on decreasingly complex logic, and that at the end he still didn't understand, says a great deal about the quality of discriminating thought among staff officers thirty years ago. I moved to Plan B, which was to assert with some authority that my assignment to an infantry battalion was mandated by the Department of the Army. But because I couldn't support this with any proof stronger than my recapitulation of a telephone call that had occurred months earlier, even the personnel officer recognized that I had no leverage. In any case, he wasn't bound by some idle comment made by another drone on a distant staff, and he and I both knew it.

In the end, I prevailed, and I prevailed because I quickly and convincingly went to plan C: begging. This was a performance of mewling and moaning not seen since talkies had been invented, and had tears been required, such was my desire to get to an infantry battalion I have no doubt that I could have generated them in any quantity required. I became the executive officer of the 2nd Battalion, 32nd Infantry.

The battalion commander was a lieutenant colonel named Sam Ebbesen, who was born in the U.S. Virgin Islands and had received his undergraduate education at the City College of New York. Colin Powell was in attendance there, too, and he and Sam became close friends. Everybody looks big to me, but Sam looked very large, tall, bulky, and imposing. Sam was the person for whom "a bear of a man" was invented. As the two officers in the command group, we must have looked positively ludicrous together. Since volume increases roughly as the cube of any one dimension, the big difference in our heights and girths produced in Sam a man who had to weigh almost three times what I did.

In those days, many soldiers smoked cigarettes, but Sam had never acquired the habit, and one day he explained why tobacco had never been for him. In the library of their home in the islands, his father, very successful, tough, and old-school, had a humidor filled with the finest Cuban Gran Coronas. When Sam was quite young, perhaps seven years old, he was in his father's library, discovered the humidor, removed a cigar, and emulated his father's lighting up. He thought it was awful, as a young boy his age undoubtedly would, but before he could put the thing down, his father caught him with the cigar and made him smoke the whole thing. Sam tried to explain that he thought the cigar was revolting, but perhaps his father thought Sam's revulsion made the boy particularly receptive to a life-changing lesson. Green and sick as a dog, that was the beginning and the end of smoking for Sam Ebbesen.

Largely because of Sam, the 2nd Battalion, 32nd Infantry was a high-quality unit. He understood the importance of delegating authority and responsibility, and to that end, he worked hard to develop the skills of junior leaders. Many people in positions of authority, in and out of the uniformed services, are extremists. They tend to be either detail-oriented, anal-compulsive nuisances or else so lackadaisical and incurious that the organization accomplishes its mission only by accident. It was a blessing that Sam was nothing like these people at all. As with all methods of leading, Ebbesen's was tailored to his personality, and that included an unrelenting desire to stay in the field with his troops and away from meetings. He knew that good performance, to say nothing of excellence, results not from sitting in an office and issuing edicts, but from being among subordinates and sharing their professional lives. He believed that the boss's job was to give direction and guidance, to lead by example, and to leave to someone else all the tasks he found uninteresting, unsatisfying, frustrating, annoying, and onerous. That someone else was Jacobs, his executive officer.

As a combination deputy commander, chief of staff, administrative and logistical boss, maintenance proconsul, and all-around dogsbody, my mission was to make sure that Sam was free to command the battalion. And when I became a battalion commander myself, I found that I had an irritating officer as my second in command, and he was charged with the responsibility to perform all those inescapably tedious functions so that I could spend my time in the jungle with my soldiers.

Leading by example is a bit out of fashion these days, particularly in government and civilian life and even occasionally in the military among those who talk a good game but are irredeemably poor excuses for leaders. Being in the thick of things may be dangerous, inconvenient, and time-consuming, but if one accepts the reports of subordinates that everything is just peachy, and there is no personal supervision to ensure that the reports are accurate, disaster is the most likely outcome.

And this is as big a failing among elected officials as it is for those who have been appointed. When conflict is unconventional or of low intensity, it is easy to visit theaters of action, receive impressive briefings in relative comfort, and become convinced by the technological spectacle alone that there are few problems and they are soluble with the resources at hand. The presence of numerous impressive-looking officers of stupendous rank assists in solidifying the conclusion. And then, when reality doesn't coincide with the appearance, people who should have known better first deny knowledge, then make excuses, and then finally castigate those who were the proximate cause of the problem.

With modern, advanced technology, aggressive leadership has become both more critical and easier to avoid than ever. In Napoleon's time, one couldn't help being on the battlefield because the short range of weapons and communication precluded the commander's being very far away from the action. As late as World War II, Korea, and even Vietnam, leaders and troops were in it together. Now, pilotless attack aircraft controlled from Virginia can destroy targets in Afghanistan, and the nature of the battle seems to require the employment of small units rather than large formations of troops. There are many benefits to advances in electronic technology, but they tend to dissolve the close relationship between the senior leaders and the people they lead. Strong leadership then becomes less impor-

tant than the superficiality of appearance, and it becomes easy for
marginal officials of modest talent to perform adequately, because
the circumstances are not taxing.

And all the while, as at Abu Ghraib and Walter Reed Army Medical Center, there suffuses the growing odor of organizational decom-
position. The tragedy is that the reprehensible circumstances in these
places came about because highly placed officers who undoubtedly
knew the principles of leadership couldn't be bothered to *practice* the
principles of leadership.

IN EVERY ORGANIZATION, particularly in military units, there is
an undercurrent of emotion that occasionally pops to the surface,
almost always in the form of violence. Someone makes a casual and
unthinking snide remark, or there is an untutored misinterpretation
of something perfectly benign, and seconds, hours, or a day later
bystanders are treated to the spectacle of two red-faced youths flail-
ing ineffectually as if they were windmills in a strong but brief gale.
Young men do get mad at one another, usually when their blood is by
volume mostly testosterone and ethanol. But internecine violence is
corrosive and cannot be abided in any unit.

Perhaps I had told Sam that I had done some amateur boxing
when I was younger, but in any case, after one of these schoolyard
tiffs between a couple of young soldiers, Sam decreed that the two
knuckleheads had to settle their differences wearing gloves and head-
gear, with the entire battalion in attendance and me as the referee. I
procured the equipment, explained to them some rudiments of the
art, and at the end of the next battalion run a few days later, Sam
announced to our five hundred soldiers that the two were going to
put an end to their nonsense in front of everyone. Like actors playing
boxers in a bad movie, the two tough guys glowered at each other,

my arm between them keeping them apart. And then I dropped my arm and directed them to box.

And what a match it was. The roar from the crowd rivaled that from one hundred thousand fans at a championship football game with a tie score and seconds to go. Despite my superficial instruction, the two didn't know the first thing about the sweet science of boxing. The fundamental punch is the jab, but I don't recall a single jab being thrown. Instead, each soldier heaved one wild haymaker after another, and in less than a minute, weighed down with sixteen-ounce gloves that had the destructiveness of eiderdown pillows, their overcooked and limp spaghetti arms were draped over each other's shoulders as they gasped for breath and leaned supportively together to keep from collapsing in an ignominious heap on the grass. The onlooking soldiers cheered deafeningly, while I, Sam, the sergeant major, and the rest of the battalion's leadership just howled with laughter.

As it transpired, we actually had quite a few soldiers in the battalion who were skilled boxers, most of them Polynesian: Hawaiians, Tongans, Chamorros from Guam and the Marianas. We decided to have two of the more accomplished fighters box a few exhibition rounds each week, after the battalion run. It didn't take long before the entire division started doing the same thing, and some months later, we organized a boxing smoker in which the best fighters from each battalion competed in the Fort Ord arena before thousands of the division's soldiers.

Sam decided to use this occasion to treat the troops to a proper social event. Today they are euphemistically called "dining facilities," but thirty years ago they were "mess halls," which was often an apt description of the product. There was always a huge quantity of food, but in those battalions in which there was no command emphasis on the quality of the chow, the stuff could be unappetizing and inedible: gray potatoes, gray meat, gray broccoli. In such units, the only food that wasn't gray was the scrambled eggs, which were green.

We were required to manage the mess account very carefully to a budget, but over a period of months we were able to save enough money to organize a magnificent dinner for the soldiers, to which they could invite their wives, families, and girlfriends, everyone dressed as formally as was possible in the circumstances. Soldiers wore their standard green dress uniforms, but with white shirts and black bow ties. Women arrived in taffeta and organza, and the battalion area looked as if it were a movie set for a costume drama or the site of America's largest mass wedding. This was an extravaganza like nothing our troops had ever seen, in or out of the Army. Among other delicacies, the groaning board offered steamship rounds of beef that were simply entire beef haunches roasted perfectly and carved to order on the spot, luscious roast turkeys with crisp, lacquered mahogany skin, and whole boiled lobsters.

I stood next to one private, a soldier who was eyeing the lobster cautiously, almost suspiciously. It occurred to me that he may have never tasted one.

"It's a lobster," I said to him. "Have one."

He made no move to sample a dish that in any restaurant in the area would have cost him his net pay for a month.

"Go ahead," I urged him. "Have one. It's delicious."

"No, sir," said the soldier, looking at me and gesturing to the lobster with his thumb. "Looks like a bug to me."

———

OUR SOLDIERS WORKED hard, and when they were in the field, sometimes for weeks without a break, they were on duty all day and night with little rest. So, back from the desert or from a month in Alaska, they went on pass and played hard, too. Most soldiers were single, and like most young men their age, they headed straight for the noisiest, smokiest dumps they could find, places that served cold beer and warm women. For some of these soldiers, the opportunity to do silly things was too compelling to resist, and they had to be collected early in the morning at the local lockup. Many of the young officers and noncommissioned officers were married, and they went home to their wives and children.

With two children and *no* wife, my social engagements consisted of laundry, dishes, and vacuuming. As at Fort Leavenworth, I would occasionally be offered a sympathy meal, but I could really make my own food, and I didn't need an evening with the same people with whom I spent the rest of the day. What I needed was a date. Dates were not impossible to come by, but the pickings were slim. If I wanted to spend quality time with pole dancers or the wives of incarcerated felons, there was no end of candidates a few miles away in Salinas, not that there is anything necessarily wrong with that, and there is plenty to be said for such relationships. But most other women were put off by the fact that I couldn't sleep over because my twelve-year-old daughter insisted that I be home by midnight.

So in one sense, being the executive officer and infernally busy all the time was a blessing in disguise. It kept me fully occupied and provided me no time to dwell on the fact that I had had a more satisfying social life when I was fifteen years old.

And I *was* intensely busy all the time and had little patience for foolishness (unless perpetrated by me) or time-wasting, ancillary tasks that did not contribute directly to the accomplishment of the mission or the welfare of the men. By any definition, I was a drudge.

One afternoon, an Australian colonel visited the battalion, accompanied by a British army captain named Sue Forbes, whom I later discovered was the British exchange officer to the 7th Infantry Division. It escaped me why the British army needed an exchange officer in the division or why the division needed an exchange officer from Britain. Indeed, to what extent the visit of the Australian contributed to the defense of either country was a mystery. I, for example, would

NEWARK PUBLIC LIBRARY
121 HIGH ST.
NEWARK, NY 14513

have been pleased to visit Australia on the government's account, but the benefit that would have accrued to my personal enjoyment would far exceed the benefit, if any, to the Republic.

But in one sense, the Australian colonel's trip was a resounding success: I got to meet Captain Forbes, a stunning, effervescent, accomplished young woman. Well, at least I *saw* her. She and the Australian colonel had been visiting Sam Ebbesen in his office, and when they departed, I caught a glimpse of her. Later that afternoon, she called to ask if Sam could attend a cocktail party in honor of the Australian at the commanding general's quarters, and I seized the opportunity to chat her up in the most shameless and adolescent fashion.

I asked her to dinner, and she accepted without a fight. This could have been very bad news. Perhaps she had a rotten personality or bad body odor and couldn't get a date. Maybe she was cheating on her husband, a professional wrestler suffering from drug-induced psychoses. Perhaps both.

Having been married most of my life, I was bereft of a single social skill that was useful in dealing with eligible young women. I knew how to find the square root of any number longhand, how to close the sale of kitchen utensils to a woman with no use for them, how to disassemble a farm animal, how to make flourless chocolate cake. But aside from asking Sue Forbes to dinner, I had no idea what was supposed to happen next. I was in uncharted, and very deep, waters.

Dressed in a dark blue, wide-lapelled leisure suit of the finest polyester, the only civilian clothing I owned that could reasonably be considered unsuitable for garden work or cleaning the oven, I showed up at her apartment in Monterey the following Friday. She ushered me into the place and asked if I'd like to have a quick drink and, thinking it was de rigueur in the home of someone from London, I asked her for some gin.

"Gin with what?" she asked.

Well, I actually had no idea what went with gin, exactly, and so I said, "Just gin."

She was startled. "Ice?"

"Uh, no. Just gin in a glass."

I was trying to be terribly British but did not realize that instead I was coming across as terribly alcoholic. I suppose I could have emulated James Bond and ordered a martini, but in the movies it looked like a lot of work to prepare and I wanted to make it easy for her. I did not realize that she would have preferred to mix a martini, or chop a cord of wood, or have her gallbladder removed than to spend much time with someone whose idea of a quick drink was a water glass full of gin, neat.

We repaired to a trendy restaurant in downtown Monterey, where I made awkward conversation, asking her, among other silly things, what she thought of me when we first met.

"I thought your trousers are too tight," she said.

"No, not *these*," I said. I meant when I saw her at the battalion earlier that week, when I was in a fatigue uniform, which was quite baggy.

She said that she didn't remember seeing me at the battalion, and that she actually met me for the first time when I showed up at her apartment that evening. She was such a petite, demure, refined young lady that it seemed unfathomable that she would accept a dinner invitation from a man she had never met.

I asked her, "Do you make it a habit of going to dinner with men you don't know?"

With a fetching smile, she said, "I have a policy of never turning down a free meal."

I suppose the tight trousers were a bonus.

———

A FEW MONTHS later, Sue brought me as her guest to a cocktail party at the British Embassy in Washington, D.C. Once a year, the embassy assembled the military exchange officers serving in the States for about a week of briefings. These sessions were mostly designed to prevent the Brits, who were exposed to a culture they considered unrelentingly churlish, callous, and brash, from going native.

When there was still a powerful Soviet Union and a wall across Berlin, it was common to ask Warsaw Pact heavies, as well as those from NATO and the nonaligned states, to balls, cocktail parties, and other classy functions. If you wanted to invite Warsaw Pact attachés only out of courtesy but didn't really want them to show up, an indication that there would be no alcohol was a sufficient deterrent, and conversely you could ensure the attendance of the Soviets and their allies by suggesting that liquor would be served in infinite variety and unlimited quantity.

The cocktail party was a glittering affair, giving officers an opportunity to wear their striking formal dress and to display impressive awards and decorations to good advantage. That nobody else knew what the decorations represented was irrelevant, as was the fact that many of them were awarded for quotidian actions such as being in a particularly impressive parade or for not having been a conspirator in a failed coup d'etat. It was the sheer decorative value that was most important. Almost everyone resembled the doorman at the old Plaza Hotel, and the entire scene looked like it had been excised from *Doctor Zhivago*.

In attendance was a man who had been something of a permanent fixture in Washington, a Red Army lieutenant general named Georgi Aleksandrovich Mikhailov, the Soviet military attaché. If you were casting a movie and needed a man who looked like everyone's idea of a Red Army general, Mikhailov was perfect. He appeared to be seven feet tall, with a twenty-eight-inch waist, an enormous head, and shoulders broad enough to land aircraft on them. He also had those gigantic Brezhnev eyebrows, the kind of foliage that looked like woolly caterpillars and protruded so far that when he walked in the rain his shoes stayed dry. And as he chomped on the crudités, I noticed that he had a mouthful of stainless steel teeth.

He was holding court on the ballroom floor, surrounded by a hedge of normal-sized people, and I was propelled by the British Army attaché or someone of similar stature to Mikhailov's side, so that I could be introduced to him.

"General Mikhailov," he said, "this is Major Jacobs."

I offered my hand to his enormous palm, and he shook it firmly but cautiously, staring humorlessly at my resplendent uniform and copious decorations. He paused, and in basso profundo voice and thick Russian accent said, "Tell me, Major Jacobs, how did you get all those medals?"

For just a beat, I wasn't sure what to say. But I have an inveterate, almost uncontrollable urge to tell the truth. Truth has an awesome power. It is important and beautiful for its own sake, but also, without it an ordered society is impossible. I am driven to deliver it, and so I often blurt out things that are wholly accurate but inadvisably impolitic.

"Sir," I said finally, "I got them for killing communists."

As he stared down at me, the thought crossed my mind that, if the whim or the vodka had moved him, he could have driven me like a tent peg through the dense hardwood floor of the ballroom.

"You are kidding, no?"

"No, sir," I said, uncomfortably craning my neck to look directly into his icy eyes. "I'm not kidding."

Then, General Mikhailov threw his head back and laughed like a hyena, and he spent the remainder of the evening wandering around the ballroom, telling knots of people how I had received all my medals for killing communists, each time laughing so that his formidable teeth glinted blindingly in the ballroom lights.

WHAT LITTLE FREE time I had I spent with Sue, but nothing lasts forever, and after about a year, she told me that her NATO visa would soon expire and that she would be reassigned elsewhere, probably to London or Hong Kong. That sounded pretty exotic to me, and I wished that the United States Army offered similar postings. To be sure, Dothan, Alabama, and Leesville, Louisiana, are lovely places, but somehow not quite the same as London and Hong Kong.

But Sue had decided that she preferred not to go, that she loved the British army but she loved me more, and she wanted to retire and marry me. And if she didn't retire and marry me, she would redeploy and I'd never see her again.

The prospect of her disappearing forever was not an attractive one, but neither was marriage. To someone who had had his fill of marriage, who believed that it is often an investment with unlimited, unmanageable risk and occasionally an instrument of torture, this was potentially big trouble. I had become averse to long-term relationships, which in my calculus was anything more than one evening. On those rare occasions that I dated a woman for a longer period, it was usually in the vain hope that the second date would not be as disastrous as the first.

I stammered as if I were suffering from a rare but debilitating aphasia, and, recognizing that I was not likely to say anything coherent, Sue gave me the weekend to think about it. And it was a miserable weekend: no sleep, pondering the awful idea of not seeing her again, but also considering the unpleasant concept of getting married. We often misuse the term "dilemma," applying it to just about any choice, no matter how small, inconsequential, or lacking in complexity. A dilemma is not merely a tough choice. It is one in which the outcome is undesirable no matter what is decided. Eggs or pancakes? Not a dilemma. Order the pancakes; you can have the eggs tomorrow. Or order them both. You've done it before and it didn't kill you.

On Monday, she called and asked what I had decided, and I said I needed more time. She said there was no more time, because the British army attaché, Brigadier Houston, was going to call from Washington that morning for her decision on retirement. Backed against the wall, out of time, out of energy, and out of excuses, vulnerable to the smile, compassion, and love of a pretty young woman, I agreed to get married. She said I wouldn't regret it.

The day for the ceremony arrived. Perhaps my old head wound had caused a temporary memory lapse, although more likely it was the result of my subconscious brain thinking about having been on parole for two years and the stark contrast of impending reincarceration, but instead of being at the Monterey County courthouse I was in the battalion's motor pool, inspecting vehicles. Sue; my daughter, Heather; and my son, David, were nattily dressed and at the courthouse, waiting for me. Sam Ebbesen, responding to a concerned call from Sue, telephoned me at the motor pool.

"Hey, XO," he said heartily, "what are you doing there?"

He knew the schedule, and I was puzzled why he would ask. I said, "Sir, I'm inspecting vehicles. This afternoon is motor stables, and I'm inspecting vehicles."

"I know what you're doing, you fool! But where are you *supposed* to be?"

It wasn't until that very second that I realized I was late for my own wedding. I arrived at the courthouse in time only because the case before our ceremony was that of a man who decided to contest a ticket for running a stop sign, thus delaying the judge. Had the defendant pled guilty, the judge's day would have been over before I arrived, and he would have left to play a round at Pebble Beach. And Sue could not have been faulted for booking the next plane to London or Hong Kong or wherever the rest of her life would take her. Tragedy, it appeared, had been averted by a misdemeanor, and I became a married man again. I had had two years on parole, but I was now a serial monogamist, no longer required, or permitted, to make another decision by myself.

SOME MONTHS LATER I was selected for promotion to lieutenant colonel, and after that, a separate Army board chose me to command a battalion. For those officers who aspire to the highest ranks in the military service, these selections are prerequisites. And it is a binomial system. Failure to be selected is a message that one should be prepared for a career that may be productive but not personally satisfying, and some people, particularly those with the ambition to be general officers, view it as a demoralizing suggestion to find another line of work.

And because a selection for anything is subjective, dependent on a number of variables including the vagaries of the selection procedure itself, the results of such boards are not perfect predictors of either intrinsic worth or future success. As with most things in life, it is advisable to maintain a realistic attitude, to understand that selection is not an occasion for self-congratulation and nonselection is a lousy reason to drink rat poison.

When it came to determining where I would command, I had some confidence, however limited, that the Army employed people who could read, and they would recognize from my record that I was a paratrooper, and they'd conclude that I should thus command an airborne battalion. Therefore, it was outside the boundaries of logic that I would run a mechanized infantry battalion, a unit that required nearly as many maintenance people as infantry soldiers and an inventory of more spare parts than General Motors. As a light-infantry officer, I had learned early in my career that if an item cannot be carried on a soldier's back or safely delivered by parachute, its utility was limited. So, I was quite enthused about the possibility of returning to the 82nd Airborne Division, or perhaps to one of the few remaining airborne battalions of the 101st Airborne Division, or even to the separate airborne battalion unobtrusively located in Vicenza, Italy, only sixty kilometers from Venice.

But I was doomed to disappointment. I was offered an infantry battalion in either Panama or Alaska. I suppose that as an extremist it was only proper that I should serve at the extremes. No delightful, temperate Vicenza for me. I could choose either steaming jungles overrun with voracious fire ants and cockroaches or else the frozen steppe with an average temperature of absolute zero.

"You're not getting an airborne command," said the latest incarnation of The Evil One. "You're going to Alaska or to Panama. Your call." I groaned into the phone receiver.

"Listen," he explained, "there's no guarantee you'll get your choice, either." How wonderful. "Alaska or Panama?"

For a man who preferred hot combat to a cold climate, the choice was an easy one. I did not have to dwell very long on recollections of a previous training exercise at Fort Wainwright, Alaska, where the availability of wild salmon and fresh game was negated by the lack of sunshine for half the year and the need for electrified dipsticks to prevent engine oil from solidifying. To some, the tradition of a softball game in the sunshine at midnight on June twenty-first may be an adequate novelty to justify two winters of ice fog and having to rescue squads of soldiers whose gasoline heaters set fire to their tents, but I found all of this inadequately charming in its own right and insufficient to compensate for being stationed only 160 miles south of the Arctic Circle.

Panama it was.

*Standing for right when it is unpopular
is a true test of moral character.*

—MARGARET CHASE SMITH

CHAPTER SEVENTEEN

THERE ARE NO longer any American military units in Panama, but in 1980 there was a whole brigade of us, scattered around the Canal Zone and charged with the mission of protecting the vital shipping lane across the isthmus. One supposes that almost any enemy might take a shot at grabbing the Panama Canal, and there were—and still are—plans to send large numbers of Americans to the area to repel or eject Russians, Chinese, or Venezuelans. But three decades ago, Jimmy Carter announced that the Canal Zone and the canal that went with it would be reverting to Panamanian control at the end of 1999, and until then we were viewed as lame-duck colonialists. And because the most significant perceived threat was not from external enemies but the Panamanians themselves, we regularly practiced our skills in defeating riots and other actions of civil violence that could be directed against sites along the canal.

I commanded the 4th Battalion, 10th Infantry Regiment. At the time I took command, it was stationed at Fort Davis, on the Caribbean side of the Canal Zone, not far from the city of Colón, but the majority of the jungle training areas, where my companies spent most of their time on small-unit tactics, were on the Pacific end of the Zone, fifty miles away. Panama writhes like a snake between Colombia to the south and the rest of Central America to the north, producing a geographical anomaly in which the sun rises over the Pacific Ocean and sets in the Caribbean Sea.

Although it dries out when the wet season is over, the Canal Zone is mostly jungle and teems with the animals that jungles typically contain, including jaguars, wild pigs, parrots, toucans, and sloths. And troops of howler monkeys. These large monkeys roar like tigers and delight in throwing things like bananas at the troops passing under them, but the animals take perverse pleasure in heaving their favorite ammunition, feces, whenever possible.

Colón was tropical and exotic, but in the steamy and run-down fashion of John Huston's Tampico in the opening scenes of *The Treasure of Sierra Madre*, it was a rough town of gangsters and petty thieves mingling among poor people trying to survive. It was a shabby, mossy backwater that looked in 1980 exactly as it had looked nearly a century before, when the French had tried unsuccessfully to cut a canal across Panama and failed, defeated by engineering expertise they did not have and driven away by yellow fever and malaria. American engineers eventually got the job done, but at a massive cost. The Panama Canal consumed hundreds of millions of dollars to build, and by some estimates more than thirty thousand people died in the French and American projects, an astonishing one-third of the total workforce.

One could argue that the most desirable aspect of Fort Davis was that it was located fifty-three miles from the rest of the brigade, and that included the brigade commander and his staff. Visiting the brigade headquarters usually required a helicopter ride and was a blessedly infrequent occurrence, as were his visits to me. Supervision, assistance, and even constructive criticism are always welcome when one is attempting to perform complicated and important missions, but these things are most pleasantly received from a great distance.

Other battalions were located painfully close to the headquarters and thus received concomitantly more help from those with an almost inexhaustible supply of it.

When I first joined the Army, the mess halls were the province of company commanders whose troops were being fed. At Fort Devens, my company had had a willful and cantankerous old mess sergeant with a leathery, lined face, and he had always sported a cigarette jammed into one side of his mouth. As he spoke, the butt would bob up and down, threatening to drop a long tobacco ash into the soup, which I was sure occurred with some regularity. When I drew KP, which seemed to happen often, he enjoyed assigning me to the worst jobs in the mess hall: scrubbing pots and pans and cleaning the grease trap.

By the late 1960s, some food service functions were being let by contract to civilian firms that supplied the mess halls' workers, and at my post, Fort Davis, the men who worked in our mess hall were all Kuna, most of them from the San Blas Islands off the Panamanian coast. This is an ancient indigenous tribe who still lived simply in huts on Fort Davis, the communal households tended by the women and children while the men worked in various jobs around post, including cleaning barracks and latrines and cutting lawns with machetes.

In many places around the world in which the U.S. Army had contractual arrangements for such services, including in the United States, performance and discipline of the workers were constant problems, and frequent written reports and meetings were required to set things right. This was not a problem with the Kuna. A single discouraging word to the chief was all that was required to remedy a problem, and it is likely that the unpleasantness of the remonstration that ensued was sufficient to get the workers' attention. After I had been in command about a year, the head of the Kuna clan on my post decided that I should become an honorary San Blas Kuna chief. The solemn ceremony was held one early evening in the clan's long Congress House, with the women and children assembled at attention, silently, against the walls.

These people were loyal, brave, and very short but immensely strong, and in the modern environment of a late-twentieth-century U.S. Army post, they looked oddly anachronistic, with colorful native dress, tattoos, and pierced body parts. Given the modern penchant of many people for body art and puncturing their skin with foreign objects, the Kuna look far less primitive than avant-garde.

CHAPTER EIGHTEEN

IN THE SUMMER of 1982, my two-year assignment as a battalion commander was over, and my family and I returned to the United States. My daughter, Heather, had graduated from high school in Panama the previous January and was beginning her freshman year in college, and David was fifteen and in high school. After sixteen years in the Army I was fairly adept at avoiding the Pentagon, but it is also likely that my file contained alert notices advising the assignment officer to avoid engaging me in a conversation on the subject unless he had a degree in rhetoric, a high threshold of pain for invective, and an unlisted home phone number. After a surprisingly civil and productive conversation about my destination after Panama, I received an interesting one-year assignment in the intelligence business, after which I reported to the National War College in Washington, D.C.

Fort McNair is a very picturesque enclave in the grubby southwestern portion of the District of Columbia, and it sits on a peninsula at the confluence of the Potomac and the Anacostia rivers. The National War College occupies an imposing Colonial Revival brick building that was designed by Stanford White and intended to house the Army War College, now at Carlisle Barracks, Pennsylvania. With a spectacular rotunda under a large dome, it is one of the most imposing buildings in Washington and can be seen easily from Reagan Airport, across the Potomac.

To educate its most promising senior officers, each service operates its own war college. In 1947, when the Defense Reorganization Act created the Joint Chiefs of Staff, the National War College was also created so that the Joint Chiefs could operate a similar institute, with the objective of educating senior civilians and officers of all services in the complicated businesses of joint operations and national security. There were roughly 160 students, evenly divided among the Army, Navy, Marine Corps, Air Force, and civilian agencies. Most of the latter were career officers from the Departments of State and Treasury and the intelligence community. For this level of schooling, the services selected only those candidates they were confident would rise to the highest ranks—generals, ambassadors, and directors—and most of them did.

Students at the National War College studied military operations, but at a high level of abstraction. A large portion of the curriculum was an examination of the complexities of the budget process and the interaction among the branches of government that produce, alter, and fuel the national security establishment. Almost all the students had service in the Pentagon or the headquarters of their agencies, and one of the most interesting, informative, and useful opportunities was the free exchange among the students about intergovernmental relations. Every student had one or more stories, either uproariously funny or infuriating and frustrating, about the dysfunction of the government structures in whose hands rest the security of our nation. That the hands were palsied and not connected to a fully functioning central nervous system may have accounted for many problems we saw, and what is most alarming is that there seems to have been little improvement over the years.

My boss, the commandant of the National War College, was a major general named Perry Smith, a 1956 graduate of West Point who opted for the Air Force and became a fighter pilot. His father-in-law was Aquilla James Dyess, a lieutenant colonel in the Marine Corps Reserve who was killed while earning the Medal of Honor for action on Kwajalein Atoll. Jimmy Dyess was also notable for being the only person in American history to have ever received both the Medal of Honor and the Carnegie Medal, awarded for civilian heroism. As a teenager in 1928, he saved two drowning swimmers off the coast of Charleston, South Carolina.

Among other qualifications, General Smith had received a doctorate at Columbia. He was a thoroughly inquisitive man, and very few things escaped his attention or interest. An iconoclast as well, he got into hot water with some of his narrow-minded superiors for inviting to speak to the National War College a woman named Petra Kelly, a founder of Germany's Green Party. The view of most people—at least those who are not intellectually constipated by large, indigestible hunks of dogma—is that one can disagree with things that controversial people have to say, as General Smith and the rest of us certainly did of Petra Kelly, but that doesn't make them any less interesting or useful. Having a breadth of intellectual experience is vital among those who have great responsibility and authority, and in our history we have seen the occasional, sad result of having leaders who were narrow-minded simpletons.

One of Perry Smith's more admirable traits was that he was constantly asking the people who worked for him how we could make things better. One afternoon, he asked some of the faculty how the program of speakers could be improved. In fact, we were already able to attract some very impressive specialists, renowned in their fields, and contemporary members of governments who had superb insights into the operation of the national security establishment. There was a steady parade of people from the National Security Council, the

Congress, the Defense Department, and so on. But the boss wasn't satisfied.

"You know," I said, "it would be interesting if we could get Richard Nixon to speak."

At the time, Nixon had not spoken or even appeared in public since he exiled himself with that famous good-bye wave from the helicopter on the White House lawn, and he was living as something of a recluse in New Jersey. Everybody agreed that it would be fascinating to hear from Nixon—if we could get him. I was not without resources, and a few weeks of gumshoe work produced a contact name and number. I placed the call.

"This is Colonel Jacobs," I told him. "We wondered if we could have Richard Nixon come speak at the National War College."

"Speak about what?" the contact asked.

"Whatever he wants."

That was all it took, and it was startling that nobody, including me, had thought of it before: find his number and invite him. Nixon came to the National War College surrounded by the usual phalanx of Secret Service agents and delivered a sweeping, masterful, extemporaneous foreign policy address to students and faculty who were transfixed by every word. Among other things, he identified the factors that adversely affected our national security situation, how to repair broken international relationships, and the strengths and weaknesses of diplomacy and other instruments of power. Nixon was spellbinding, and after answering only some of the dozens of questions that students and faculty wanted to ask, he left the auditorium and proceeded into the rotunda under the dome. The students, these middle-aged potential generals and ambassadors, followed him as if they were schoolchildren and formed a circle around him, continuing to pepper him with questions.

Meanwhile, the head of the Secret Service detail kept looking at his watch and muttering, "Mr. President, sir, we really must go...."

"No, no, I'm going to stay here," Nixon said. "I want to talk to these guys."

He carried on with the dialogue for what must have been at least half an hour, and then, suddenly, he stopped speaking and pointed his index finger directly at me.

"Hey, I know you," Nixon said. "Don't I know you?"

"Yes, sir," I said. "Seventeen years ago. You decorated me with the Medal of Honor."

Then Richard Nixon walked across the open circle of the rotunda and gave me a powerful hug. It was really quite astonishing that after nearly two decades, the man remembered a brief encounter among thousands of appearances, ceremonies, and official functions. And years later, long after Nixon's death, I happened to meet someone who had been close to him for a very long time, someone who knew him at least as well as anyone else, and I told him about the incident and how affectionate the old man had been.

After a second or two of pregnant silence, he shook his head and said, "That's the most amazing story I've ever heard."

"How so?"

"Because he was the *coldest* man I ever met in my life."

I said, "Well, he wasn't cold that day at the War College."

As a MAJOR additional duty, each faculty member was assigned students to advise, and one of mine was Eric Shinseki, who eventually rose to become the Chief of Staff of the Army. General Shinseki gained national attention when, just before we began the invasion of Iraq, he testified before Congress that we needed at least "several hundred thousand" troops to make sure that we held the country.

It is worth revisiting precisely what Shinseki said, when pressed by Michigan senator Carl Levin, in those televised hearings:

I would say that what's been mobilized to this point, something on the order of several hundred thousand soldiers, are probably, you know, a figure that would be required. We're talking about post-hostilities control over a piece of geography that's fairly significant with the kinds of ethnic tensions that could lead to other problems.

Despite his honesty, foresight, and prescience, Shinseki's assessment was flippantly dismissed just two days later by Defense Secretary Donald Rumsfeld:

What is, I think, reasonably certain, is the idea that it would take several hundred thousand U.S. forces, I think, is far from the mark.

Also dismissing it was Rumsfeld's deputy, Paul Wolfowitz:

But some of the higher-end predictions that we have been hearing recently, such as the notion that it will take several hundred thousand U.S. troops to provide stability in post-Saddam Iraq, are wildly off the mark. First, it's hard to conceive that it would take more forces to provide stability in post-Saddam Iraq than it would take to conduct the war itself and to secure the surrender of Saddam's security forces and his army. Hard to imagine.

A lack of understanding can make almost everything hard to imagine, particularly when the facts do not coincide with implicit, unfounded assumptions. For his troubles, Shinseki became an almost instant lame duck when the Secretary of Defense announced more than a year in advance that he was not going to renew Shinseki's appointment and left him to twist in the wind for the remainder of his career.

But if they have done nothing else, the events of the past five years have demonstrated conclusively and sadly that General Shinseki was entirely right. Yes, we needed at least 250,000 troops merely to make sure that we held the objective, and if we had to do it today, we might conclude we required more, perhaps 100,000 more. Just as Shinseki and I and thousands of others have learned from experience in actual ground combat, and as every infantryman knows: it takes more resources to hold an objective than to take it. An assertion that it takes fewer can only come from people with no understanding of how wars are actually fought and won.

There has been much criticism of the civilian leadership for the misadventure in Iraq, and all of it is deserved. The assertion that our national security was at risk from Iraq was nonsense. So was the conclusion that Iraq was such a threat that we could shortchange the more important and pressing effort against terrorists in Afghanistan. History will be thorough in judging the complicity or acquiescence of all the players in this tragedy, including the president, the vice president, and many others, but there is plenty of blame to go around, and it will eventually be apportioned fairly.

Perhaps we must learn to expect very little from people with very little expertise. After all, nobody expected George W. Bush to be a military genius, and I have met no one who expected Rumsfeld to be one, either. What the Defense Department touted as a revolutionary and more effective form of modern warfare was merely a lame attempt to accomplish a big job with insufficient strength and poor understanding of warfare.

We have a system in which military leaders serve civilian bosses, because we do not want people in uniform to run the country. We have seen it attempted elsewhere, and it is rarely successful and never very pretty. So American service members are inculcated with the notion of the superiority of civilian authority, and they are very uncomfortable acting contrary to that notion. Officers have the responsibility to contribute to the plans and the decisions to execute those plans, but they are taught that, once the decision is made, they must obey—unless, of course, the order is immoral or illegal. And this works extremely well at nearly every level of command. Nearly, but not at *every* level.

As in every other area of operations, there was an existing plan to go into Iraq. The Iraq war plan that was extant before the invasion, based on Desert Storm, stipulated months of advance preparation and weeks of heavy air bombardment. According to James Fallows, a national correspondent for *The Atlantic* and author of *Blind into Baghdad*, although Rumsfeld wanted to use only about 75,000 troops for the invasion force, the Army thought the number should be *five times* greater. And there are reliable accounts of Rumsfeld's personally eliminating units from deployment lists.

But if the Secretary of Defense wants to do something contrary to the best judgment of the general officers appointed to render advice, something so egregious that experienced military people know instinctively, if not from experience, that it is foolhardy or worse, who is left to prevent disaster?

Only those general officers. Professional military men know how many troops are needed to perform missions, and the plans must be reviewed and certified annually. If Tommy Franks or Dick Myers or any other officer at the top of the chain of command thought that the plan was unworthy, each had an obligation to his uniform, to the nation, and to the troops they sent to war to ensure that the plan was not executed. And if they thought that the plan was a good one, then they were fools. In either case, they failed this country.

Civilian control was established to prevent military domination, and the rules for following lawful orders are clear. Who would have thought that our real danger was the civilian hijacking of the military apparatus, snatching it from officers who were either too inept or too pusillanimous to resist? In this regard, one might hear an attempted justification asserting that it is more effective to be inside than outside the organization. Of course, if you're outside, certainly you can't affect anything. But if you're not effective *inside*, you might as well be outside.

To employ the military instrument of power *knowing* it was inadequately resourced is a bit like baking a chocolate cake and having all the ingredients except chocolate. You'll get *something*, but it won't be what you want. It's much better to wait until you have all the ingredients.

Or better yet, skip dessert altogether.

You'll live longer.

CHAPTER NINETEEN

LATE IN 1986, after I had been at the National War College for three years, I got a call from Bob Kerrey, whom I knew from before he was elected governor of Nebraska. Bob had by then nearly finished his term and was contemplating a run for the Senate. He reported that he was coming to the East Coast that weekend and asked if I was free to join him first in New Jersey for a cocktail party and then in Boston to dedicate a veterans' memorial.

I agreed eagerly, mostly because of a rule I had established when I arrived in the capital: never reject the opportunity to avoid spending weekends in suburban Washington, D.C. There is nothing inherently *wrong* with suburban Washington, D.C. It is generally neat and clean and populated with pleasant people who work hard to keep our national government running. But then, maybe that's why I preferred not to hang around there if I could avoid it.

The cocktail party was a black-tie affair, and, still on active duty, I had to get my dress blue uniform cleaned and pressed and then spend about half an hour attaching the various insignia, ribbons, and other accouterments to the jacket. There is a lot of sartorial and haberdashery work involved in being a colonel, which is why the British army provides its senior officers with batmen.

The affair was held at a very posh golf club in New Jersey and was actually a fund-raiser for Bill Bradley, who was already in the U.S. Senate. And the fund-raiser was being underwritten by a fellow named Tom Kane, who ran his own institutional bond firm. From Xavier High School and Fordham University, Kane had joined the Marine Corps, where he became an A-4 attack aircraft pilot and flew sixty-three combat missions during the Vietnam War. After his Marine Corps service, he began a successful career on Wall Street.

About an hour into the cocktail party Kane introduced himself to me, and he also took me around to meet a large number of the people who worked for him at his firm, Printon Kane & Company. These were very nice people, full of energy and blessed with good humor and a limitless capacity for martinis.

"Jacobs," Tom Kane said finally, after I had met dozens of his colleagues, "when are you going to retire from the Army?"

"Retire? I haven't thought much about it," I said. "I have just over twenty years—I guess I could retire anytime."

"Look," he said, jabbing a finger in my chest, "you need to retire from the Army and come and work for me. I'll pay you a lot of money to learn the bond business."

Bob and I left for Boston the next morning, and when I returned home on Sunday night, Sue asked me about the fund-raiser at the club. I mumbled something about how a former Marine named Kane had told me he wanted me to work for him and learn the bond business.

Sue asked, "What's the bond business?"

"I have no damn idea, but he'll pay me three times what I'm making as a colonel in the Army. It's time to retire." Sue, who had argued strenuously for years that I had already done my bit and should start making a proper living, was very happy indeed.

Just days later, in the first week of November 1986, I submitted my retirement request. Our checkered relationship notwithstanding, the Army spent considerable effort trying to convince me to stay, and ultimately I received a call from the Chief of Staff of the Army himself, who asked me to reconsider. But I explained that I had three children, one of whom had already finished college and another who was enrolled at Virginia Tech, and at the rate I was shoveling money out the door, in two years I would be bagging groceries in the commissary to augment my meager salary.

"I'm forty-two years old," I told him. "I'm making forty thousand dollars a year. I love the Army, but it's really about time I did something for my family."

I retired on February 1, 1987.

OLD HABITS ARE tough to shake, and I found myself still driven to polishing my shoes before going to bed and to awaking at 5:00 a.m. without an alarm clock, as if I had never left the Army. Otherwise, of course, the lifestyle was very much different, and after years of privation it was not hard to get used to regular meals and the luxuries of having two bathrooms and a house larger than a walk-in closet. I discovered the security of *not* running out of money before the end of the month and the miracle of valet parking, both phenomena I hadn't known existed. I was startled to discover that there actually were people who made a living from painting houses, fixing plumbing, and repairing roofs, and that I would no longer have to attempt these things myself. This was a new and exciting world.

And the work was significantly different, too. In many ways, structuring and selling investments to institutions like banks, insurance companies, and pension funds was very different from defending the country. But by almost every objective measure, it was easier to devise, buy, and sell investments than to kill people. Now, it may seem that the complexities of finance are unfathomable, that the state of the economy is often such that the business of business seems too much for even its practitioners to understand. Perhaps economists and finance professionals should be cut some slack, and maybe without their hard work things would be very much worse. But it is difficult these days to generate sympathy for executives of large financial houses when they profess ignorance of risk that is obvious to anyone who takes the time to look for it, risk that is accurately measurable by anyone using techniques available to a first-year MBA student.

To an infantry soldier, determining the volatility of a derivative transaction or the risk-adjusted return of a large portfolio of mixed assets is far easier than devising a plan to destroy a well-entrenched battalion and then motivating a bunch of petrified twenty-year-olds to do it. No, the banking business isn't brain surgery, and as an experienced neurosurgeon once said, even brain surgery isn't brain surgery. Success in anything takes some luck, of course, but it mostly takes diligence, dedication, and hard work. For example, in order to sell securities and do a number of other things related to investments, one must pass a demanding all-day examination to earn a license. The examination tests the applicant's knowledge of every financial instrument, law, operation, and calculation, a lifetime of banking knowledge in one sitting. Even fresh out of the Army and with banking experience limited only to making mistakes in my checkbook, concentrated study was all that was required to answer correctly hundreds of abstruse questions about things like the relationship between duration and yield and the provisions of the Securities Exchange Act of 1934. Like many others who knew almost nothing before they studied, I passed the exam on the first try.

Shortly before he died, Vladimir Horowitz, probably the greatest pianist of the twentieth century, was asked about the origin of his talent, suggesting that virtuosity was an inchoate trait.

"No," said Horowitz with a huge sigh, "it's just a lot of practice."

"WHAT ARE YOU idiots doing?" screamed Tom Kane. It was Monday, October 19, 1987, about nine months after I had retired from the Army, and he had just stormed out of his office onto the trading floor. "Are you all *nuts*? You're sitting around doing nothing? Buy every bond you can!"

It was Black Monday, the day of the single largest drop in Wall Street history, a loss of more than five hundred points, almost 23 percent of the value of the Dow Industrial Average. There were margin calls on every equity portfolio, savings were wiped out, businesses ruined. But because stocks were crashing, bonds—securities that deliver a fixed return—were skyrocketing, as investors flew to quality and security. Just about all the bonds we would buy were likely to rise dramatically in value. They did, and Kane and the firm and everyone associated with it did very well in a rotten market.

Like many of the people he hired, Tom Kane is a larger-than-life character whose intelligence, energy, and wry wit were the perfect ingredients for success. Not satisfied with half measures, he did everything in a big way, educated as he was in the Jesuit tradition—and a jet pilot, too. He owned two airplanes and a beautiful Rolls-Royce. When not traveling, he would lead a contingent of friends to one of his favorite restaurants for drinks and dinner, and the party usually didn't end until well after midnight.

Back then, almost everyone drank a bit too much, and Kane didn't want to drive. So one night he instructed me to stay sober, drive him home, take his Rolls to my house, and collect him on the way to the office in the morning. I had just moved with my wife and Zachary, our young son, into a comfortable but relatively modest house in a new subdivision. The sight of a very expensive, classy Rolls-Royce parked in the driveway of a house that was worth less than the car aroused the suspicions of the neighbors, who must have concluded that I was involved in drugs or smuggling or was otherwise mobbed up. It was not an easy task convincing them to leave me alone, since the police were inherently skeptical, my story sounded farcically improbable, and the Rolls wasn't registered to me.

Tom Kane surrounded himself with people who were reliable and straightforward, many of them veterans of military service where these traits were essential for survival and success. Among them was Tom O'Grady, one of the few remaining Runyonesque characters anywhere. He once said to me that the tax laws ought to be amended to permit him to declare his bookie as a dependent. O'Grady grew up in Jersey City, the son of a fireman who died young, and he was one of only a few hundred youths actually drafted into the Marine Corps during the Vietnam era. He had had a low draft number and was called to report to the reception station on White-hall Street in Manhattan. With too few people to handle too many inductees, the place was a noisy, disorganized mess, and O'Grady loudly registered his displeasure. A female Marine NCO was evidently not amused and directed O'Grady to a corner where she was collecting loudmouths. Satisfied that she had culled them all, she then had her new crop of Marines, almost all of whom eventually found themselves in Khe Sanh, a most unpleasant place to be at the beginning of 1968.

O'Grady's mother, Catherine, had a heart condition, and a few years ago she underwent a triple bypass. She was in the hospital for a while, and when she was to be released, O'Grady left home about midmorning to collect her and bring her home. Late that afternoon, I got a call from Irene, his wife.

"Hey, have you seen O'Grady?" she asked.

"No, was I supposed to see O'Grady?"

"He went to pick up Grandma Cath from the hospital and bring her home this morning, but he's not back yet. I thought maybe he was at your place."

Irene had been married to O'Grady for a long time, and she knew both him and his mother very well. If she had thought more clearly, she could have easily determined where he was and so saved herself some aggravation.

O'Grady had collected his mother from the hospital right on time and was on his way to her home in Jersey City. She was very wobbly, still had the surgical clips holding her chest together, and was not in particularly good shape. Not far from her apartment, however, she pointed to the row of storefronts they were passing.

"Tommy boy, I'm thirsty. What do you say we stop and get a couple of drinks?" So that's where they turned out to have been. Instead of going home, the amazing O'Grady and Grandma Cath, complete with assorted surgical appliances still attached, had bellied up to the bar for an afternoon—and evening—of restorative beers.

Usually, the first opportunity to go home that soldiers get, they go home, because they're sick to death of being away. I was no different. Having been away from home for a good portion of my twenty years in the Army, I preferred to spend as little time on the town as possible. But in the bond business, late-night forays were difficult to avoid. Soon after I started my new career, we were out late, and I was ready to call it a night, but I had to wait for a ride home. The participants were the usual suspects from the firm, people with street names like the Hammer, the Raccoon, and Cement Head. I started looking anxiously at my watch, and O'Grady asked, "What's the matter?"

"It's past midnight," I said. "I think I better call my wife."

"Now why would you want to do that?" he asked.

"I want to tell my wife that I'm going to be late."

"She already knows that," he said.

"I better call her anyway."

"Let me take you through this," O'Grady said. "If you call her right now, what's going to happen?"

"She's going to chew my ass."

"Right. And what time do you think you're going to get home?"

"I don't know. At this rate, three in the morning."

"Also right. And what's going to happen when you get home?"

"She's going to chew my ass again."

"Exactly. Don't call her now. When you get home, she'll give you crap once, and it will be over with. Why get your ass chewed twice?"

Wittgenstein, eat your heart out.

DESPITE THE PHYSICALLY debilitating social life, I was doing very well at Printon Kane & Company, but about a year after I arrived, I encountered an opportunity to found a finance company in California. The idea was to start a securitization business, to package consumer loans into fixed-income investments for purchase by pension funds, insurance companies, and other institutions. If it sounds confusing, it did to me, too, but it really wasn't all that difficult, and success in the business was merely a function of ensuring we had good people, good procedures, and good supervision. The rest was just numbers, making sure that we had lots more quality assets than we needed for all but the most hideous economic situations. And if the worst happened, everyone would have far bigger problems than a few nonperforming loans. Tom Kane thought it was a great idea and provided the seed capital.

When I got home, Sue said, "How was work today?"

"Well, I have to go to California," I said.

"When?"

"Tomorrow."

"When are you coming back?"

"Coming back? Never thought about that. I guess I don't know."

For a man who was always concerned that his wife wouldn't speak to him if he got home after midnight, I was very nonchalant about leaving home for an indeterminate, and perhaps even interminable, period of time. In the next fifteen months, until we sold the company, I think I saw my family maybe half a dozen times. The business was fraught with headaches, setbacks, and mistakes, and we ran out of money at one point, but the enterprise yielded to the components of most successes: clear thinking and hard work.

Back in New Jersey with my wife and young son, it didn't take very long before I became a bored and boring nuisance. I spent quite a bit of time surveying my backyard, which was mostly crabgrass and chickweed, and my front yard, which was mostly chickweed and crabgrass. I washed and polished my car so often that I had the rust in a high state of shine. When the dishwasher had accumulated two juice glasses and a spoon, I ran it off, and I think I reorganized the cupboards once a week.

Seeing that the Rolls-Royce had long since disappeared, and that I seemed to be hanging around home without much to do, the chap who lived across the street from me, a managing director of Bankers Trust, came to see me one evening.

He said, "*My* wife says that *your* wife says if you don't get out of the house, she's going to kill you." I said that I had noticed a bit of tension since I returned from California.

"Jack, what do you know about the EMS?"

"The Emergency Medical Service?"

He chuckled. "No, the European Monetary System."

"Never heard of it," I said.

"We're starting up an institutional hedge fund at Bankers Trust, and you ought to be involved in it." I knew nothing about hedge funds, institutional or not. And I didn't know that the Europeans even had a monetary system. And I couldn't determine what contribution I could make to all this, except that I had had plenty of responsibility and I was very much older and at least marginally wiser than the average person on Wall Street.

"I don't know..."

He said, "You need to get out of the house, man."

I DIDN'T FIT the profile at all. People who went into the banking business generally had MBAs or were certified financial planners, or at the very least had already been in the finance business for a long time. I was, to say the least, a nonstandard hire. Beyond my Rutgers degrees, what were my qualifications? Basically, I had spent my life killing people and teaching other people to kill people. There was nothing but complex dynamic tension in trying to live a moral life as a warrior, and on the surface it seemed difficult to reconcile with a productive life as a civilian. But if I was still an emotional adolescent, combat service had bestowed on me an intellectual maturity that one found rarely among civilians.

So I joined Bankers Trust and again had to leave my family behind, heading for London, where I stayed for the next five years. The business was a huge success, and I became a managing director and was also given responsibility for the bank's foreign exchange options business worldwide. But that merely increased the number of places I had to visit and reduced to nearly zero the amount of time I spent at home. If I returned from Europe on Saturday morning, I had a few hours to repack my bags, catch a plane to Tokyo, and arrive for a meeting on Monday. One year, I was away from home more than 220 working days, and that was just about all the working days that year. The enormous fun of spending time with my Japanese traders and eating raw blowfish at a geisha house or singing "Suki-yaki" at their favorite bar in Roppongi was negated by the annoyance of the plane rides and the loneliness in hotel after hotel. There is just so much raw sea cucumber I can eat before longing for a steak.

Of course, I *could* have ordered a steak in Tokyo, but it would have cost the same as a new car.

CHAPTER TWENTY

As with bachelorhood, sentience, and continence, everything ends, and in 1994, after five years, I left Bankers Trust. Eventually things ended for Bankers Trust, too, as it was absorbed into Deutsche Bank and ceased to exist. I became immediately eligible for a tiny pension and found it humorously ironic that I was receiving an annuity from a German bank.

Now in yet another retirement, and several standard deviations from the mean age of Americans, I was not inundated with phone calls enticing me to work, and I was essentially unemployed. But in an effort to preclude a reprise of five years earlier, when I had spent enough time at home to drive my household to exasperation, I needed to stay busy doing *something*. Of course, there are major benefits to idleness, including an opportunity to view again those favorite, beloved episodes of *Leave It to Beaver*, to learn the game of bridge, and to acquire a protective layer of adipose tissue that would be useful if chocolate ice cream were ever outlawed and unavailable. For a while, I attempted to learn the game of golf but found that, like playing the piano, it is a skill best acquired in youth. From time to time, friends and I would try to play a round, and we eventually discovered that the least frustrating game was "71," in which, upon reaching that score, no matter what the hole, we retired to the clubhouse. Such was our skill that I do not recall ever playing the back nine.

But one of the biggest advantages of having a bit of free time is the ability to make some small contribution to the community at large, and I sought to get involved in a variety of charitable enterprises. Talking to civic groups, at libraries, and in schools are extremely satisfying things to do, but surely the greatest leverage comes from talking with young people.

I had some trepidation about addressing teenagers, since I despised the times when decrepit people like me spoke to my classes when I was young. There are few things more enervating than listening to some old coot blab at length on a subject of little immediate interest to young people. For all I know, when I was young I attended a lecture delivered by President Eisenhower, but the teenage brain is so structured that anything important is blocked, and only that information of no consequence makes an impression. In high school, we were visited by a famous radio disk jockey, and to most of the students it was so memorable that few have forgotten it forty-five years later. Meeting Albert Einstein, Mohandas Gandhi, or Abraham Lincoln was likely to produce far less excitement.

The inclination is to visit comfortable suburban high schools situated on green, manicured campuses, places to which the children either are delivered in large white SUVs or else drive their own Mercedeses. These are Lake Wobegone Edens, where all the children are above average, taking advanced placement courses exclusively, and suffering only to the extent that they must choose which among a number of Ivy League colleges they will attend. Visits to these schools are usually benign experiences, and students typically have a reserved, casual, and polite interest in leadership, current events, and the proud American history of military service. It is not exactly preaching to the converted, but neither is it an efficient delivery of influence to parts of society that really need it. Well-fed people do not require food as desperately as those who are undernourished.

And to visit intellectually malnourished children, those who have little information, motivation, or hope, one must go to the inner cities. And for some time that was where I went. But by the time that sociologically needy children are of high school age, they have already built a firewall of cynicism that is nearly impenetrable. This is depressing, and of course one must persevere, but I have found that the most fruitful venues to affect children at risk are middle schools, where there is still a flame of inquisitiveness, and where cynicism has not yet hardened into impermeability.

To be honest, school principals and business executives find that the attractiveness of an address by Jack Jacobs is not Jack Jacobs at all, but instead my decoration. This is not a bad thing, however. Recipients of the Medal of Honor feel strongly that the award is less a recognition of individual effort than it is representative of the sacrifice and patriotism of *all* those who have served, many of whom did not survive to talk about it. And as time marches inexorably on, and as the number of living recipients of the award gets smaller, the mission of the remaining recipients—to educate the nation and particularly our youth about service to our republic—becomes more critical.

Every day, we lose more than a thousand veterans and with them the wisdom of age and the lessons of history. American culture puts a huge premium on youth and beauty and even on inexperience and naïveté, but it is hard to see how any of these traits have utility in making us prosperous and safe. To be sure, it is more pleasant to hear platitudes from vibrant, attractive people with hairless, sculpted bodies than it is to hear the unvarnished truth from someone with a leather face and less glibness than experience, but older people are more likely to speak with authority.

And with passion, too, for the older we get the more we recognize that, when the day is gone, it is gone forever and it can't be retrieved. So there is an urgency to the things that mature people say, which is why they talk incessantly and won't shut up. So much of their lives have already passed that they don't have enough time left to recount the lessons in it. And they are worried that you aren't listening, which is why they tell the same stories, and deliver the same aphorisms, over and over again.

If it seems that we keep making the same mistakes, it is because we pay insufficient attention to people who have been through it all at least once before. In the end, we will survive rather than perish not because we accumulate comfort and luxury but because we accumulate wisdom.

The person who has nothing for which he is willing to fight, nothing which is more important than his own personal safety, is a miserable creature and has no chance of being free unless made and kept so by the exertions of better men than himself.

—JOHN STUART MILL

EPILOGUE

WHEN I WAS decorated in 1969, there were 450 living recipients of the Medal of Honor. Today, there are only about one hundred, and the average age is near eighty. Statistically, in five years there will only be fifty or sixty still alive, and in less than fifteen years there will be none of us left. There has not been a living Medal of Honor recipient from any conflict since the war in Vietnam.

Perhaps now resigned to the verity that time waits for no one, recipients get together as often as possible, but forty years ago, when men now long gone were still young and were going to live forever, we gathered only every other year. At the first Medal of Honor Society dinner I attended, my tablemates included Charles "Commando" Kelly, the first recipient in Europe in World War II; the flamboyant marine aviator Pappy Boyington; and the World War I ace Eddie Rickenbacker, who sat to my immediate right. I was twenty-six and passing dinner rolls to a man who had piloted a biplane in dogfights against the Kaiser's "Flying Circus," before my father was born. And it is even more astonishing that also in attendance was Bill Seach, who was born in England in 1877 and had received the Medal of

Honor for, among other exploits, leading a bayonet charge during the Boxer Rebellion in China in *1900*. These men, proud representatives of both their nation and the valor of their fallen comrades, are all gone now.

Today, the oldest living recipient of the Medal of Honor is John Finn, who was decorated for action on Pearl Harbor Day. Born in 1909, John joined the Navy in 1926, and, loquacious as we all tend to be when we finally grasp that we have too many stories and not enough time, he will transfix anyone who cares to listen with tales of what it was like to grow up before the First World War and to ply the Yangtze River as a young sailor aboard an American gunboat.

In 1941, he was stationed in Kaneohe Bay, with a squadron of Navy patrol planes. Rudely rousted from bed by the cacophony of the Japanese bombs destroying the fleet anchored at Pearl Harbor, John raced from his quarters, sped to the hangars that housed his aircraft, and manned a .50-caliber machine gun mounted on an exposed section of a parking ramp. For the next two hours, Finn, in the open and suffering from more than twenty shrapnel wounds in his back and stomach, blasted at the attacking enemy planes, hitting many of them and not relinquishing his post until the attack was over. Even when we were young, those of us who were raised on stirring John Wayne war movies assumed that there was more than a little hyperbole and cinematic license in them. But for forty years I have known a man whose real-life exploits render the movies limp, pallid, and ineffectual in contrast. Art can often approximate life, but it has a hard time doing it justice.

Not long ago, I asked John what he was doing at the precise moment when the Japanese attacked Pearl Harbor.

"Truth be told, my boy," John said, "I was in bed with a good-looking gal."

I asked if he ever saw her again.

"See her again?" said John. "She was my wife for sixty years!" Then he slapped his knee and bellowed with laughter.

RECIPIENTS OF THE Medal of Honor really have little in common. They have been from every state, economic station, and ethnic group. But they have shared a strong sense of duty and of purpose and the motivating burden of personal responsibility at the perilous point of decision. They feared death, but their biggest fear was failing themselves, their friends, and their nation, and thus they have been no different from the tens of millions of the other men and women who have served in uniform.

When the Japanese attacked on December 7, 1941, most Americans did not know where Hawaii was, let alone Pearl Harbor. And yet on the very next day, thousands of Americans rallied to the nation by offering their services in its defense. During World War II, almost every household made some contribution to the effort, and nearly half a million Americans sacrificed their lives so that hundreds of millions of others could live.

Today, a small number of brave and dedicated young Americans have answered the call, and whatever else one can argue about the merits of recent uses of military power, it is impossible not to revere the patriotism of these volunteers. More Americans were killed in New York on September 11, 2001, than were lost on December 7, 1941, and yet the response was a small fraction of that after Pearl Harbor. What is interesting, and more than a little distressing, is that the number of people wearing the uniform is only a bit more than 1.5 million on active duty, and that this represents only about one-half of one percent of Americans.

One may reasonably inquire why, if the war in Iraq is so unpopular, there aren't riots in the streets as there were during the war in Vietnam. One answer is that our service members are all volunteers, and no one else has to serve. This country has been going about its business almost as if nothing catastrophic has occurred, while the sacrifice has come from only a few citizens. Those of us who don't serve have thus outsourced our defense to those who do. One could argue persuasively that if all citizens had a stake in the protection of our freedom, the arbitrary use of the military instrument of power, as a *first* resort, would be very difficult to engineer.

Other than paying taxes and having a measure of sympathy and support for the troops, it is difficult to see what the polity is doing to defend itself. Like military units and corporations, societies survive only if all its members participate in nurturing it, and the survival of the American democratic experiment is not enhanced by the asymmetrical distribution of sacrifice we have now. It is dangerous when there is a wide gulf between a society and those who protect it, and participation is the only way to narrow the gulf.

If you have been getting something for nothing for a long time, it's tough to convince you to pay for it. But pay Americans must. In the years since the end of World War II, we have experimented with a number of schemes for producing the force we have needed, but none has been based on the notion of shared sacrifice. It is arguable whether the current volunteer system or one in which we relied on a draft is worse, but suffice it to say that they are both bad. We don't need *selective* service. We need *universal* service. But there is great political danger in merely suggesting that all Americans contribute in a meaningful way to our collective defense, and so no politician who wants to keep his job will do it. Consequently none does, and we are the poorer for it.

A society coheres only when it shares beliefs and experiences, and humans rarely value things that are acquired at no cost. With a minuscule percentage of people making a contribution to our defense, we will not be successful in protecting a country of more than three hundred million people, worldwide obligations, and threats from a variety of malefactors who want to see us destroyed.

Some of us are fortunate to spend some time with the few who have served and bear the scars to prove it. Yes, visiting badly wounded troops makes you self-conscious, uncomfortable, frustrated, angry, and guilty. But it also generates pride that our society can produce such magnificent young people. They have an unquenchable optimism, a certainty that they will overcome the rotten luck and physical constraints, and a conviction that they will prevail. With the same dedication they displayed in volunteering to be our proxies, and in taking care of each other on the battlefield, these splendid citizens take pride in working hard every single day to accomplish simple things that the majority of us take for granted.

The United States of America would be a much better place if we would emulate them.

Official Citation

For conspicuous gallantry and intrepidity in action at the risk of his life above and beyond the call of duty. Capt. Jacobs (then 1st Lt.), Infantry, distinguished himself while serving as assistant battalion adviser, 2nd Battalion, 16th Infantry, 9th Infantry Division, Army of the Republic of Vietnam. The 2nd Battalion was advancing to contact when it came under intense heavy machine gun and mortar fire from a Viet Cong battalion positioned in well-fortified bunkers. As the 2nd Battalion deployed into attack formation its advance was halted by devastating fire. Capt. Jacobs, with the command element of the lead company, called for and directed air strikes on the enemy positions to facilitate a renewed attack. Due to the intensity of the enemy fire and heavy casualties to the command group, including the company commander, the attack stopped and the friendly troops became disorganized.

Although wounded by mortar fragments, Capt. Jacobs assumed command of the allied company, ordered a withdrawal from the exposed position and established a defensive perimeter. Despite profuse bleeding from head wounds which impaired his vision, Capt. Jacobs, with complete disregard for his safety, returned under intense fire to evacuate a seriously wounded adviser to the safety of a wooded area where he administered lifesaving first aid. He then returned through heavy automatic weapons fire to evacuate the wounded company commander. Capt. Jacobs made repeated trips across the fire-swept open rice paddies evacuating wounded and their weapons. On three separate occasions, Capt. Jacobs contacted and drove off Viet Cong squads who were searching for allied wounded and weapons, single-handedly killing three and wounding several others.

His gallant actions and extraordinary heroism saved the lives of one U.S. adviser and 13 allied soldiers. Through his effort the allied company was restored to an effective fighting unit and prevented defeat of the friendly forces by a strong and determined enemy. Capt. Jacobs, by his gallantry and bravery in action in the highest traditions of the military service, has reflected great credit upon himself, his unit, and the U.S. Army.

Congressional Medal of Honor Citation
Jack H. Jacobs
Presented on October 9, 1969

ACKNOWLEDGMENTS

A perusal of nonfiction works will reveal that they begin with a section in which an impossibly large number of people are thanked for their help in producing the book. This is only right, since nothing worthwhile is ever done alone. Usually most of these people have been peripheral to the enterprise, but they are cited because their feelings would be hurt by not being identified, and mentioning someone's name costs nothing anyway. One tries to be all-inclusive at great risk, however, because the author may forget to thank one person and incur his wrath forever. But it is a quiet and desperate life (apologies to H.D.T.) that is lived without danger, and so I will take a stab at it.

It would be boorish not to mention the hairdressers and the makeup artists at NBC because, although they didn't help me with the book, they succeed in making me look presentable, a worthy achievement in its own right. Similarly, Bob at Long Hill Auto has kept my nine-year-old Subaru in the peak of condition, and it still runs flawlessly after more than 130,000 miles. Thanks, Bob.

Accolades must be heaped without limit upon a generation of long-suffering public school teachers, all of whom endeavored, with at least middling success, to make me and my cohort reasonably familiar with the written word. I was graduated from high school with almost nine hundred others, and even the man who finished dead last in the class was capable of reading an article in the *New York Times* and writing an intelligent paragraph about it. His essay would not be elegantly written, but each sentence would contain a subject and a predicate and end with the appropriate punctuation mark. We should consider ourselves lucky to get the same today from only some of those with university degrees, let alone from every high school graduate.

There is a large number of people who were children fifty or sixty years ago, friends of mine in the streets of New York, from whom I learned the most elemental skills: the finer points of stickball and stoopball, where babies come from, the maximum effective volume of a water balloon, how to make a zip gun. But from these pals I also received a most important concept: the inviolability of the community. There is simple elegance in the truth that your comrades deserve every measure of your devotion. I don't know what has happened to my friends from Public School 83, but I thank them for giving me the gift of brotherhood and hope that it has been as valuable to them as it has been to me.

Special thanks are due to Ivan Kronenfeld, my friend and the most unlikely of Renaissance men. It was at his insistence that I wrote a memoir, and he persisted despite my first refusing and then ignoring his entreaties. But he is tougher than I, and he prevailed. His is a most successful technique, espoused by Sun Tzu and practiced with great success by Mao Tse-tung: jab, run, jab, rope-a-dope, jab again and again—and eventually wear the poor guy down. This book was his idea, and so if it isn't any good, blame Ivan.

Many thanks also to: Frank Weimann, an author's dream agent; Natalee Rosenstein, an editor with patience to spare; Michelle Vega, whose confidence was infectious; Perry and Connor Smith, my friends and skilled, honest critics; Dave Murphy and Shanta Covington, two young television producers with much important to say and plenty of time left to say it; and Nathalie Casthely, friend and acting first sergeant.

Being asked to read a friend's manuscript must rank in unpleasantness with undergoing a painful medical or dental procedure. It places one in the unenviable position of choosing either to feign interest and thus be uncomfortably disingenuous, or else to accept the burden with good grace and realize that misery awaits. No fair weather friends, Brian Williams, Tom Brokaw, Bob Kerrey, Barry McCaffrey, and Nelson DeMille are tough warriors, and they all accepted the challenge of wading through a very rough draft. Thank you for your fortitude.

The trial of writing a book visits upon one's family an extra burden that often exceeds the capacity of friendship or even of love. Sue, thanks for your willingness to let me commandeer your computer, for your encouragement, and most of all for your formidable patience when my already unbearable irascibility was magnified by the press of deadline.

And to those patriots, many now gone, who served with me when we wore the cloth of this Republic, I offer thanks for your guidance and confidence, your humor and comfort, your honor, valor and sacrifice. We savor freedom today because of you.

—Jack Jacobs
New York
1 July 2008

I want to thank Jack Jacobs for the unflagging enthusiasm, energy and humor that made it a constant pleasure to work on this book. Without our mutual friend Ivan Kronenfeld, who made the *shidduch*, I would never have had the opportunity of hearing firsthand the wit of a singular American patriot. Thanks also to our editors at Berkley, Natalee Rosenstein and Michelle Vega; to my literary agent, Sloan Harris, and Kristyn Keene, at ICM. For their support and inspiration, I'm indebted to my parents, Jack and Marcia, and to my daughter, Lena Century.

—Douglas Century

INDEX